Perennial Wisdom for the Spiritually Independent

Selected Books in the
SkyLight Illuminations Series

The Art of War—Spirituality for Conflict: Annotated & Explained
Bhagavad Gita: Annotated & Explained
The Book of Job: Annotated & Explained
Celtic Christian Spirituality: Essential Writings—Annotated & Explained
Chuang-tzu: The Tao of Perfect Happiness—Selections Annotated & Explained
Confucius, the Analects: *The Path of the Sage—Selections Annotated & Explained*
Dhammapada: Annotated & Explained
The Divine Feminine in Biblical Wisdom Literature: Selections Annotated & Explained
Ecclesiastes: Annotated & Explained
Ghazali on the Principles of Islamic Spirituality: Selections from The Forty Foundations of Religion—*Annotated & Explained*
The Gospel of Philip: Annotated & Explained
The Gospel of Thomas: Annotated & Explained
Hasidic Tales: Annotated & Explained
The Hebrew Prophets: Selections Annotated & Explained
The Hidden Gospel of Matthew: Annotated & Explained
The Imitation of Christ: Selections Annotated & Explained
John & Charles Wesley: Selections from Their Writings and Hymns— Annotated & Explained
Maimonides—Essential Teachings on Jewish Faith and Ethics: The Book of Knowledge & the Thirteen Principles of Faith—Annotated & Explained
The Meditations of Marcus Aurelius: *Selections Annotated & Explained*
Native American Stories of the Sacred: Annotated & Explained
Philokalia: *The Eastern Christian Spiritual Texts—Annotated & Explained*
Proverbs: Annotated & Explained
The Qur'an and Sayings of Prophet Muhammad: Selections Annotated & Explained
Rumi and Islam: Selections from His Stories, Poems, and Discourses— Annotated & Explained
The Sacred Writings of Paul: Selections Annotated & Explained
Saint Augustine of Hippo: Selections from Confessions *and Other Essential Writings—Annotated & Explained*
Saint Ignatius Loyola—The Spiritual Writings: Selections Annotated & Explained
The Secret Book of John: The Gnostic Gospel—Annotated & Explained
Sex Texts from the Bible: Selections Annotated & Explained
Tanya, the Masterpiece of Hasidic Wisdom: Selections Annotated & Explained
Tao Te Ching: Annotated & Explained
The Way of a Pilgrim: The Jesus Prayer Journey—Annotated & Explained
Zohar: Annotated & Explained

Perennial Wisdom for the Spiritually Independent

Sacred Teachings— Annotated & Explained

Annotation by Rami Shapiro

Walking Together, Finding the Way ®
SKYLIGHT PATHS®
PUBLISHING
Woodstock, Vermont

Perennial Wisdom for the Spiritually Independent:
Sacred Teachings—Annotated & Explained

2013 Quality Paperback Edition, First Printing
© 2013 by Rami Shapiro
Foreword © 2013 by Richard Rohr

Library of Congress Cataloging-in-Publication Data

Shapiro, Rami M.
Perennial wisdom for the spiritually independent : sacred teachings-annotated & explained / Rami Shapiro.
    pages cm
Includes bibliographical references.
ISBN 978-1-59473-515-8
1. Religions—Comparative studies. I. Title.
BL80.3.S527 2013
204—dc23
                                    2013021007

10 9 8 7 6 5 4 3 2 1

Cover Design: Walter C. Bumford III, Stockton, Massachusetts
Cover Art: © majeczka/Shutterstock.com

Manufactured in the United States of America

SkyLight Paths Publishing is creating a place where people of different spiritual traditions come together for challenge and inspiration, a place where we can help each other understand the mystery that lies at the heart of our existence.

SkyLight Paths sees both believers and seekers as a community that increasingly transcends traditional boundaries of religion and denomination—people wanting to learn from each other, *walking together, finding the way.*

SkyLight Paths, "Walking Together, Finding the Way" and colophon are trademarks of LongHill Partners, Inc., registered in the U.S. Patent and Trademark Office.

Walking Together, Finding the Way®
Published by SkyLight Paths® Publishing
A Division of LongHill Partners, Inc.
Sunset Farm Offices, Route 4, P.O. Box 237
Woodstock, VT 05091
Tel: (802) 457-4000   Fax: (802) 457-4004
www.skylightpaths.com

This book is dedicated to Peter Santos and Michael Gelinas, my high school Asian Civilization teachers, who were the first to introduce me to the world's religions; to Huston Smith and Teresina Havens, my first gurus, who taught me how to uncover the Perennial Wisdom woven into every religious tra- dition; to my rebbe, Rabbi Zalman Schachter–Shalomi, who taught me to be "a Jewish practitioner of universal truth"; and to Eknath Easwaran, whose practice of Passage Meditation continues to guide me day by day.

Contents □

Foreword ☐

You can call it the collective unconscious; you can call it globalization; you can call it the Spirit of God; but why is it that so many of us are saying very similar things today when we are all from different traditions, countries, ethnicities, educations, and religions? This is really quite amazing and to my knowledge has no precedent in human history.

What a joy it is to write a few words in support of, and strong encouragement for you to read, this excellent book! Who would have thought that a Franciscan priest in New Mexico, trained in classic Catholic theology, would even be invited to do such a thing? Or even want to do it? Yet I read Rabbi Shapiro's words and all I keep saying is "Yes," "Of course," "Makes total sense," and "This fits my own experience and education!"

The things we used to argue about or use as reasons to dismiss one another now so often seem boring, limited, historically bound, and frankly prejudicial. Why should we be trapped inside of other peoples' history, other peoples' categories, or past arguments that are not really ours?

We are rediscovering the *philosophia perennis*, the early nineteenth-century phrase that pointed to an idea of a shared universal truth, and at a rather quick pace—God seems urgent at this point in our tragic history. Some of us call it the "wisdom tradition" which keeps showing itself in all of the world religions throughout history. This wisdom cannot be dismissed as mere syncretism—a word we Catholics loved to use for anyone who was trying to broaden our vocabulary and experience—or as lightweight thinking, sophisticated skepticism, or just wrong! That is too easy.

Too many of God's holy people keep saying the same thing—although admittedly from the more mature levels of consciousness—that we cannot continue to dismiss all holy people as "fuzzy thinkers." And, of course, they each say it in their own in-house language, culture, and century, which probably did magnify the problem.

Some have called these folks mystics, prophets, and saints, although even that word "mystic" got mystified in common usage, because we did not know how to think contemplatively, non-dually, or how "to teach spiritual things spiritually," to quote Paul from his sermon on wisdom (1 Corinthians 2:1–16). I am convinced Paul learned the core of this from his own Jewish tradition and was trying to teach it to what would become another religion called Christianity—which most of us would now agree, neither Jesus nor Paul ever foresaw or intended! (Don't hate me, Christians!)

Most were not ready for Paul's non-dual way of thinking, and most Christians and Jews have interpreted his thinking in an entirely dualistic way, and even in antagonism to his own beloved religion of Israel. "The mystery of the crucified" that Paul often speaks of is not a statement about Jesus being victimized, or a pro-Christian rallying cry, but a metaphor for the universal pattern of disorder inside of order, tragedy inside of holiness, surprise inside of consistency, the last being first, death inside of life, and the fly in every ointment. This is a universal pattern and truth, as old as the Hindu Scriptures, Confucian aphorisms, and the books of Exodus and Job.

But we Christians used Paul in a contentious, dualistic, and either-or way. We used his strong metaphor to blame, hate and separate, because that is what the unconverted self prefers. You can almost define the ego as that part of you which loves to take sides. The longer and more vigorously it justifies its side, the more it feels like this is surely truth, and soon my truth easily and quickly morphs into *the* truth and even the *only* truth. That is the devious darkness of the ego. We end up not with orthodoxy but with egocentricity.

This is invariably what happens when you have not been exposed to perennial philosophy, when you are not taught how to distill the big patterns out of the momentary arguments where everyone takes sides, when you cannot distinguish between the small, separate self and the self created by God and one with God, from all eternity. Rami Shapiro will guide you well here. Read on!

Fr. Richard Rohr, OFM

Center for Action and Contemplation

Albuquerque, New Mexico

Preface □

Perennial Wisdom for the Spiritually Independent is shaped by four factors: the swift increase in the number of spiritually independent Americans who, when asked in surveys to identify their religious affiliation, check the box labeled "None"; the perennial wisdom or perennial philosophy taught by the world's great mystics; Eknath Easwaran's practice of Passage Meditation, which I share here with the permission and blessing of his Blue Mountain Meditation Center; and the Five Questions at the heart of almost every spiritual quest for meaning and meaningful living.

Spiritually Independent, Not Spiritually Disinterested

A recent Pew Research Center survey on American religious life records that "one-fifth of the US public—and a third of adults under thirty—are religiously unaffiliated today, the highest percentages ever in Pew Research Center polling."[1] Given that the label offered to the spiritually independent survey taker was "None," it isn't surprising that these religiously unaffiliated individuals are often called *Nones*. The label is decidedly negative, however, and implies a lack of spiritual or religious interest, when in fact just the opposite is true. Most of these so-called Nones are not dismissive of God or spirituality but simply find religious labels and affiliation too narrow and constraining. This is why I choose to call this growing segment of the population by the far more positive and accurate term *spiritually independent*. People who are spiritually independent share the same existential questions as almost every other human being but do not confine their search for answers to any one religion. The answers they do find are often those taught by the great mystics of the world's religions—answers that emerge over and again through-out human history and across human cultures and that have come to be called the perennial philosophy or perennial wisdom.

Perennial Philosophy: It's Fourfold

The term "perennial philosophy" was coined by Agostino Steuco (1497–1548) and refers to a fourfold realization: (1) there is only one Reality (call it, among other names, God, Mother, Tao, Allah, Dharmakaya, Brahman, or Great Spirit) that is the source and substance of all creation; (2) that while each of us is a manifestation of this Reality, most of us identify with something much smaller, that is, our culturally conditioned individual ego; (3) that this identification with the smaller self gives rise to need-less anxiety, unnecessary suffering, and cross-cultural competition and violence; and (4) that peace, compassion, and justice naturally replace anxiety, needless suffering, competition, and violence when we realize our true nature as a manifestation of this singular Reality. The great sages and mystics of every civilization throughout human history have taught these truths in the language of their time and culture. It is the universality and timelessness of this wisdom that makes it the perfect focus for the spiritually independent seeker.

Passage Meditation: Meaningful Memorization

In his work with American students in search of a spiritual practice suited to the American psyche, Shakespeare scholar and spiritual mentor Eknath Easwaran (1910–1999) drew on his experiences in the college classroom. He found that asking students to memorize passages from Shakespeare aided their understanding of the text and allowed them to more deeply contemplate its meaning for their lives:

> The secret of meditation is simple: you become what you meditate on. When you use an inspirational passage every day in meditation, you are driving the words deep into your consciousness. Eventually they become an integral part of your personality, which means they

will find constant expression in what you do, what you say, and what you think."[2]

He called this practice Passage Meditation. In Passage Meditation you choose texts that articulate your deepest insights and values, commit them to memory, and then silently repeat them to yourself during formal meditation sessions. Internalizing texts through memorization is like planting seeds in a garden. The seeds are plunged deep into the ground, watered, and allowed to germinate and blossom of their own accord. In Passage Meditation, seed texts are worked deep into your psyche through memorization, watered by daily repetition during formal meditation practice, and allowed to shape your thoughts, feelings, and actions as they become your constant companions. *Perennial Wisdom for the Spiritually Independent* is an anthology of perennial wisdom texts designed for Passage Meditation.

The Five Questions: The Heart of the Spiritual Quest

Perennial Wisdom for the Spiritually Independent is organized around five questions at the heart of almost every spiritual quest: (1) *Who am I?* (2) *Where did I come from?* (3) *Where am I going?* (4) *How shall I live?* and (5) *Why?* Each chapter is introduced by a brief essay clarifying the question and then presents a selection of teachings from a variety of religions that speak to the question at hand. Most, though not all, of these texts are drawn from the SkyLight Paths SkyLight Illuminations series, which features sacred texts of the world's faith traditions with facing-page commentary, thus providing the reader with a trusted source for learning more about the books I used. Some of the texts are from the Bible, and most of these are my own translations. On the rare occasion when I do use a translation from the Jewish Publication Society (JPS) or the New Revised Standard Version (NRSV), I cite these sources. These texts are not definitive answers to the questions posed, but seeds that, when well planted and nourished through the practice of Passage Meditation, will blossom into answers uniquely your own. That is the goal of

Perennial Wisdom for the Spiritually Independent: not to draw you into a fixed wisdom tradition, but to draw out of you the wisdom that surpasses all tradition.

Perennial wisdom isn't unique to any specific system of thought or belief, but rather a set of teachings common to all of them. Each articulation of perennial wisdom takes on the flavor of the system in which it rests. Mistaking the flavor for the substance leads us to imagine differences where none exist. *Perennial Wisdom for the Spiritually Independent* deliberately mixes these texts and teachings to allow each to deepen the wisdom revealed in the others and to help you weave your own tapestry of truth out of these culturally diverse threads of universal wisdom.

Personal Note

I have worked with perennial wisdom since the late 1960s and have practiced Passage Meditation since the early 1980s. My experience with both convinces me that all diversity is part of a greater unity; that my sense of a separate self is a functional necessity rather than an absolute reality; that all my suffering is rooted in mistaking my limited and labeled self (male, Jewish, white, American) as my truest Self; and that I can, with practice, shift my awareness from that limited egoic self to the infinite divine Self that is all Reality.

I wrote this book to share with you what works for me. I believe that if you memorize the texts that speak to you and cultivate their transformative potential through Passage Meditation, you will find yourself transformed into what Saint Francis called "an instrument of divine peace" and what the Bible calls "a blessing to all the families of the earth" (Genesis 12:3).

Acknowledgments □

As always, I want to thank my editor, Emily Wichland, for both her support of this project and her expert guidance in bringing it to fruition. While my mind is forever kicking up an endless stream of brilliant ideas, it is those few that Emily is willing to commit to that I know have the potential to shine the brightest. Thanks also to Kaitlin Johnstone who assisted Emily in editing this book, and who caught several embarrassing errors that otherwise would have made it into print. And lastly, thanks to my son, Aaron Shapiro, whose bibliographic and research skills produced the annotated bibliography and annotated biography sections found at the back of this book. He brings me much *nachas* (joy).

☐ What Is Perennial Wisdom?

Twenty-five hundred years ago the Indian sage Siddhartha Gautama said:

> Don't believe anything secondhand. Don't believe anything because it's written in ancient books. Don't believe anything because "everyone" knows it's so. Don't believe anything because the sages proclaim it. Don't believe anything because of habit. Don't believe anything arising in your own mind, mistaking imagination for Truth. Don't believe anything on the authority of your guru or priest. What you yourself feel is true, what you experience and see for yourself, what is helpful to you and others, in this alone believe, and with this alone align your behavior.[1]

This might well be the manifesto of the spiritually independent. Be your own authority. Determine for yourself what is true. Take responsibility for your actions and the quality of your life. There is no one to turn to; there is no one to follow; there is no one to blame; there is just you in this moment.

Fair enough. But is it really enough? What do you know that isn't shaped by the knowing of others? What do you believe that isn't influenced by scriptures, habits, cultural norms, scientific models, personal bias, and the rest? Is it possible to strip yourself of all of this and see what is without a filter or distorting lens?

The story of the Buddha rests on the assumption that this is possible and that Siddhartha Gautama, the historical Buddha, did it. After years of training in the austerities of his native Hinduism, Siddhartha was no closer to Truth than before he began. Then something changed. He took responsibility for his own awakening. He ceased to walk the path his teachers followed and simply sat down. He sat beneath a large and already ancient fig tree in Bodh Gaya, India, and observed what he could of the world within and without. And then the lens shattered, and he knew what was so. He awoke.

The story of the Buddha carries a challenge that the stories of other founders of religion often don't. There can be only one Abraham, only one Moses, only one Jesus, only one Muhammad, and only one Krishna. Each of these individuals was called by God or was God, so there is no expectation that you can become another Moses or Muhammad or Jesus or Krishna. But you can be a Buddha, at least theoretically.

It was this possibility of personal awakening, the chance that I too could become a Buddha, that drew me to Buddhism in the late 1960s. It was this expectation that drew me to take the four Bodhisattva Vows:

> Sentient beings are innumerable; I vow to save them all.
> Desires are inexhaustible; I vow to extinguish them all.
> The Dharmas [teachings] are endless; I vow to learn them all.
> The Buddha Way is unsurpassed; I vow to attain it.

It was the hope that I could keep these vows that kept me sitting crossed-legged on a *zafu* (meditation cushion) for years and, more recently, on a chair or on a rock formation—a stone *zafu*, if you like—jutting out in the midst of a small rapids in Stones River about a mile from my home. But like most vows I have taken, these too never panned out.

Yet I still believe.

I believe because what I have heard makes sense to me. I believe because what I believe appears not in one or two sacred books, but in almost all of them across time and cultures. I believe because what I believe seems to be what sages have taught for millennia in cultures both long dead and still thriving. I believe because what I believe seems to arise in the heart/minds of gurus, rabbis, roshis, pastors, imams, priests, poets, scientists, swamis, and brilliant people of no rank and title over and over again throughout human history. Because it does, I trust it. Because I trust it, I seek to find it in myself and for myself. This search seems beneficial to me, making me kinder and more just, which makes my search of benefit to others beyond myself. So it is to this that I align my behavior.

The "this" I am talking about is called the perennial philosophy or perennial wisdom. I prefer the second term, because it is more concrete. Philosophy means the love (*philo*) of wisdom (*sophia*). It isn't the love of wisdom that we will explore in this book, but wisdom itself. This wisdom is called "perennial" because just as a perennial flower cycles through periods of birth, thriving, death, and rebirth, so this wisdom keeps appearing and disappearing in almost every human civilization. The heart of this wisdom is simple: everything is a manifestation of the One Thing, call it God, Tao, Brahma, Krishna, Allah, Great Spirit, or any other name you wish.

The Four Points of Perennial Wisdom

I take my understanding of perennial wisdom from the English writer and philosopher Aldous Huxley:

> *Philosophia perennis*—the phrase was coined by Leibniz [the German philosopher Gottfried Wilhelm Leibniz, 1646–1716]; but the thing—the metaphysic that recognizes a divine Reality substantial to the world of things and lives and minds; the psychology that finds in the soul something similar to, or even identical with, divine Reality; the ethic that places man's final end in the knowledge of the immanent and transcendent Ground of all being—the thing is immemorial and universal.[2]

Huxley offers a more ordered, and I would say more helpful, definition in his introduction to Swami Prabhavananda's 1944 translation of the Bhagavad Gita. There he lays out what he calls the "four fundamental doctrines" of the perennial wisdom:

> First: the phenomenal world of matter and individualized consciousness—the world of things and animals and men and even gods—is the manifestation of a Divine Ground within which all

partial realities have their beginning, and apart from which they would be non-existent.

Second: human beings are capable not merely of knowing about the Divine Ground by inference; they can also realize its existence by a direct intuition, superior to discursive reasoning. This immediate knowledge unites the knower with that which is known.

Third: man possesses a double nature, a phenomenal ego and an eternal Self, which is the inner man, the spirit, the spark of divinity within the soul. It is possible for a man, if he so desires, to identify himself with the spirit and therefore with the Divine Ground, which is of the same or like nature with the spirit.

Fourth: man's life on earth has only one end and purpose: to identify himself with his eternal Self and so come to unitive knowledge of the Divine Ground.[3]

This is an excellent summary of perennial wisdom, but not necessarily the most clear. Here is another version of the same four points taught by the German mystic Meister (Master) Eckhart (1260–1327), as set forth by the contemporary Indian scholar Eknath Easwaran:

First, there is a "light in the soul that is uncreated and uncreatable": unconditioned, universal, deathless; in religious language, a divine core of personality which cannot be separated from God. Eckhart is precise: this is not what the English language calls the "soul," but some essence in the soul that lies at the very center of consciousness. As Saint Catherine of Genoa put it, "My me is God: nor do I know my selfhood except in God." In Indian mysticism this divine core is called simply *atman*, "the Self."

Second, this divine essence can be *realized*. It is not an abstraction, and it need not—Eckhart would say *must* not—remain hidden under the covering of our everyday personality. It can and should be discovered, so that its presence becomes a reality in daily life.

Third, this discovery is life's real and highest goal. Our supreme purpose in life is not to make a fortune, not to pursue pleasure, nor to write our name on history, but to discover this spark of the divine that is in our hearts.

Last, when we realize this goal, we discover simultaneously that the divinity within ourselves is one and the same in all—all individuals, all creatures, all of life.[4]

Given the centrality of these four points to this collection of teachings and commentaries, let me add my own version of the perennial wisdom to that of Huxley, Eckhart, and Easwaran.

Everything Is a Facet of the One Thing

Think in terms of white light shining through a prism to reveal the full spectrum of color perceivable by the human eye: red, orange, yellow, green, blue, indigo, and violet. Each of these colors is part of the original whole and cannot be separated from it—turn off the light source and the colors disappear. Now apply this metaphor to the world around and within you. Everything you see, think, feel, and imagine is a part of and never apart from the same Source. We call this Source by such names as God, Reality, Brahman, Allah, One, Krishna, the Absolute, and the Nondual. The list of names is long; the reality to which they all point is the same.

You Are That

Everything is a manifestation of God—everything. That means you. To know God is to know yourself; to know yourself is to know God. The quality of knowing I'm talking about isn't knowledge about something other than yourself, because you cannot be other than God, the only being there is. Knowing God isn't knowing through theological speculations about God but rather knowing God directly, the way a ray of sunlight knows the sun. When you know God directly, you know God as yourself. But—and this is a huge but—you do not imagine you alone are God. Knowing you are God is knowing everything else is God as well. Knowing that you and everything else are God is knowing that there is no you or anything else—only God.

Absolute and Relative, and That Which Embraces Them Both

Imagine you are a wave on a vast shoreless sea. Imagine further that you come to realize that you and all the other waves of this sea are in fact nothing other than the sea waving, extending itself in time and space. You are still you—a wave—and yet so much more than you—the sea itself. Knowing yourself as a wave is knowing the relative world, the world of seemingly separate beings. Knowing yourself as the sea is knowing the absolute world, the world of the One who is all these seemingly separate waves. But there is still another level of knowing—the unlabeled knowing that knows both sea and wave, both the absolute and the relative. This knowing and the knower who knows it cannot be known; it cannot become the known; it cannot become an object. It is the eternal subject, the knower that cannot be known, the subject that cannot be made an object of knowing.

There is no name for this knower or this knowing. Any name would make it an object, and hence no longer the knower. This is where all language breaks down. Even the word "silence" is insufficient to describe what we are talking about, because what we are talking about cannot be talked about, and hence cannot be described. And yet it is the truest Self, the truest you, God.

If this makes your head hurt, rest assured you are not alone. Just ask yourself, who is it who knows your head is hurting? Damn! You almost had it.

Know God. No God.

It is popular today to speak of a purpose-driven life or to speculate about why you are here. The answer provided by perennial wisdom is simple: to know God in, with, and as all reality, or, more simply, to know yourself as God. This is like a wave waking up to the fact that it is nothing but the ocean in extension. This doesn't mean that you, or any given wave, are any less unique, precious, and worthy of utmost respect and dignity, only that all the rest of life is worthy of the same because all life is the same.

Knowing God as the Whole and the Part, and knowing that there is a knowing behind this knowing that is the greater Godhead of which nothing can be said, frees you from imagining that any one name of God is truer than any other name. Krishna, Brahman, YHVH, Allah, and the myriad other names of God are all God to the extent that these names point beyond themselves toward the Unnamed; and Krishna, Brahman, YHVH, Allah, and the myriad other names of God are not God to the extent that they point only to themselves and their constituents.

Because you know all the names of God can be of value, you are free to explore the sacred literatures of the world to cull the wisdom they have to offer. Because you know that no name is exclusively God, you are free from having to surrender yourself to any one name or system of belief. This is the essence of what it is to be spiritually independent. You are open to wisdom from whatever system of belief it may come, and yet free from having to believe in that system as a whole in order to benefit from its wisdom.

God Is One, Gods Are Not

As Lao Tzu, the sixth-century author of the Tao Te Ching, says in his opening poem, "The tao that can be named is not the eternal Tao." While theologians will argue otherwise, for our purposes, Tao and God, along with other names such as Brahman, Krishna, Allah, Great Spirit, and Emptiness, all point toward that Absolute Reality of which all things are a part. I am not concerned with the theological or philosophical nuances of each name in the context of its culture of origin. For me, and for this book, all names are pointers to That which is beyond naming.

In saying this, I am lifting these names of God out of their cultural contexts. So before leaving this subject let me be clear that I am not saying that all Gods are the same, only that from the perspective of the mystics and the perennial wisdom all names of God point beyond themselves and "toward" that which cannot be named or pointed toward.

For example, in the context of Islam, Allah is "one without second." Allah has no son. Allah chooses Muhammad as his final prophet, and the

Qur'an as his final revelation. The God of Christianity in the context of Christianity, however, is completely other than Allah. The Christian God has a son, knows nothing of Muhammad, and never reveals the Qur'an.

Similarly, the Jewish God knows nothing of Jesus and has nothing to do with the New Testament the Christians regard as the Word of God. Krishna, God for many Hindus, on the other hand, has nothing to do with the Hebrew Bible, the Greek New Testament, or the Arabic Qur'an. If you wish to understand him, you need to read the Bhagavad Gita, the revelations of Lord Krishna to Arjuna, about which the Jewish, Christian, and Muslim Gods know nothing.

It is wrong to claim that all Gods are the same or that all Gods are variations of the One God. They aren't. Each God arises in its time and place and reflects the values of that time and place, or at least the values of its priests, prophets, sages, and gurus. If you want to understand Allah, study Islam. If you want to understand Krishna (or Brahman, Vishnu, Shiva, Ganesha, Saraswati, and the rest of the Gods of India), study the many schools of Hinduism. Just take care not to water down each religion so that it is indistinguishable from the others. Rather, treat each religion and each God as it asks to be treated, allowing it speak to you within its own context and with its own authenticity and integrity intact. If this were a book about religion, this is precisely what I would do.

But *Perennial Wisdom for the Spiritually Independent* is not a book about religion. It is an anthology of texts and teachings that articulate the perennial wisdom. In the context of this book, we are sifting through scriptures and teachings of many cultures looking for those teachings that step beyond the limits of any culture and point to the Reality that cannot be named.

Think of this book as a compass. The needle of a compass always points northward, but northward is not a place. You cannot arrive at northward; you can only travel northward. Take one step northward. Take a second step, and the prior step, which was once northward, is now southward. Take a third step and both previous steps are southward when a moment ago each was northward. This is so because there are no fixed points on the spiritual path. There is only a direction; there is only the journey and never the arrival at a fixed destination. Moving northward is moving from the conditioned to the unconditioned, from fear to love, from a constricted heart to an open heart, and from a closed mind and clenched fist to an open mind and open hand.

There is so much more one can say about perennial wisdom, and I urge you to consult the bibliography and learn more about it. But to go on here would be to distract us from the purpose of *Perennial Wisdom for the Spiritually Independent*: to plant the seeds of this wisdom in your mind and heart by memorizing, repeating, and contemplating the teachings of the sages collected in this book. So let's get to it.

Who Am I? ☐

Was there ever a time when you weren't you? I often ask this of my comparative religion students. It may seem an odd question to ask, and it causes some confusion in class, but let's consider it for a moment.

Perhaps, like many of my students, you believe that you consist of a soul as well as a body and that the soul will outlive the body and is in fact immortal. If it is immortal, your soul not only lives on after your body dies, but lived before your body was born as well. If you existed prior to your birth, is the "you" you were then the same "you" you are now, and will it be after your death?

Because this kind of questioning requires more than a snap response, I ask my students to write down their answers before sharing them with the class. Here is one that, while being more articulate than many, is representative of most:

> If my soul is the real me, then the me I take myself to be—the embodied me, the me that is female, born to Mexican parents, raised a Catholic, and pursuing a BA in psychology—is like a costume my soul wears when playing this role in the greater drama of the world. So the answer to the question, *Is the me I was before I was born and the me I will be after my death the same me I am now*, must be "no." Just as an actor is the same before and after the play, so my soul is the same before and after my life. And just as the actor plays a role different than her real life, so my soul plays a role—a me—that is different from itself.

This is a fairly standard response. Most people imagine that their soul is other than their body, but that doesn't put an end to our investigation. In fact, it opens us up to even more questions. Here, as best as I can recall, is the ensuing conversation I had with this young woman and her classmates.

"If being a Catholic woman of Mexican heritage is the role your soul plays, is your soul female, Hispanic, or Catholic?"

"No."

"Is it a different gender, ethnicity, or religion?"

"No."

"So the soul is without gender, religion, ethnicity. Does it have any other identifying characteristics? Does it have a certain age, height, weight, or any of the things we use to define or identify ourselves?"

"No."

"And this soul is the real 'you,' the 'you' you were and will be, and in fact still are beneath the costume of gender, race, ethnicity, religion, and the rest?"

"Yes."

"Then who are you, really?"

My student waits for the class to stop laughing, then takes a deep breath and says, "Nobody."

"You're nobody? How can that be?"

"Well if I have no identifying characteristics—no body, no gender, no race, no ethnicity, no religion, no nationality, no likes or dislikes— then I'm nobody, for the only way we know ourselves to be somebody is through these things that I'm pretty sure my soul doesn't have. So I'm nobody."

Not everyone agrees with this position, of course, but it is the answer most closely associated with perennial wisdom.

Nobody or Somebody

There are two fundamental and fundamentally different views of Self or soul. The first sees the soul, our true Self, as free from all labels, and hence "nobody." The second sees the soul, our true Self, as necessarily labeled and hence "somebody."

If you believe you are somebody, then you must also believe that other people and other beings are somebody else. The universe is populated by myriad somebodies. This is the view held by most people: my "I" is separate from and other than your "I," my self is other than your self.

If you believe you are nobody, however, do you still believe there are somebodies? Or if you are nobody, do you believe there isn't anybody at all? I raise this question with my students, and my original nobody from Mexico volunteers to go into this with me.

"If your true Self or soul is without any distinguishing characteristics whatsoever," I ask her, "how can you distinguish your true Self or soul from any other?"

Silence. I try again.

"Does your soul have a shape?"

"No."

"Without a shape, does it have a boundary? Is there an inside or an outside to your soul, your true Self?"

"No."

"OK. So there's no end to you, no limit, no boundary beyond which you might say that isn't me or that is someone else."

"I guess. Right."

"And there are no identifying characteristics to this infinite expanse that is you, right?"

"Right."

"So how can you be other than any other soul? How can there be more than one soul at all?"

Again, silence, but this time only for a moment.

"There can't be any other soul," she says hurriedly. "There isn't any other soul. There is just that one Self that dresses up as all of us!" She was flushed and very animated. "There is only one soul," she said, "and we are it!"

Nobody or Everybody

I usually discourage hand raising in my classes, preferring instead to have a more free-flowing conversation, but I noticed an older student sitting in the front row off to my far left, raising his hand and supporting his raised elbow with his other hand. I know this student is a veteran of the Iraq War, having served multiple tours of duty. He rarely says anything in class but often talks with me privately afterward.

"Which camp are you?" I ask him as I motion for him to put his hand down. "Are you somebody or nobody?"

"Nobody."

"And you want to add something?"

"Yeah. I get there is only one soul or Self or whatever you want to call it. And it isn't anything in particular because it has to be everything in general. It has to be her and me and you, everyone. Animals, too, most likely. Everything. But if it's everything, how does it differ from God? It doesn't. It is God. The soul is just another name for God."

"'Atman is Brahman' is how Hinduism puts it," I said. "The soul is God."

A forest of "somebody" hands fly into the air. I don't call on anyone in particular but wave them all down and invite them to work out for themselves the order of response.

"I'm not God," one somebody says.

"God is other, the Other," another somebody adds.

"God is the Creator and we are the creation, separate and not equal," a third says.

I notice one student plowing through his well-worn Bible. I ask him what he's looking for.

"Look, I thought I was in the somebody camp, but all these nobody passages of the Bible are racing around in my head."

"Care to share?"

"Yeah. I mean Jesus says, *I am the vine, you are the branches* (John 15:5). There really isn't a division between vine and branch even though we can tell the difference between vine and branch. And Jesus says, *I am in my Father, and you are in me, and I am in you* (John 14:20). Again no separation of the Self and God. And Saint Paul defines God in Acts as that *in whom we live and move and have our being* (Acts 17:28). I'm not saying that I'm switching camps, but it makes you think ..." His voice trailed off.

Why It Matters

By this point, if I'm lucky enough to have the conversation go this well and get this far, I'm usually pressed for time. I'm also eager to have my students internalize this discussion and carry it on outside of class. To do this I ask them to write down their answers to one final question and bring their answers with them to our next class session: "What are the consequences in this life of being somebody or being nobody? What difference might it make if I think I'm somebody or if I think I'm nobody?"

For continuity's sake, here is what our female psychology major wrote:

> I think the consequences couldn't be clearer. If I believe I'm somebody, not psychologically but spiritually, not temporarily but eternally, and if I think my soul can be saved or damned, then I'm going to do all I can to get saved, and that would include separating myself from all those who are damned and who through their thoughts or actions might lead me to be damned as well. But if I'm nobody, or now maybe I'm God, then I'm everybody, and there is nobody to be separated from, nobody to fear, and nobody to war with. Being somebody would make me anxious of the other. Being nobody is peace because there is no other.

I Is God

There is no other; there is only God: not our "Father who art in heaven," but the singular Reality that is everywhere and everyone; even you. See if this is true for you.

As you read these words, become aware of yourself doing so. Notice your body sitting in a chair or on the couch. Without changing your posture, become aware of your posture. Now answer this question: Is the you that is aware of yourself sitting also sitting?

Now observe yourself reading. Notice your eyes scanning the page or the screen. Notice how you translate the letters you are scanning into words, and the words into sentences, and the sentences into paragraphs. Notice how meaning arises in you while you read. Now answer this question: Is the you that is aware of yourself reading also reading?

Or stop reading and just notice your thoughts. Is the you that is noticing these thoughts also thinking them?

When I do this exercise, I find that the "me" that is doing is not the "I" that is noticing. The "me" that is doing is male, Jewish, early sixties, and American, while the "I" that is noticing all the doing isn't any of these things. As my student said, this "I" is nobody. It doesn't have a gender, race, religion, ethnicity, nationality, age, job, obligations, or anything else that is attached to the "me" I normally take myself to be. This observing "I" isn't separate from me, and there doesn't appear to be any place where this "I" resides. It isn't anywhere or anything. In fact, it isn't an "it" at all, for as soon as I try to observe it, what I observe is no longer it, and the one observing is again nothing.

The real "I" is an eternal subject that cannot be observed, for in so doing it is reduced to an object, and another subject arises to observe it. I am the eternal subject, the limitless "I" without labels. And so are you.

Tat Tvam Asi

This is the first and foundational insight of perennial wisdom, *tat tvam asi*, as the Hindu Chandogya Upanishad (6.8.7) put it some twenty-five hundred years ago: You are That; you are the Subject that embraces and transcends all objects. You are not other than what you observe, but you are always greater than what you observe.

One more question: How many of these "I's" are there? Is your "I" different from mine? Let's go into this slowly.

You and I both know what it is to be hungry. While you and I may differ as to what it is we prefer to eat in order to satisfy our hunger, the experience of "I'm hungry" isn't different. I'm not talking about the intensity of our hunger or the context in which our respective hungers may arise. I'm asking, is my "I" that is aware of hunger different from your "I" that is aware of hunger? I suggest it isn't.

How could it be? If my "I" and your "I" are both unlabeled, free of all identifying characteristics, how can we distinguish my "I" from your "I"? If the "I" is limitless, without boundaries, how can there be room for more than one "I"?

If the "I" that is aware of the body's hunger isn't male or female, if it doesn't belong to any religion, ethnicity, race, or nationality, if it lacks shape and even location, then what is it? My experience is that this "I" is nothing and nobody. It is awareness without form, it is knowing rather than knower.

Of course I am talking about the "I" as if it could be made into an object of conversation, and once this is done, the "I" about which I am speaking is no longer the knowing itself. "The tao that can be named is not the eternal Tao," as Lao Tzu put it.

When we talk about the "I" or try to observe the "I," the "I" being observed is no longer the observer; what was subject is now object. But the observing "I" is never object, and only subject. Look for yourself to see if this is true.

Observe the observer. What happens? The observing "I" is nobody, while the observed "I" is somebody—you. So which are you? The observer or the observed? You are both. You are nobody and somebody. You are the eternal and the temporal. You are the absolute and the relative. You are God.

Of course "God" is only a word, another label, no more applicable than any other. The true "I" is without labels. It is very difficult for us to speak without falling into the trap of making an object of the eternal Subject. That is the limitation of language, and we will run into it over and over again. But we can use words to point beyond themselves toward the ineffable, and that is what you must do as you read the texts and commentaries that follow.

But what benefit is there in knowing this? What benefit is there in realizing the Subject that is nobody and everybody?

I Is Free

Once, during a retreat I was leading, the conversation turned to the eternal "I," which of course meant that we had turned the Subject into an object, but bear with me. A psychiatrist told us this story:

> I was interning at a hospital and working with a very depressed young man. Certainly drug therapy was called for, but I wanted to try something else before prescribing pills. I listened attentively to his story. He was very good at detailing his depression and spoke clearly, with a level of understanding that suggested he had been in therapy before, which he had.
>
> When he finished speaking, I said, "Is the person telling me this story of depression himself depressed?"
>
> The young man just stared at me.
>
> "Think about your depression, and then notice if the you that is thinking about your depression is also depressed."
>
> He closed his eyes and sought an honest answer to my question. "No," he said. "He's not."
>
> "He's not? Who's he?"
>
> "Me," he said, "I'm not. I mean the me that was telling you about my depression wasn't depressed, but was just telling you about another me that was, that is, depressed."
>
> "Great," I said. "Let's use the you who isn't depressed to help the you who is depressed."
>
> His eyes grew wide, and he smiled with a mixture of surprise and joy. He was ready to get well.

The "I" that says "I'm depressed" is not the eternal "I," the infinite observing "I" that is the real you. Yet we tend not to notice this. In fact, we assume just the opposite to be true: when I say I'm sad, or happy, or hungry, I assume that the "I" that is speaking is in fact sad, or happy, or hungry. But if I look more closely, this isn't the case at all. The "I" that notices sadness or depression is not sad or depressed; the "I" that notices joy or guilt, hunger or lust, isn't actually feeling any of these states. This "I" is witnessing everything but isn't caught up in anything.

The "I" that cannot be watched, seen, observed, or noticed, the "I" that can only watch, see, observe, and notice, is the "I" at the heart of the question first asked in my class. This "I" isn't the "you" that is named or gendered. It doesn't have a race or ethnicity. It isn't bound to any nation or religion. Don't take my word for it—look and see for yourself. Of course you see this "I" as male or female, Jew or gentile, black, brown, red, yellow, or white, but remember: the "you" you are seeing isn't the you that is doing the seeing. So try again. And again. And again. You cannot see the seer. And because you can't see it, it can't be named, labeled, or identified in any way. It simply is.

This is the "I" Saint Paul calls "Christ Jesus," in which "there is no Jew or Greek, slave or free, male or female" (Galatians 3:28). This is the "I" the Hebrew prophet Isaiah called *YHVH* (be-ing, from the Hebrew verb *h-y-h*, "to be"), who says, "I form light and create darkness; I make peace and create evil. I, the Be-ing of all being, do all these things" (Isaiah 45:7). This is the "I" of Jesus who says, "I and the Father are one" (John 10:30). This is Allah, "the First and the Last, the Manifest and the Unmanifest, who is fully aware of all things" (Qur'an 57:3). This is Krishna, who says, "I am the Father of the universe and its Mother ... I am the Goal, the Sustainer, the Lord, the Witness, the Home, the Shelter, the Lover, and the Origin; I am Life and Death ... I am Death and Immortality, I am Being and Not-being" (Bhagavad Gita 9:17–19).

God, the Absolute, the Real, is the "I" that cannot be made into an object. Because it cannot be made into an object, it cannot be named. Again, as Lao Tzu, the sixth-century author of the Tao Te Ching, says in his opening poem, "The tao that can be named is not the eternal Tao."

Of course, in speaking of God this way I am naming it. So I'm betraying the point even as I try to make the point. This is where all language breaks down, and why Lao Tzu says, "One who knows doesn't speak; one who speaks doesn't know" (Tao Te Ching, chapter 56).

To avoid getting tripped up by the limits of language as you read this book I suggest you keep in mind the Hindu saying *neti, neti. Neti, neti* means "not this, not that," and comes from a passage of the Avadhuta Gita: "*Tat tvam asi* [thou art that] affirms the eternal Subject; but of every object you perceive say *neti, neti*, the Absolute is not reduced to this, the Absolute is not reduced to that" (Avadhuta Gita, 1.25, my translation). Whenever you find yourself making an object of "I" or God, remind yourself: *neti, neti*—not this, not that, but the nameless Subject that embraces and transcends them all.

So, who am I? Nobody, everybody, nothing, everything, God, Allah, YHVH, Brahman, Christ, Buddha, Tao, Great Spirit, and the knowing that embraces and transcends them all.

1 The speaker here is *Chochmah*, Wisdom, God's daughter (*Chochmah* is a feminine noun in Hebrew). Wisdom represents the eternal "I." What she says of herself, you can say of yourself. You arise from God the way sunlight arises from the sun, the way a wave arises in the ocean. This is not the "I" that can be named, but the eternal Tao, the unnamed manifesting in and as the named.

2 While often translated as "Word," Logos is Wisdom, Tao, the ordering principle of all Reality. In fact, in one Chinese translation of John, Logos is translated as Tao. In Christianity, Logos incarnates as Jesus; in the perennial wisdom, Logos incarnates as you and all things.

3 The "I" that is your true Self and the true Self of all beings predates time and creation the way an acorn predates an oak and is yet the product of it. This is one of the great paradoxes of Reality: it is endless creativity giving rise to itself over and over and over again.

4 The *I am* of Jesus is the eternal "I" of all things. The *I am* is eternally present, without past or future, beginning or end. The power of now isn't to be in the moment, however, but to realize you are the moment, and the moment is fleeting, emptying even as it forms, forming even as it empties. Jesus isn't saying he is older than Abraham, which is what his audience seems to think he is saying. He is saying that the "I" embraces time and yet is never trapped in it.

5 The eternal "I" is birthless and deathless, without beginning and end. It is pure subjectivity that can never become an object. Objects come and go, but witnessing abides eternally. You are this witnessing.

God is my Source,
and I am God's first creation.[1]
(PROVERBS 8:22, *THE DIVINE FEMININE IN BIBLICAL WISDOM LITERATURE:*
SELECTIONS ANNOTATED & EXPLAINED, P. 3)

In the beginning was Logos,
and Logos was with God,
and Logos was God.[2]
(GOSPEL ACCORDING TO JOHN 1:1)

Before time—I am. Before beginnings—I am.
There were as yet no oceans when I was born,
no springs deep and overflowing.
I am older than mountains.
Elder to the hills, the valleys, and the fields.
Before even the first lumps of clay emerged—I am.[3]
(PROVERBS 8:23–26, *THE DIVINE FEMININE IN BIBLICAL WISDOM LITERATURE:*
SELECTIONS ANNOTATED & EXPLAINED, P. 3)

Before Abraham was—I am.[4]
(GOSPEL ACCORDING TO JOHN 8:58)

Before time,
at the beginning of beginnings,
God created Me.
And I shall remain forever.[5]
(WISDOM OF JESUS BEN SIRACH 24:9, *THE DIVINE FEMININE IN BIBLICAL WISDOM*
LITERATURE: SELECTIONS ANNOTATED & EXPLAINED, P. 21)

6 The eternal "I" is that Reality from which all things flow. To the extent you identify with the temporal and conditioned "I" of ego, you know hunger and thirst. To the extent you identify with the eternal "I," there is no hunger and thirst.

7 How can you come to that which you already are? Moving from point A to point B takes time, but the eternal "I" is already and always present. It isn't anywhere but everywhere, so how can you *come* to it? Jesus is speaking to your lesser "I," the "I" that doesn't yet know the greater Self. This "I" imagines it must go somewhere and be someone. But the truth is different: all you need to do is realize what is, not arrive at what is to be.

8 Can you believe in the eternal "I" without making it an object? Again Jesus is speaking to the lesser "I" of ego. If you believe there is a greater "I," you are more apt to discover it, but the "it" you discover is nothing other than yourself.

9 Jeremiah calls you to trust rather than believe. Trust is being with what is as it is. This is all you have to do.

10 Trust in Reality alone. Don't imagine anything other than what is, and you will discover you are what is, and what is *is* God.

11 When you trust what is rather than seek to control what is, every-thing happens in its season; everything ripens as it must in its own time. There is nothing you need do to make things right. Things are as they are because they cannot be other than they are. And that's true of you as well. Know this and all fear will end.

Then Jesus declared, "I am the bread of life.[6]
One who comes to me[7] will never hunger,
one who believes[8] in me will never thirst."

(GOSPEL ACCORDING TO JOHN 5:35)

Blessed are you who trust in Me,[9]
and in Me alone.[10]
You are like trees rooted near water.
Your leaves are evergreen and yield fruit in its season.
You have no fear of drought.[11]

(JEREMIAH 17:7–8, *THE HEBREW PROPHETS:*
SELECTIONS ANNOTATED & EXPLAINED, P. 63)

[12] The light mentioned here is the light of wisdom, the capacity to suc-
cessfully navigate the world in all its complexity. "Wisdom is superior
to foolishness as light is superior to darkness" (Ecclesiastes 2:13). Light
allows you to navigate the dark, but it would be folly to imagine that
you would be better in a world of light alone. Following Jesus, realizing the eternal "I," you navigate the dark places with the light of wisdom. The dark is no less dark, but the obstacles over which you might
stumble are illumined and your balance is maintained.

[13] The gate is the moment you awaken to, in, and as the eternal "I."
Jesus, not the man but the Christ Mind he manifests (1 Corinthians
2:16), has become a gate to this awakening. Entering the gate, entering Jesus, what Saint Paul calls putting on the Mind of Christ (Philip-
pians 2:5), is realizing what Jesus is and who you truly are.

[14] To be saved is to be released from the object-driven world of ego
and into the pure subjectivity of the witnessing "I," a state Hindus call
sat-chit-ananda, pure being, pure consciousness, pure bliss.

[15] Enter *and* exit? Having awakened as Christ Mind, *sat-chit-ananda*,
why would you want to leave? The truth is you can't leave. There is
nowhere to go. But this doesn't mean you are no longer able to function in the relative world of self and other. The eternal "I" is the Whole
of which the lesser "I" is a part. Putting on the Mind of Christ allows
you to operate in all worlds justly and kindly. Knowing all things as the
One Thing, you treat all things with respect and all beings with love.

[16] God is the endless process of birthing, dying, and rebirthing. Knowing you are a manifestation of this process, you embrace all of it with
equanimity. Imagining you are apart from this process, equanimity is
lost and death is a constant worry. Of course the lesser "I" will die, but
the greater "I," the divine and eternal "I," never does.

When Jesus spoke again to the people, he said,
"I am the light of the world.
One who follows me will never walk in darkness,
but will have the light of life."[12]

(GOSPEL ACCORDING TO JOHN 8:12)

I am the gate;[13]
one who enters through me will be saved.[14]
Such a one will enter and exit, and find pasture.[15]

(GOSPEL ACCORDING TO JOHN 10:9)

I am the resurrection and the life.
Those who believe in me will live,
even though they die;
and whoever lives and believes in me will never die.[16]

(GOSPEL ACCORDING TO JOHN 11:25–26)

17 The vine is God, the branches are extensions of God. When you know you are an extension of God, your actions are shaped by godliness; you naturally engage the world with justice and love.

18 This is true because there is nothing apart from the Whole.

19 God is all there is. Do not imagine separation where none exists. But if you do, then go about gathering in the Divine. In time you will discover that you are gathering in the Self that is not other than you, only infinitely greater than you.

20 You are the absolute and the relative. You are the ever-existing whole out of which the temporarily existing parts arise and return. The key isn't to deny the parts but to embrace them as parts of the whole.

I am the vine; you are the branches.
Those who remain in me and I in them,
will bear much fruit;[17]
apart from me you can do nothing.[18]

(GOSPEL ACCORDING TO JOHN 15:5)

I am you and you are I,
and in whatever place you are,
I am there,
and I am sown in everything.
And in whatever place you wish,
you may gather me,
but when you gather me, you gather yourself.[19]

(GOSPEL OF EVE IN EPIPHANIUS, AGAINST HERESIES 26.3.1, *THE LOST SAYINGS OF*
JESUS: TEACHINGS FROM ANCIENT CHRISTIAN, JEWISH, GNOSTIC
AND ISLAMIC SOURCES—ANNOTATED & EXPLAINED, P. 113)

Blessed are you who existed before you came into being.
For you who exists, did exist and will exist.[20]

(GOSPEL OF PHILIP 49, *THE LOST SAYINGS OF JESUS: TEACHINGS FROM ANCIENT*
CHRISTIAN, JEWISH, GNOSTIC AND ISLAMIC SOURCES—
ANNOTATED & EXPLAINED, P. 109)

21 Don't imagine that God, Allah, Tao is all this or all that, all good or all loving. God is simply everything and its opposite. God is the good and the bad, the loving and the cruel; it is all God, for God is all there is. Imagining God to be less than all is to imagine a world of competing opposites instead of realizing the world as a dynamic and creative dance of interdependent polarities. Trapped in a false and limited dualism, you will spend your time seeking what you call good and desperately trying to avoid what you call evil. Because each goes with the other, however, you cannot achieve this goal. The challenge isn't to have one and not the other, but to navigate both with compassion: "Shall we not accept the good as well as the bad from God?" (Job 2:10).

22 The breath of God is God extending in time and space. In the Jewish tradition, this breath is called *Chochmah*, Wisdom, God's daughter. Later, in the Christian tradition, it is called Logos, Jesus, God's Son. It is the same Wisdom, spoken of here as a woman, there as a man. Whether manifest as woman or man, Wisdom is the same.

I am the One Who Is;
there is nothing else.
Beside Me, there is no god....
I form light and create darkness;
I make peace and create evil—
I, the One Who Is, do all these things.[21]

(ISAIAH 45:5–7, THE HEBREW PROPHETS:
SELECTIONS ANNOTATED & EXPLAINED, P. 83)

I am the breath of the Most High,
blanketing the earth like mist,
filling the sky like towering clouds.
I encompass distant galaxies,
and walk the innermost abyss.
Over crest and trough,
over sea and land,
over every people and nation
I hold sway.[22]

(WISDOM OF JESUS BEN SIRACH 24:3–6, THE DIVINE FEMININE IN BIBLICAL WISDOM
LITERATURE: SELECTIONS ANNOTATED & EXPLAINED, P. 21)

23 The Tao of the Chinese is the Hebrew's *Chochmah*, the Greek's Logos, the Christian's Christ, the Hindu's Kali. She is the Mother of all life, and the way of the living.

24 To name the eternal "I" is to make it an object. To make it an object is to lose it altogether. Yet we must speak, and when we do, we need names. So we call the Unnamed "Tao," "Allah," "God," "Brahman," "Great Spirit," "YHVH," but the name is never the named. The problem with so much religion is that it mistakes the named for the Unnameable; it makes a fetish of the word rather than surrendering to the silence in which the Unnamed is realized. The spiritually independent use names lightly, knowing that no name can express the Nameless.

25 In this context, "great" means infinite. The Tao is the endless dance of life—passing, receding, returning, and passing again: birthing, aging, dying, rebirthing over and over again. You are one with this process: both a temporary expression of this endless creativity and the endless creativity itself.

26 *Ehyeh asher Ehyeh* means "I will be what I will be." You cannot name that which is forever becoming. You cannot reduce eternal process to a fixed state. What God offers us here is a "name" that is no name. God is saying, "If you must name Me, do so in a way that undermines the very act of naming."

There is something formlessly created
Born before Heaven and Earth
So silent! So ethereal!
Independent and changeless
Circulating and ceaseless
It can be regarded as the mother of the world[23]
I do not know its name
Identifying it, I call it *Tao*[24]
Forced to describe it, I call it great
Great means passing
Passing means receding
Receding means returning
Therefore the Tao is great[25]

(TAO TE CHING, CHAPTER 25, *TAO TE CHING: ANNOTATED & EXPLAINED*, P. 51)

Moses inquired of God, "When I approach the Israelites
and they ask me for Your Name, what shall I tell them?"
And God replied, "*Ehyeh asher Ehyeh.*
Tell them *Ehyeh* sent you."[26]

(EXODUS 3:14)

27 *Elohim*, literally "Gods," is here coupled with a singular noun. In this way Torah seeks to lift you out of the temptation to limit God to the One or the Many and helps you realize that God is that which embraces and transcends both. If you are so inclined, you may read *Elohim* as the Trinity, the three-in-one God of many Christians. Or, following *gematria*, Hebrew numerology, you may note that the numerical value of *Elohim* (eighty-six) is identical to the numerical value of *ha-teva*, nature, and read *Elohim* as the creative force of nature, plural because creation is multiform, and yet singular because all the living manifest the singularity of life. However you choose to understand the Name, remember that the Reality for which it stands is in and of itself unnamable.

28 *Adam*—pronounced "ah-dahm"—means "earthling," and is derived from *adamah*, "earth." Adam is one way *adamah* becomes conscious. You are the consciousness of life awakening to itself as the extension of God.

29 You are the image and likeness of God the way a wave is the image and likeness of the ocean.

30 Notice the intent of God is to create you in the divine image and likeness, but in the actual act of creating there is no mention of likeness. Why? Likeness is the act of actualizing your potential as the image of God. You are born as the image of God, but you must cultivate the image and actualize the likeness; you awaken as God through acts of godliness.

And *Elohim*[27] said,
"Let us make *adam*[28] in our image,
after our likeness."[29]

And Elohim created *adam* in the divine image,
in the image of *Elohim* was *adam* created,
male and female *Elohim* created them.[30]

(GENESIS 1:26–27)

31 This is Krishna speaking to Arjuna in the Hindu Bhagavad Gita. As with Jesus earlier, Krishna is not referring to the form Arjuna sees beside him in his chariot, but to the eternal, infinite, and formless Self that is all reality.

32 You cannot cease to be because you are that which is endless being. Your form will end, your memories will fade, but the Self, the eternal "I," endures forever. Just don't imagine that this "I" belongs to you or is different from that of others. There is only one "I," only one Absolute Life manifesting as all the living. You are that, and that is you, and everything else.

33 The wise have no delusion, but that doesn't mean they escape the process of birth and death. The key is not to escape anything, but to see everything as the endless flowing of God.

34 We endure the opposites of life best when we see them as complementarities. If you cease to image you can have hot without cold, or love without loss, you will embrace hot and cold, and love and loss with equanimity.

35 You are that Spirit. There is no "other," there is only This—God, Tao, Spirit, Brahman, Allah ... you!

There was never a time when I was not,[31]
nor you, nor these princes were not;
there will never be a time when we shall cease to be.[32]
As the soul experiences in this body,
infancy, youth, and old age,
so finally it passes into another.
The wise have no delusion about this.[33]
Those external relations which bring cold and heat,
pain and happiness,
they come and go; they are not permanent.
Endure them bravely, O Prince![34]
The hero whose soul is unmoved by circumstance,
who accepts pleasure and pain with equanimity,
only this one is fit for immortality.
That which is not, shall never be;
that which is, shall never cease to be.
To the wise, these truths are self-evident.
The Spirit, which pervades all that we see, is imperishable.
Nothing can destroy the Spirit.[35]

(BHAGAVAD GITA, 2:12–17, *BHAGAVAD GITA: ANNOTATED & EXPLAINED*, P. 13)

36 Don't mistake this teaching for the conventional understanding of reincarnation. Krishna is not saying there is a separate and eternal "you" that moves through one life after another. There is no "you" separate from the "I" of God. Rather, Krishna is saying that your body is a robe of the eternal "I." When this body dies, the ego dies with it. But the eternal "I" cannot die. Just don't imagine you—the egoic, named, gendered, labeled you—are That, only know that That is you. The distinction is crucial to awakening. Just as a wave is not all of the ocean, while the ocean is all of the wave, so the self is not all of the Self, but the Self is all of the self. If you imagine that the "I" of ego is the eternal "I," then you imagine that ego lasts forever. This is not the case. Ego dies when the brain dies. But you are more than this. You are the "I" of the awakened Buddha, the resurrected Christ, the One who is the many. You are not reincarnated. God is recycled.

37 Awakened saints and sages throughout history and across every culture know this distinction. They know that while they see, hear, touch, smell, eat, move, sleep, and breathe, it is simply God doing this through them as them. You can test this for yourself. Do you know how to see, or do you just see? Can you make your ears hear, or do they just hear? What if you had to digest your food by consciously making your digestive tract function? Would you know what to do? You cannot make your nails grow or stop them from growing. If you can't control your body, how can you imagine you are in control of anything else?

As you discard your threadbare robes
and put on new,
so the Spirit throws off Its worn-out bodies
and takes fresh ones.[36]

(BHAGAVAD GITA, 2:22, *BHAGAVAD GITA: ANNOTATED & EXPLAINED*, P. 15)

Though the saints see, hear, touch,
smell, eat, move, sleep, and breathe,
yet they know the Truth,
and they know that it is not they who act.[37]

(BHAGAVAD GITA, 5:8, *BHAGAVAD GITA: ANNOTATED & EXPLAINED*, P. 43)

38 Rest in this sense is what the Chinese call *wei wu wei*, noncoercive action. This is the quality of swimming with the current and cutting with the grain. This rest isn't non-doing, but doing in harmony with Reality as it presents itself moment to moment.

39 Love in this context isn't the love of one for another, but the love of the One who is the other. This is the love of the eternal "I" that is your greatest Self. Your "sunken nature" is the egoic alienated "I" that inhabits a dying world where you desperately cling to form even as it crumbles in your hand.

40 Love is "goodness of will." Your prayer is not "My will be done," but "Your will be done," being careful not to pretend that these wills are one and the same. "My will" is always for the "I" of self in opposite to another. "Your will" is always the eternal "I" that acts for the benefit of self and other.

41 Finding rest isn't a matter of grueling discipline. Finding rest is a matter of surrendering to the weight of the loving and eternal "I." The challenge here is not to do something, but to at last allow something to be done of its own accord—*wei wu wei*.

42 Too many of us turn spiritual practice into serious work, when in fact it is nothing more than letting gravity do what it must.

Our true place is where we find rest.[38]
We are borne toward it by love, and it is your good Spirit
who lifts up our sunken nature from the gates of death.[39]
In goodness of will is our peace.[40]
A body gravitates to its proper place by its own weight.
This weight does not necessarily drag it downward,
but pulls it to the place proper to it:
thus fire tends upward, a stone downward.[41]
Drawn by their weight, things seek their rightful places.
If oil is poured into water, it will rise to the surface,
but if water is poured onto oil, it will sink below the oil:
drawn by their weight, things seek their rightful places.
They are not at rest as long as they are disordered,
but once brought to order, they find their rest.
Now, my weight is my love,
and wherever I am carried, it is this weight that carries
me.[42]

(SAINT AUGUSTINE, CONFESSIONS XIII.9.10, SAINT AUGUSTINE OF HIPPO:
SELECTIONS FROM CONFESSIONS AND OTHER ESSENTIAL WRITINGS—
ANNOTATED & EXPLAINED, P. 95)

43 The mind that wavers is not the Mind of Christ, the singular and eternal "I" that is all beings. The mind that wavers is the lesser "I" of ego. The lesser "I" quakes at the sight of God, for it desperately clings to the notion that God is other. This lesser "I" is like a candle flame in a breeze, clinging to the wick so as not to be extinguished.

44 This teaching has two meanings. First, whatever the narrow mind of ego rests upon becomes the object of its desire. If your mind rests on hunger, food is the treasure. If your mind rests on wealth, money is the treasure. If your mind rests on fame, notoriety is the treasure. Second, whatever the spacious mind of Self rests upon becomes your treasure. But spacious mind rests solely on God, seeing self and other as manifestations of That, so the treasure of spacious mind is God and the infinite manifestations of God. But this is still not the greatest treasure.

45 The greatest treasure is the Self that cannot be made an object, the "I" that embraces and transcends both narrow mind and spacious mind. This is the mind in between (and around, and within) soul and spirit. Soul is narrow mind that knows itself to be apart from God. Spirit is spacious mind that knows itself to be a part of God. But the greater "I" is that which knows itself to be God, part and whole.

46 You are born human rather than Jewish, Buddhist, Muslim, or the rest. These labels are given to you at birth or chosen later in life, and you are trained to embody them according to the standards set by those who define them. The key to spiritual awakening is to drop the label and see what is as it is.

Mary said,
"I saw the Lord in a vision
and I said to Him,
'Lord, today I saw you in a vision.'
He answered and said to me,
'Blessed are you who did not waver at the sight of me.[43]
For where the mind is, there the treasure is.'[44]
I said to him,
'Lord, how does someone see the vision,
through the soul or through the spirit?'
The Savior answered and said,
'Not through the soul nor through the spirit,
but through the mind that is between the two.
That is what sees the vision.'"[45]

(GOSPEL OF MARY 7:1–6, THE LOST SAYINGS OF JESUS:
TEACHINGS FROM ANCIENT CHRISTIAN, JEWISH, GNOSTIC AND ISLAMIC SOURCES—
ANNOTATED & EXPLAINED, P. 101)

Every newborn is born
into a state of natural inclination [to worship One God],
and it is our parents who make us into
a Jew, Christian, or Magian.[46]

(MUHAMMAD, THE QUR'AN AND SAYINGS OF PROPHET MUHAMMAD:
SELECTIONS ANNOTATED & EXPLAINED, P. 63)

47 The Hebrew command translated "go" is *lech lecha*, literally "walk toward yourself." The self toward which you are commanded to walk is the truest Self, the Self that is God, the eternal "I" that is all things.

48 To realize this "I," you must strip away the conditioning of nationality, ethnicity, religion, and parental bias. Only when you stand without labels of any kind are you standing in the land God wishes to show you: the land of the radically free.

49 Paradoxically, the person of no rank, the person without a label, often becomes famous among the labeled. Meant to stand as models to be followed, they all too often become idols others choose to worship.

50 Those who bless the unlabeled will become unlabeled; those who fear the unlabeled will become all the more labeled.

51 You are not called to freedom for your own sake, but for the sake of "all the families of the earth," all living beings. You become free only to free others. In this you take on the vow of the Bodhisattva: "Though sentient beings are innumerable, I vow to save them all."

52 The empty, the unformed, the unmanifest, the unlabeled, and hence the ineffable is central to the functioning of life. But so too is the full, the formed, the manifest, the labeled, and the named. Don't imagine that one is opposed to the other or that either can function in isolation from the other. A window or doorway needs the frame no less than the space the frame defines. Without the clay, a cup holds no water; without the spokes, a wheel cannot roll. Do not take "unlabeled" as your label. Drop all labels. When you are free from all labels, even the label of being unlabeled, you are free to wear any label, putting it on and taking it off as the needs of the moment demand.

Now the Ineffable One said to Abram,
"Go[47] from your country
and your kindred
and your father's house
to the land that I will show you.[48]
I will make of you a great nation,
and I will bless you,
and make your name great,
so that you will be a blessing.[49]
I will bless those who bless you,
and the one who curses you I will curse;[50]
and through you all the families of the earth
shall be blessed."[51]

(GENESIS 12:1–3)

Thirty spokes join in one hub
In its emptiness,
there is the function of a vehicle
Mix clay to create a container
In its emptiness,
there is the function of a container
Cut open doors and windows to create a room
In its emptiness,
there is the function of a room
Therefore, that which exists is used to create benefit
That which is empty is used to create functionality[52]

(TAO TE CHING, CHAPTER 11, *TAO TE CHING: ANNOTATED & EXPLAINED*, P. 23)

53 Jesus is talking about the birthless and deathless "I" that is the ground of your very being. This is the "you" that existed before you were born, and the "you" that continues after you die. But it isn't the "you" you think you are. This is because it cannot be made an object of thought. You cannot know the "I," you can only be the "I."

54 The "original face" of Ch'an (Zen) master Huineng (b. 638) is Jesus's "I am" who exists before existence. You cannot know this face with your ordinary mind, though it isn't other than your ordinary mind. You cannot know it when you are trapped in the opposites of good and bad, in desiring one thing and avoiding another. Only when you are open to all without grasping and releasing can you be the birthless one that is your true face.

55 The Self Jesus wants you to know is Huangpo's original face, the face that is yours before your parents labeled it "Jew or gentile, slave or free, male or female" (Galatians 3:28). Unless you know this Self, you are ignorant of yourself.

56 What is within you is the intuition that you are the eternal "I." Nurture this and you are rescued from the alienation and anxiety that mark the lesser self.

57 Jesus is speaking as the eternal "I," the source and substance of all Reality. Everything comes from this, and everything returns to this, and everything is this. Everything: wood and rock, the One and the many, self and other.

Jesus said: Blessed is one who existed
before coming into being.[53]

(GOSPEL OF THOMAS 19A, *THE GOSPEL OF THOMAS: ANNOTATED & EXPLAINED*, P. 27)

When your thoughts are not tied
to positive or negative,
good or bad,
what is your original face?[54]

(HUINENG, *THE PLATFORM SUTRA*)

Jesus said: If you know everything else
but do not know yourself, you know nothing.[55]

(GOSPEL OF THOMAS 67, *THE GOSPEL OF THOMAS: ANNOTATED & EXPLAINED*, P. 89)

Jesus said: When you give rise to that which is within you,
what you have will save you.
If you do not give rise to it,
what you do not have will destroy you.[56]

(GOSPEL OF THOMAS 70, *THE GOSPEL OF THOMAS: ANNOTATED & EXPLAINED*, P. 93)

Jesus said: I am the light above everything.
I am everything.
Everything came forth from me,
and everything reached me.
Split wood, I am there.
Lift up a rock, you will find me there.[57]

(GOSPEL OF THOMAS 77, *THE GOSPEL OF THOMAS: ANNOTATED & EXPLAINED*, P. 99)

58 The Greek philosopher Plotinus (204–270) taught that there is a single source from which all things arise and into which all things return. He called this "the One." You are this One manifest as your unique self, but to know the One you have to drop the illusion that you are other than the One. This is what Plotinus means by ceasing to be an individual: ceasing to cling to the labels that mark you as one thing or another. When you no longer identify as this *or* that, you will discover you are this *and* that. This is the supreme awakening of perennial wisdom.

59 Saint Catherine of Genoa (1447–1510) realized the original face of Huangpo, the One of Plotinus, and spoke of it as Me: not the egoic "I" of narrow mind, but the singular One, the eternal "I" of spacious mind. This "I" is you, and everything else as well.

60 The first "I" Saint Paul mentions is the named, the labeled, the "me" of ego rather than the Me of God. This "I" is not false or illusory. It is a necessary function of the One manifesting in and as the world. Honoring this "I" by seeing to your own welfare is not wrong. But do not imagine that this "I" is permanent or self-sufficient. It is neither. The lesser "I" of you is a facet of the Greater "I" of all. Know the one and cherish it; know the One and live from it.

61 Can God desire? Yes: God desires to be God. God desires to be God the way the sun desires to shine, or a river desires to flow, or an acorn desires to oak and the oak desires to acorn. God desires only to be God, and, as Rabbi Aharon HaLevi Horowitz (1766–1829) says, to be God means to manifest the world in all its diversity. God doesn't choose to create the universe; creating the universe is what it is to be God.

62 This is a central teaching of perennial wisdom: the Oneness of God includes the multiplicity of creation. Everything is a unique manifestation of God—everything: the good and the bad, the just and the unjust, the right and the wrong, the things you crave and the things you despise. It is all God, for if anything existed that was not God, God would not be God.

Each being contains in itself the whole intelligible world.
Therefore All is everywhere.
Each is All, and All is each.
You as you are now has ceased to be the All.
But when you cease to be an individual,
you raise yourself again and penetrate the whole world.[58]
(PLOTINUS, CITED IN ALDOUS HUXLEY, *PERENNIAL PHILOSOPHY*, P. 5)

My Me is God,
nor do I recognize any other Me
except my God.[59]
(SAINT CATHERINE OF GENOA, CITED IN ALDOUS HUXLEY,
PERENNIAL PHILOSOPHY, P 11)

I live, yet not I but Christ lives in me.[60]
(SAINT PAUL, GALATIANS 2:20)

God's only desire is to reveal unity through diversity.
That is, to reveal that all of reality is unique
in all of its levels and in all of its details,
and nevertheless united in a fundamental oneness.[61]
(RABBI AHARON HALEVI HOROWITZ, *SHA'AREI HA-YIHUD VE-HA-EMUNAH*, IV.5)

The main point of creation ...
[is] to reveal the wholeness of God
from the opposite perspective....
For it is the nature of completeness
to include all opposites in the One.[62]
(RABBI AHARON HALEVI HOROWITZ, *AVODAT HA-LEVI, VA-YEHI*, FOL. 74A)

63   Who are you apart from what you imagine yourself to be, apart from the costumes you wear to be the person you are expected to be? What if you awoke tomorrow without the faintest memory of who you are? Who would you be? While the named you might be lost, would the Original You, the Me, the eternal "I" be any less or any different?

Once Chuang Chou dreamt he was a butterfly,
flitting and fluttering about as butterflies do.
He had a wonderful sense of pleasure and felt greatly alive.
He had no idea that he was Chou.
Suddenly he woke up
and could clearly sense that he was Chou.
But then he did not know whether he was Chou
who had just dreamed that he was a butterfly
or whether he was in reality a butterfly
who was now dreaming that it was Chou.
Still, Chou and the butterfly
have to be somehow separate—or do they?
This is what we call the changes things undergo.[63]

(CHUANG-TZU, CHAPTER 2, *CHUANG-TZU: THE TAO OF PERFECT HAPPINESS—
ANNOTATED & EXPLAINED*, P. 75)

64 You create yourself from the past. Habit defines you. The roles you play define you. Imagine a soccer player who, when the game was over, still refused to use his hands and sought to do everything with his feet and head. It sounds silly, yet that is how we all live: engaging today by yesterday's standards. What would it be like to meet each moment free?

65 So closely identified are we with our labels, our roles, and the costumes that come with them that we forget the greater Self, the "I" that wears them all without being restricted to any. You can no more find your Self by searching than you can hear your ears by listening. You are the Self. It isn't a matter of finding what you lack, but of realizing who you already and always are.

66 Notice that the Buddha says you are the result of what you have thought, not simply what you are thinking at this moment. What you think now is shaped by what you thought earlier. The quality of your thought determines the quality of your life. But it is not enough to merely purify your thoughts. This is a start, but such work is endless, for thoughts are ceaseless. Besides, by the time you realize your thought is evil, it has already been thought. What you need to learn is to observe thought without clinging to what is thought. When you rest in the eternal "I," you can watch thoughts arise without insisting that you are the thinker. Free from owning the thoughts you observe, you can choose which to actualize and which to leave alone. This is living freely.

67 It is easy to get lost in theories and theologies. Job isn't speculating about the existence of God; he sees God in his own flesh. See God in yourself as yourself, and there is no need to theorize.

Rabbi Hanoch taught,
There was once a man whose memory was so poor
that he could not find his clothes in the morning.
This fact made him afraid to go to sleep at night
until one evening he hatched a plan
and wrote down where he placed each item of clothing
as he undressed for bed.
The next morning he used his list to dress:
Cap—there it was. Pants—there they were.
Item by item he dressed himself effortlessly,
and then a great fear overtook him:
Here is my hat and here my pants, but where am I?[64]
Where did I leave myself?
He searched and searched but could not find himself.
So, too, Rabbi Hanoch said, it goes with us.[65]

(MARTIN BUBER, *THE WAY OF MAN ACCORDING TO THE
TEACHINGS OF HASIDISM*, P. 30, ADAPTED)

All that we are is the result of what we have thought.
It is founded on our thoughts.
It is made up of our thoughts.
If you speak or act with an evil thought, pain follows you,
as the wheel follows the foot of the
ox that draws the wagon.[66]

(DHAMMAPADA 1:1, *DHAMMAPADA: ANNOTATED & EXPLAINED*, P. 3)

In my flesh I see God.[67]

(JOB 19:26, *THE DIVINE FEMININE IN BIBLICAL WISDOM LITERATURE:
SELECTIONS ANNOTATED & EXPLAINED*, P. 103)

68 You are the "I" of the five senses, the nonpersonal "I" of the body feeding data to the brain that then seeks to maximize its own survival by using the world as a means to its own ends.

69 You are the "I" of intellect, the personal "I" that takes itself to be the stories it tells and the labels it wears.

70 You are the "I" of the Great Atman, the interpersonal "I" that knows the many as the One.

71 You are the "I" of the Unmanifest Brahman, the transpersonal "I" that knows the One as the many.

72 Beyond all these is the "I" that embraces and transcends body, mind, Atman, and Brahman. This is the "I" that embraces part and whole within itself as itself. This is Huangpo's "original face," Saint Catherine's "Me," Saint Paul's "Christ." This is the One and Only that is each and every. This is you, but you are never it, for here there is no it, only "I am."

73 This is the exclamation of the awakened: God is I, and I am God. While Abulafia (1240–c. 1291), Jesus (4 BCE–33 CE), and al-Hallaj (858–922) each articulates this realization in his own way, the realization itself is the same. It is sad, and yet not incidental, to note that all three men were persecuted for their teaching. Abulafia was hounded by the rabbis who sought to silence him and his teaching, Jesus was crucified by the Romans in Jerusalem, and al-Hallaj was publicly dismembered by the Islamic authorities in Baghdad. The history of perennial wisdom within the Abrahamic faiths is often marred by violence perpetrated against its teachers. The reason for this is simple: perennial wisdom requires no clergy, supports no religious institution, and bows to no ecclesiastical authority, and so those who promote it are often seen as the enemy by those whose power, prestige, and authority depend on the very structures perennial wisdom calls into question.

Beyond the senses is the brain.[68]
Beyond the brain is the intellect.[69]
Beyond the intellect is the Great Atman.[70]
Beyond the Great Atman is the Unmanifest Brahman.[71]
Beyond the Unmanifest Brahman is the I,
all-pervading Subject impossible to objectify.[72]

(KATHA UPANISHAD 2.3.7–8)

For now the awakened one is no longer separated from
God,
and behold you are God, and God is you;
for you are so intimately adhering to God that
you cannot by any means be separate from God,
for you are God. So now that I, even I, am God.
God is I and I am God.

(ABRAHAM ABULAFIA, CITED IN MOSHE IDEL, THE MYSTICAL EXPERIENCE IN
ABRAHAM ABULAFIA, PP. 126–127)

I and the Father are one.

(GOSPEL ACCORDING TO JOHN 10:30)

I am Truth.
There is nothing wrapped in my turban but God.
There is nothing in my cloak but God.[73]

(MANSUR AL-HALLAJ)

Where Did I Come From? □

There are two basic answers to the question *Where did I come from?* Either you came from somewhere else or you came from right here. The first answer I call "I am Alien," and the second answer I call "I Belong."

I Am Alien and I Am Bad

Several years ago during an interfaith discussion on population control, I listened to Father Steve, a local Catholic priest with whom I had shared several interfaith panels in the past, explain why his church opposes contraception even in countries where overpopulation leads to abject poverty and rampant disease. Father Steve said that each of us is a soul temporarily inhabiting a physical body, and that the soul comes from heaven and doesn't really belong to this world or to the body that houses it.

Each soul, he said, has a right to be born, and all unborn souls stand in line in heaven waiting for their turn to be sent down to earth. Because no soul can come to earth until there is a fertilized egg capable of housing it, when we prevent conception we prevent that soul from entering the world, and thus postpone the births of innumerable souls standing in line behind it.

At first I thought he was joking, but I was wrong. Nor was he speaking metaphorically. When asked if we are to take literally the idea of billions upon billions of souls cuing up in heaven waiting for the next available egg, he said, yes, that is in fact what is happening, and contraception does a terrible disservice to these patient souls, which is why the church opposes it; that and the fact that until they are born they cannot be baptized and saved. So, Father Steve proclaimed, "Contraception actually impedes salvation!"

"But if they are already in heaven," a woman in the audience stood up and asked, "why would they need to be saved? Why not just stay in heaven and be happy?"

"Original sin," Father Steve blurted out and then stopped for a moment to organize his thoughts. The questioner took advantage of his hesitation and said, "You mean souls are sinful even before conception? How can that be? God makes souls, so are you telling me that God is responsible for original sin?"

Father Steve smiled condescendingly at the woman. I had seen him do this on other occasions. He used the look to silence people he considered hecklers. Neither impressed nor cowed, the woman remained standing and was about to say something else when Father Steve unexpectedly turned and handed me the microphone. The woman shifted her gaze to me as if I was supposed to answer this Catholic conundrum. I too should have smiled, though not condescendingly, and demurred. Always willing to muck around with other people's theologies, however, I foolishly set out to answer the woman's question instead.

"Yes," I said, "God is responsible for sin. How could it be otherwise? God is responsible for everything. This is what God says in Isaiah 45:7: 'I create darkness, I create light, I make goodness, I make evil, I the Infinite One do all this.'"

"Then why does God punish us for sin," the woman said, "when it is God who is responsible?"

"That is the genius of the Christian story," I said. "First God blames Adam and Eve for sin and threatens them with death. But sin continues. Then God blames all humanity for sin and kills all humans with the exception of Noah and his family. But sin continues. Then God chooses the Jews and threatens them with big sticks and entices them with big carrots to give up sin and live just and righteous lives, but sin continues. Finally God realizes that it is God rather than humanity that's the problem, and hence it is God rather than humanity that must be punished. So God does the only logical thing: God becomes an innocent human and dies on the cross. Of course, the church says God died for our sins, but a deeper reading of the Christian story is that God had to die for God's own sins."

I doubt my answer satisfied the questioner, but she did sit down. I glanced over at Father Steve. He was staring at his hands pressed palms down on the table. I think he trembled a bit. The moderator wisely changed topics.

Just Passing Through

My point in sharing this story is not to impress you with my mastery of Catholicism; I clearly lack that. My point is simply to say that once we posit the notion that we come from somewhere else, we are forced to ask and answer questions that in the end cannot be adequately answered: If I am a spirit from elsewhere embodied in an earthly form, this body and the world it inhabits isn't really my concern, so why should I care about it or take care of it? Why not just let it die that I might go back to where I came from? If my soul is the real "me," what am I to make of the physical "me" I seem to be at this moment? Is this a false me? If it is false, how do I free myself from it? If I do free myself from it, who is the "me" doing the freeing, and how does it relate to the "me" that is freed?

I once asked these questions of an Egyptian imam who said, "You're making this too complicated. We are fundamentally alien to this world. We are here to do God's will, but we don't really belong here, and we won't stay here. We come from heaven, and when we have accomplished our set tasks, we will return to heaven."

"But what am I to make of the self I seem to be while on earth?"

"This is a false self. It is like a mask the soul wears and has no value when it is removed, and has little value even when worn. Your appetites and desires, your lusts and hungers, these are all distractions to be surrendered. Your very will is to be surrendered to Allah that you might achieve the goal God has set for you and then go home."

Both Father Steve and the imam subscribe to the alien theory of self: you are from somewhere else, somewhere better, somewhere more real and true. You don't really belong here. You are here only for a time and then you get to go elsewhere—ideally back to where you came from or, if you fail in your mission, perhaps somewhere else. Religions that teach that we come from somewhere else are eager to help us get somewhere else, and while they don't recommend suicide, they are often not adverse to martyrdom. To die in the act of affirming your faith is often seen as one of the quickest routes to getting out of here and back to there. There is always better than here.

This approach to the question *Where did I come from?* creates within us the dis-ease of alienation, and often does so with catastrophic results. As an alien stranded in this world, I'm never quite at home here, and therefore I never take full responsibility for what happens here. As an alien, I see the world around me as other and have little if any concern over its fate. As an alien trapped in a human body, I feel disconnected from this body and often abuse it. As an alien, I am fearful of other humans. Not only am I alienated from "here," but I am also alienated from "them," with "them" being anyone who doesn't think or feel as I do. The "I Am Alien" story is at the heart of so many of our political, economic, social, and environmental problems. Because it is the "I Am Alien" story that produces and sustains these problems, it is only when we opt for a different story that we can fix these problems. Perennial wisdom offers the alternative story we need, the story I'm calling "I Belong."

I Belong

"I Belong" says you didn't come into this world from somewhere else, you grew out of this world right here. You aren't an alien soul imprisoned in a physical body and exiled from your true home to wander in this alien environment, you are a natural expression of this environment. You emerge from "here" the way an apple emerges from an apple tree: you belong.

Once while exploring the "I Belong" story and the apple tree analogy with a synagogue confirmation class, a young woman challenged me, saying, "So we humans are no different or better or more valuable than fruit?"

"The point of the analogy isn't to reduce us to fruit," I said, "but to say we are as natural to this world as an apple is natural to an apple tree."

"We are different, and we are better," she said.

"We are different just like your liver is different from your lungs, but can you say one is better or more valuable than the other? Without either you would be dead. The point of 'I Belong' is to say that all beings are a part of a single system of being."

Another student jumped in, "Then we're just a part of nature like Darwin said. We are just a by-product of natural selection, an accident. Nature is dumb, and we're dumb."

"On the contrary," I said. "Nature isn't dumb. Nature is intrinsically intelligent. Nature learns through experiment, trial, and error. But she learns. And what she learns is how to become more and more conscious and more and more compassionate. We humans, far from being dumb, are, at least in this place and at this moment, the way the universe becomes self-conscious. We are a way—maybe the way—life comes to know itself, to understand itself, maybe even to improve itself."

Some of the students complained that I was teaching Intelligent Design, a pseudo-science they associated with fundamentalist Christianity.

"Not at all," I said. "The Intelligent Design people assume nature is dumb and that the only way it can produce what it does produce is if there is an outside Intelligence—God, if you like—who designed things according to a master plan. Some scientists believe similarly, though they remove the idea of an Intelligent Designer and assert that intelligence is an accident. I'm saying that nature herself is intelligent because nature herself is a manifestation of God."

The Universe Is My Body

My position, and the position of perennial wisdom, is that we arise from "here," and "here" is intrinsically intelligent. Consciousness isn't an accidental by-product of matter; matter and consciousness are both attributes of "here." The apple isn't stapled onto the apple tree; it is a natural manifestation of it. Some of the kids in this confirmation class, however, would have none of it.

"What you're saying, Rabbi, makes no sense to me," another young woman said as she stood up. "Look," she said pointing to her body, "this is me. Just this. I'm not a part of anything; I am who I am, and who I am is this!"

"I'm not denying that you are your body," I said, "I'm only suggesting you are more than your body as well. Will you humor me for a moment and answer some questions?"

"Sure."

"Thanks. So we agree you are your body. Can we agree that your lungs are part of your body and that if we suddenly removed them from your body, you'd die?"

"OK."

"What is the function of your lungs?"

"They get rid of carbon dioxide and take in oxygen and get it to the cells of the body."

"Does your body make the oxygen your lungs need?"

"No, oxygen is produced by trees and plants and the ocean through photosynthesis."

"OK. So if there were no trees or plants or oceans, there would be no oxygen, and if there is no oxygen, your lungs couldn't do their job and you would die."

"Pretty much."

"So why not admit that trees and plants and the oceans are as essential to you as your lungs? Why not recognize them as parts of your body as well? Don't answer. I'm not trying to trick you. Just consider it. Of course, trees, plants, and oceans don't exist in isolation; they need the earth and sky, so these too are part of your body. As you said a moment ago, photosynthesis is essential to our survival, so the sun is absolutely necessary and should also be understood as a part of your body no less so than your lungs, heart, or brain. The sun is where it is in relation to the earth because our solar system is the way it is, and our solar system is the way it is because our galaxy is the way it is, and our galaxy ... you see where this is going? The entire universe is your body!"

"Damn, I'm huge!" a boy called out from the back of the room.

"More huge still," I said scanning the class to identify him. "Beyond the visible universe is dark matter and dark energy, the invisible structure and dynamism of reality, and—and now I'm leaving the realm of science for the realm of religion—and beyond all this, but in no way separate or other than all this is God, the infinite field of creativity in which the universe is happening. The Hindus have a saying that gets to the heart of who we are. In Sanskrit, it's *Tat tvam asi*; in English, You are That! You are the entirety of being and becoming. You are an expression of the infinite just like an apple is an expression of the apple tree."

Two Questions, One Answer

By now you should have noticed that the answer to *Where did I come from?* is intimately connected to the question *Who am I?* In fact, who you are and where you come from share the same answer from opposite directions.

In my conversation with the young woman in confirmation class, we moved outward from the smaller self, the physical self, to the cosmic or divine Self, and did so in a manner that I hope made clear to both her and you that there is no separation between the two. You are God, and God is you.

Now reverse the direction and move from the infinite to the finite and you see where you came from. You came from the very infinite reality that you are right here and now. The apple comes from the apple tree and is the apple tree; the wave comes from the ocean and is the ocean; you come from God and are God—just not all of God or ocean or apple tree.

Our first question leads us out from self to Self, from the finite to the infinite. Our second question leads us back from Self to self, from the infinite to the finite.

When you answer the question *Where did I come from?* with the realization that I came from here, and you come to understand that "here" is the result of 13.8 billion years of evolutionary creativity, you come to know that "I belong here" is an expression of this creativity.

The alienation of self and other, person and planet, ends. You suddenly realize that you are the way God cares for the world you encounter. You are the way God feeds the hungry, clothes the naked, frees the captive, and heals the sick. God is the hungry, the naked, the captive, and the ill that you serve. This is what Jesus reveals when he says, "I was hungry and you fed me, I was thirsty and you gave me drink, I was a stranger and you welcomed me, I was naked and you clothed me, I was sick and you took care of me, I was imprisoned and you visited me" (Matthew 25:35–36). This is what he meant when he said, "What you do for the least of these, you do to me" (Matthew 25:40, 25:45).

When you answer the question *Where did I come from?* with "I am alien," you are prevented from realizing the greater you, the organic you, the you that is the universe manifest as you in this moment and in this place. When you answer the question with "I belong," you quickly move beyond the isolated egoic "I" to the "I" of universe and then to the "I" of God, the eternal Subject that is all the objects we perceive around and within us.

1 Every element of reality is a manifestation of God.

2 God is both "inferior," that is, the least inclusive, and "superior," the most inclusive. God is Life manifest in and as the living. There is nothing alien to God and nothing alienating to the godly.

3 Many of us are trained to think of God as Father, the creator, but God is also Mother, the womb from which all things emerge. This teaching balances the previous one: God is not only the substance of reality, but its source as well. God is the "highest," the most inclusive: there is nothing that is other than God.

4 God is every pearl and also the string, that which binds us together as a single strand. Religions often seek to divide us into competing camps, but God knows no divisions, only the nonduality of each thing (each pearl) as a manifestation of the One Thing, God.

5 God is not only the beings of the world, but the doings as well. Indeed, there is nothing static, nothing fixed and unchanging; nouns are necessary to grammar but not to reality. There are only verbs, only happenings, doings, be-*ings*. God is the activity of the universe, and besides activity there is nothing else.

6 God is womb and seed, source and substance. God is eternal Life forever birthing, dying, and rebirthing within a birthless and deathless whole. In the Bible we learn that God is a verb, *Ehyeh* (Exodus 3:14), the Is-*ing* of all reality. Whenever you make a noun of God, you are making an idol. Look carefully and you will see that the idols you worship are in fact products of your own imagination, reflecting your lesser self back to you. When you worship an idol—an *ism*, creed, ideology, or theology—you are always worshipping yourself.

Earth, water, fire, air, ether, mind, intellect, and
personality—
this is the eightfold division of My Manifested Nature.[1]
This is My inferior Nature;
but distinct from this, O Valiant One!
know that My Superior Nature
is the very Life which sustains the universe.[2]
It is the womb of all being;
for I am That by whom the worlds were created
and shall be dissolved....
There is nothing higher than Me;[3]
all is strung upon Me as rows of pearls upon a thread....[4]
I am the Fluidity in water, the Light in the sun
and in the moon.
I am the mystic syllable OM in the Vedic scriptures,
the Sound in ether, the Virility in humanity.
I am the Fragrance of earth, the Brilliance of fire.
I am the Life Force in all beings....[5]
I am the eternal Seed of being;[6]
I am the Intelligence of the intelligent,
the Splendor of the resplendent.
(BHAGAVAD GITA 7:4–10, BHAGAVAD GITA: ANNOTATED & EXPLAINED, PP. 59, 61)

7 God is all that is and more. This more is the unseen, the unknowable, pure potential. Take care not to reduce God to nature, and take care not to separate nature from God. Nature is the face of God visible to us through our senses and technologies. God includes and transcends the world we can know.

8 We are not conscious of our place of abiding because we are only partially conscious of who we truly are. We are like waves imagining a world without oceans. We are like sunlight imagining a world without suns. We insist on being "other"—other than God, other than nature, other than our neighbor. But there is no "other," there is only the One.

9 God is greater than the sum of God's parts. God is Brahman, Vishnu, and Shiva—the Creator of all, the Preserver of all, and the Destroyer of all, yet God is not limited to creating, preserving, and destroying. God is both ocean and wave, and that quality of wetness that embraces and transcends them both. This is what is meant by "outside," the endless more of God.

10 When you rest in God, you rest in your truest nature, your truest Self. When you rest in God, you realize you are the image of God, God reflected in time and space. When you rest in God, you realize that you are the branch and God the vine (Gospel of John 15:5)—an extension of God in time and space. When you rest in God, you are your Self.

11 God is the source and substance of all things. God is the doing that gives us the sense of being, and the being that seems to be in the process of becoming. There is nothing that isn't This, for This is all there is.

The whole world is pervaded by Me,
yet my form is not seen.
All living things have their being in Me,
yet I am not limited by them.[7]
Nevertheless, they do not consciously abide in Me.[8]
Such is My Divine Sovereignty that
though I, the Supreme Self,
am the cause and upholder of all,
yet I remain outside.[9]
As the mighty wind, though moving everywhere,
has no resting place but space,
so have all these beings no home but Me.[10]

(BHAGAVAD GITA 9:4–6, *BHAGAVAD GITA: ANNOTATED & EXPLAINED*, P. 71)

I am the Father of the universe and its Mother....
I am Life and Death....
I am Death and Immortality;
I am Being and Not-Being.[11]

(BHAGAVAD GITA 9:17–19, *BHAGAVAD GITA: ANNOTATED & EXPLAINED*, P. 73)

12 Religions imagine a zero-sum world of winners and losers, the Chosen and the not chosen, the Saved and the Damned, the True Believer and the Infidel, the Wise and the Ignorant, the Awakened and the Sleeping. In these worlds, God is limited to the superior of the two states. But in the real world, the non-zero world where God is all and transcends all, there are no winners or losers. Every thing is equally God, but not everyone is equally aware of this. To worship God as All is to awaken to God as All, and in that awakening is the great home-coming: at last realizing that God is that in whom you live, and move, and have your being (Acts 17:28).

13 Just as the same lump of clay can take on infinite form and remain itself unchanged, so God takes on infinite form while never being other than God.

I am the same to all beings.
I favor none, and I hate none.
But those who worship Me devotedly,
they live in Me, and I in them.[12]
(BHAGAVAD GITA 9:29, *BHAGAVAD GITA: ANNOTATED & EXPLAINED*, P. 75)

Behold My celestial forms,
by hundreds and thousands,
various in kind, in color, and in shape.
Behold the Powers of Nature:
fire, earth, wind, and sky;
the sun, the heavens, the moon, the stars;
all the forces of vitality and of healing;
and the roving winds.
See the myriad wonders revealed to none but you.
Here, in Me living as one....
behold the whole universe,
movable and immovable,
and anything else that you would see.[13]
(BHAGAVAD GITA 11:5–7, *BHAGAVAD GITA: ANNOTATED & EXPLAINED*, P. 87)

14   This is the Self speaking. Can you imagine yourself speaking like this? Seeing God in all things is a step toward awakening. Seeing all things in God is another. You might begin with seeing God in all and then progress to seeing all in God. Or you might begin with seeing all in God and then progress to seeing God in all. In the end there is no first step, next step; there is only arriving at the place of knowing in which you rest—albeit unconsciously—even now.

15   The eighth-century Indian philosopher Shankara wrote in his poem the *Vivekachudamani*:
> The world is an illusion.
> Only Brahman [God] is real.
> Brahman is the world.

Many on the spiritual path come to accept the first two stanzas of this verse: the world is *maya*, a magician's illusion, unworthy of our care and attention. Only God is worthy of our engagement. But Shankara moves beyond the dualism of God and the world, and reveals that God, while greater than the world, is not alien to the world. The world is the play (*lila* in Sanskrit) of God. When we learn to play in the world, we discover God playing as the world.

O Almighty God!
I see in You the powers of Nature,
the various Creatures of the world....
I see You, infinite in form,
with, as it were, faces, eyes, and limbs everywhere;
no beginning, no middle, no end;
O Lord of the Universe, whose Form is universal![14]
(BHAGAVAD GITA 11:15–16, *BHAGAVAD GITA: ANNOTATED & EXPLAINED*, P. 89)

The human body is the playground of the Self;
and that which knows the activities of Matter,
sages call the Self.
I am the Omniscient Self
that abides in the playground of Matter;
knowledge of Matter and of the all-knowing Self is wisdom.[15]
(BHAGAVAD GITA 13:1–2, *BHAGAVAD GITA: ANNOTATED & EXPLAINED*, P. 105)

16 Note it is bliss that is immortal and not you. The limited "you" identified with your particular physical and psychological form is temporary. It is but a wave in the ocean, rising and then falling, and never to
rise again. It is the waving that is eternal and not the wave. Bliss is
eternal because bliss is the waving of the universe, it is the quality of
lila, divine play, that is the nature of God as that which creates and
that which is created.

17 While God is unaffected by the world, God nonetheless delights in
the world. Imagine yourself watching a very scary horror movie. You
chose to attend the film because it's scary and because there is delight
to be had in being scared. You know what you're watching isn't as real
as you are, yet you suspend disbelief in order to enjoy the film. When
the movie is over, so is the fear it generated, and you return to being
yourself.

   The same is true of God. God knows that the world is God's own
play but suspends this knowledge in order to play more joyfully. When
the game ends—when you die, when the universe dies—God is no less
God for having died in and as the world. To the extent you identify
with your character alone, you are needlessly frightened. To the extent
you identify with the Absolute alone, you live without affectation in
a state that is needlessly cold and emotionless. The key is to see both
the relative and the absolute as God, and thus scream in terror at the
scary parts, grieve unrestrainedly at the sad parts, and laugh freely at
the funny parts, neither holding back nor holding on.

18 The presence of God is in your own heart. The Way of God no less
so: "It is not in the heavens, that you should say, 'Who among us can
go up to the heavens and get it for us and impart it to us, that we may
observe it?' Neither is it beyond the sea, that you should say, 'Who
among us can cross to the other side of the sea and get it for us and
impart it to us, that we may observe it?' No, the thing is very close to
you, in your mouth and in your heart, to observe it" (Deuteronomy
30:12–14).

I will speak to you now
of that great Truth which you ought to know,
since by its means you will win immortal bliss;[16]
That which is without beginning,
the Eternal Spirit which dwells in Me,
neither with form nor yet without it.
Everywhere are Its hands and Its feet,
everywhere It has eyes that see, heads that think,
and mouths that speak;
everywhere It listens; It dwells in all the worlds;
It envelops them all.
Beyond the senses,
It yet shines through every sense perception.
Bound to nothing, It yet sustains everything.
Unaffected by the Qualities, It still enjoys them all.[17]
It is within all beings, yet outside;
motionless yet moving; too subtle to be perceived;
far away yet always near.
In all beings undivided, yet living in division,
It is the upholder of all, Creator and Destroyer alike;
It is the Light of lights, beyond the reach of darkness ...
the Presence in the hearts of all.[18]
(BHAGAVAD GITA 13:12–17, *BHAGAVAD GITA: ANNOTATED & EXPLAINED*, P. 107)

19 Saint Augustine is warning you not to mistake the menu for the meal. The word "river" is not wet, and the word "God" is not That to which it refers. Because God is the eternal Subject, and all names refer to objects, no name can speak of God. God is the ineffable, the unnameable. You cannot speak of God, though you can speak to God. You speak to God when you realize God in, with, and as all reality. Then you are speaking not so much to the other, but to the Greater manifest in and as the other.

20 Yet names do have power. Allah, God, YHVH, El, Tao, Brahman, Great Spirit, Krishna, and the rest of the menu of names we use for Reality awaken something in you. Just as the name of your favorite food may trigger a hunger for that food, so the name of God in any of its forms may trigger a desire for awakening and unity.

21 In the previous text, Krishna told you that God is present in your heart, and now Saint Augustine tells you that there is a word there as well. What is this word? It is a question: "Now there was a great wind, so strong that it was splitting mountains and shattering boulders before the Ineffable, but the Ineffable was not in the wind; and after the wind an earthquake, but the Ineffable was not in the earthquake; and after the earthquake a fire, but the Ineffable was not in the fire; and after the fire a sound of sheer silence. When Elijah heard it, he wrapped his face in his mantle and went out and stood at the entrance of the cave. Then there came a voice to him that said, "What are you doing here, Elijah?" (1 Kings 19:11–13). The God-question in your heart is always this: What are you doing here at this very moment? Are you acting for God and godliness or for self and selfishness?

Look, I utter a word when I say, "God";
what a short word I have uttered,
three letters, one syllable!
Is that really all that God is,
just three letters and one syllable?
Or, rather, is what is understood by these letters
cherished all the more insofar as the word
is so insignificant?[19]
What happened in your heart when you heard "God"?
What happened in my heart when I was saying "God"?[20]
Something great and supreme occurred to our mind;
it soars utterly above and beyond
every changeable, carnal, and merely natural creature....
So what is that thing in your heart,
when you are fixing your mind on some substance
that is living, everlasting, almighty, infinite,
present everywhere, everywhere whole and entire,
nowhere confined?
When you fix your mind on all this,
there is a word about God in your heart.[21]

(SAINT AUGUSTINE, HOMILIES ON THE GOSPEL OF JOHN 1.8, *SAINT AUGUSTINE OF HIPPO: SELECTIONS FROM CONFESSIONS AND OTHER ESSENTIAL WRITINGS—ANNOTATED & EXPLAINED, PP. 71, 73*)

22 Anything you say about God is less than God. All speech is about something; God is about nothing. God isn't and cannot become an object. God is the eternal Subject, the I that speaks but can never be spoken about. And yet we cannot help but try. Just know that what you say about God isn't God.

23 As the Zen teaching puts it, the different names are like fingers pointing to the moon. But there is a difference between pointing to the moon and naming Truth or God. No one murders another because she says "luna" rather than "moon," yet people do kill one another because we insist on using different names for God. This is a madness that stems from ignorance and arrogance: ignorance in that we do not experience the real God beyond naming, and arrogance in that we imagine God can be named and we can name It.

24 No name can contain that which is beyond naming. Any sound you make—Tao, God, Allah, Brahman—is just noise if the name is meant to be more than a placeholder for that which is beyond all names.

So what are we to say about God?
If you have fully grasped what you want to say,
it isn't God.
If you have been able to comprehend it,
you have comprehended something else instead of God.
If you think you have been able to comprehend,
your thoughts have deceived you.
So God isn't this, if this is what you have understood;
but if God is this, then you haven't understood it.
So what is it you want to say,
seeing you haven't been able to understand it?[22]

(SAINT AUGUSTINE, SERMON 52.16, *SAINT AUGUSTINE OF HIPPO: SELECTIONS FROM CONFESSIONS AND OTHER ESSENTIAL WRITINGS—ANNOTATED & EXPLAINED*, P. 73)

Truth is one. Different people call it by different names.[23]

(RIG VEDA 1:64:46)

The Tao that can be spoken is not the eternal Tao
The name that can be named is not the eternal name
The nameless is the origin of Heaven and Earth
The named is the mother of myriad things
Thus, constantly without desire, one observes its essence
Constantly with desire, one observes its manifestations
These two emerge together but differ in name
The unity is said to be the mystery
Mystery of mysteries, the door to all wonders[24]

(TAO TE CHING, CHAPTER 1, *TAO TE CHING: ANNOTATED & EXPLAINED*, P. 3)

25 Why walk humbly with *your* God? Micah isn't talking about God, the Ineffable, but your idea of God, the idol you create with your words and worship in your mind. Walk humbly with this, knowing that it isn't God but a reflection of your own egoic projection of God.

26 When you are divided within yourself, that is, when you identify with the self rather than Self, you are blind to the presence of God. Only when you are whole can you recognize the greater Whole that is with you and that is you.

27 When you awake to God within and as yourself, you awake to God within and as everything.

28 Everything is a mirror reflecting the face of God, though no two reflections ever look alike. This is the nature of the One who is the many.

29 The differences among people are real, but not absolute. They have a purpose: to spark curiosity and encourage meeting. While it is commonplace for us to fear the stranger, what God wants is for us to love the stranger as oneself (Leviticus 19:34), that is, to love the stranger as a part of oneself, the Self that is God.

30 There is a hierarchy among humanity: the wise, the God-conscious, are "higher" than the foolish, who are unconscious of God: "The wise have eyes in their heads, whereas the foolish walk in darkness. [But] the same fate awaits them both" (Ecclesiastes 2:14). The eyes of the wise are open. They see the Divine in, with, and as all reality, and because of this they are better able to navigate the contingences of life. But this doesn't mean they escape these contingencies. The wise and the foolish face the same challenges and the same end—death. Be wise not to win a reward upon death; be wise in order to live more gracefully while alive.

Walk humbly with your God.[25]

(MICAH 6:8)

Where there are three they are godless.
Where there is one alone, I say, I myself am with you.[26]
Split the wood and I am there;
pick up the stone and you will find me there.[27]

(PAPYRUS OXYRHYNCHUS 1, *THE LOST SAYINGS OF JESUS: TEACHINGS FROM ANCIENT CHRISTIAN, JEWISH, GNOSTIC AND ISLAMIC SOURCES— ANNOTATED & EXPLAINED*, P. 37)

God spoke to Israel, saying,
"Though you have seen Me in various forms,
I am still one, the ever-same God."
Rabbi Levi taught,
"God appeared to the Israelites as a mirror,
and each face that looked saw itself reflected back to it."[28]

(*PESIKTA DE-RAV KAHANA* 109)

O humanity,
We created you from a single pair of a male and a female,
and made you into races and tribes
so that you may come to know each other.[29]
Verily the most honored of you in the sight of God
is the most God-conscious of you.[30]

(QUR'AN 49:13, *THE QUR'AN AND SAYINGS OF PROPHET MUHAMMAD. SELECTIONS ANNOTATED & EXPLAINED*, P. 143)

31 The predecessor of God? What can come before God, the birthless and deathless One of which you and all life are a part? What precedes God is what precedes your thoughts about God. Lao Tzu is showing you how to speak humbly about your god. "It *seems* to be the source of all things. It *seems* to exist." The use of the word "seems" reminds him, and us, that all this is mere talk and appearance. If there is something, can you say it came from somewhere? Can you say the Tao has parents? As long as you operate with words, images, or language of any kind, you are trapped in a logic that doesn't apply to Reality. God didn't come from anywhere; God is everywhere. And God is you. You didn't come from anywhere. You are here, or, perhaps more accurately, here is you.

The Tao is empty
When utilized, it is not filled up
So deep! It seems to be the source of all things
It blunts the sharpness
Unravels the knots
Dims the glare
Mixes the dusts
So indistinct! It seems to exist
I do not know whose offspring it is
Its image is the predecessor of God[31]

(TAO TE CHING, CHAPTER 4, *TAO TE CHING: ANNOTATED & EXPLAINED*, P. 9)

32 The only language that points to Truth is the language of paradox that ultimately destroys the logic of language altogether. How can you look at what cannot be seen? How can you listen to what cannot be heard? How can you reach for that which cannot be held? How can the formless have form? So all saying is reduced to sputtering. Sadly, we all too often enshrine our sputterings and insist that we accept what was never meant to be accepted.

33 The enigmatic is the liberating paradox of authentic God-talk. Knowing that God cannot be spoken about, and yet knowing we are compelled to speak nonetheless, the wise use words to undermine words. They use words to reduce you to silence. This is the genius of authentic spiritual teaching: rather than provide you with a verbal foundation on which to build your theology, perennial wisdom pulls the verbal rug out from under you over and over and over again, until at last you are reduced to silence and all theology ends. With the ending of theology comes the realization of God. When you no longer focus on your idea of what should be, you can at least see what is.

34 Though you cannot name the Nameless (yet this too is a name— drop it!), you can work with Reality nonetheless. You don't have to name God to act godly.

Look at it, it cannot be seen
It is called colorless
Listen to it, it cannot be heard
It is called noiseless
Reach for it, it cannot be held
It is called formless
These three cannot be completely unraveled
So they are combined into one
Above it, not bright
Below it, not dark
Continuing endlessly, cannot be named
It returns back into nothingness
Thus it is called the form of the formless
The image of the imageless[32]
This is called enigmatic[33]
Confront it, its front cannot be seen
Follow it, its back cannot be seen
Wield the Tao of the ancients
To manage the existence of today[34]
One can know the ancient beginning
It is called the Tao Axiom

(TAO TE CHING, CHAPTER 14, *TAO TE CHING: ANNOTATED & EXPLAINED*, P. 29)

35 All life arises from the womb of the Life. Tao is that womb, the Mother of us all.

36 Once again, Lao Tzu uses his words humbly, conditionally, as pointers to the Ineffable rather than as idols to be enshrined and worshipped.

37 Tao is not static. Like the biblical names *YHVH* (the *Is-ing* of all reality) and *Ehyeh* (I will be), Tao is a verb doing double duty as a noun. Forget this and you misunderstand the world around and within you. Nouns are static, fixed, and yet there is nothing in nature that is not fluid and flowing. Every seven years almost every cell of your body has died, and yet "you" still exist. This is what is meant by passing. Like a wave in the ocean, you arise and then recede, returning to the ocean. "You" never arise again, yet the ocean keeps waving. What passes for you is the name only. You still respond to the name you were called when you were four, and yet there is nothing left of that four-year-old you except the name and the stories you tell about it. When you identify with the story, you lose contact with your true Self, the flowing divine energy of Tao or God. There is nothing wrong with telling stories of your past; just don't allow them to define who you are in the present.

38 "She" is Divine Wisdom, *Chochmah*, Logos, Tao, the activity of the Divine that is the happening of all that happens. She does not leave Herself, because there is nothing happening outside Herself.

39 Friends of God and prophets of God are those who awaken to Wisdom, the Way of God within and without. A friend of God is one who furthers God's ends: creating a world rooted in justice, compassion, and humility. The prophets of God are those who warn you when you are acting from ignorance and undermining the world you are called to create. A lover of God—or better, God's beloveds—are those who reside in Wisdom, who take refuge in the Way of God by acting godly. Befriend the friends of God and support their efforts. Seek out the prophets of God and heed their warnings. Make yourself a beloved for God by opening to Wisdom and resting in Her.

There is something formlessly created
Born before Heaven and Earth
So silent!
So ethereal!
Independent and changeless
Circulating and ceaseless
It can be regarded as the mother of the world[35]
I do not know its name
Identifying it, I call it *Tao*[36]
Forced to describe it, I call it great
Great means passing
Passing means receding
Receding means returning
Therefore the Tao is great[37]

(TAO TE CHING, CHAPTER 25, *TAO TE CHING: ANNOTATED & EXPLAINED*, P. 51)

Although She is one,
She does all things.
Without leaving Herself
She renews all things.[38]
Generation after generation She slips into holy souls,
Making them friends of God, and prophets;
for God loves none more
than they who dwell with Wisdom.[39]

(WISDOM OF SOLOMON 7:27–28, *THE DIVINE FEMININE IN BIBLICAL WISDOM
LITERATURE: SELECTIONS ANNOTATED & EXPLAINED*, P. 33)

40 The Tao, too, does all things without being other than she is. Tao and *Chochmah* are one; Tao and Logos are one; Tao and Wisdom are one.

41 The work of Tao is the happening of the world, the clothing of potentiality in actuality, the moving of possibility into probability.

42 Twice Lao Tzu reminds us that Tao does not rule over us. There is no abeyance to Tao, no worship of Tao, only wise participation in Tao. You participate wisely when you identify the current of the river and swim with it. You participate wisely when you study the grain in wood and cut with it. You may swim against the current and cut against the grain—Tao allows all things—but the result is poor and you exhaust yourself needlessly.

43 From angels to insects, the same energy manifests. Do not imagine one is high and the other low; the distinction doesn't exist in God. Know instead that some are more knowing and others less knowing. The more knowing embrace the lesser, knowing all is God. The least knowing ignore the more knowing, being incapable of perceiving beyond their own level. Be careful of the middle knowers. They often seek to rule over the lower and worship the higher—both traits leading to disaster.

44 Nothing is hidden from God because nothing is other than God. God doesn't read your mind; God is your mind. God doesn't survey your thoughts—God is the thought, the thinker, and thinking itself.

The great Tao is like a flood
It can flow to the left or to the right
The myriad things depend on it for life, but it never stops
It achieves its work, but does not take credit[40]
It clothes and feeds myriad things, but does not rule over
them[41]
Ever desiring nothing
It can be named insignificant
Myriad things return to it but it does not rule over them[42]
It can be named great
Even in the end, it does not regard itself as great
That is how it can achieve its greatness

(TAO TE CHING, CHAPTER 34, *TAO TE CHING: ANNOTATED & EXPLAINED*, P. 69)

All beings,
from the holiest angel to the tiniest mosquito,
exist by virtue of God's truth.[43]
Since God is Self-knowing
and recognizes God's greatness, majesty, and truth,
God knows everything.
There is nothing hidden from God.[44]

(MOSES MAIMONIDES, *MISHNEH TORAH*, LAWS OF FOUNDATIONS OF THE TORAH
2:9, *MAIMONIDES—ESSENTIAL TEACHINGS ON JEWISH FAITH AND ETHICS:
THE BOOK OF KNOWLEDGE AND THE THIRTEEN PRINCIPLES OF FAITH—
ANNOTATED & EXPLAINED*, P. 13)

45 The Divine Truth as it is *is* reality itself. You may imagine differently. You may imagine a truth that is other than the Whole, and that separates you from the Whole. You may imagine a truth that promotes your species, your tribe, your religion, your ethnic group, your race, your gender above all others, when in fact Truth is all of these and none of this.

46 In order to know a thing, you have to first separate yourself from it. You know only objects, and you know them as other. Even when you seek to know yourself, you do so first by separating the knower from the known. You make an object of the self that you might examine it. But who is examining whom? Can the self be divided from itself and still be that self? God knows no division. God knows the Whole and the part, the One and the many, and knows them all as God. Even the act of knowing is part of God's "god-ing." God is a verb, reality is God god-ing.

47 What Maimonides says of the nature of God and God's truth is what all the great saints and sages of every tradition say about Truth: silence alone does it justice.

The Holy One, blessed be,
recognizes and knows divine truth as it is.[45]
God does not know by means of an external knowledge
that is separate from God,
the way we know things,
because we and our knowledge are not identical.
But as for the Creator, blessed be, God's knowledge and
existence are absolutely One.
God is the Knower, the Known,
and the Knowledge itself—One.[46]
The mouth has not the power to verbalize this adequately,
nor the ear to comprehend this,
nor the heart to understand it fully.[47]

(MOSES MAIMONIDES, *MISHNEH TORAH*, LAWS OF FOUNDATIONS OF THE TORAH
2:10, *MAIMONIDES—ESSENTIAL TEACHINGS ON JEWISH FAITH AND ETHICS:
THE BOOK OF KNOWLEDGE AND THE THIRTEEN PRINCIPLES OF FAITH—
ANNOTATED & EXPLAINED*, P. 13)

48 There can be nothing other than the Whole, and nothing outside of it. Nothing can be like God because nothing can be other than God.

49 Do not imagine "perfect" in opposition to "imperfect." God is perfect in the sense of whole, complete, lacking nothing. When Jesus taught, "Be perfect as your Father in heaven is perfect" (Matthew 5:48), he wasn't commanding you to be morally perfect or without flaw, but to be whole as God is whole, to see imperfection as the complement to perfection, to see the broken as necessary to the unbroken, and to know that all of this is God.

God is One in His Essence without partner,
singular without likeness to anything,
absolutely independent with no opposite,
solitary with no peer.[48]
God is beginninglessly pre-eternal with nothing before God,
unchanging and eternal with no beginning.
God's Existence endures with no terminus.
God is perpetual, without end.
God is all-sustaining, with no cessation,
everlasting, never passing.
God was and shall remain characterized
by all qualities of perfection.[49]
God does not come to an end with the passing of time.
Indeed, God is the First, the Last, the Manifest, the Hidden,
and God knows all things.
(AL-GHAZALI, BOOK 1: THE FIRST FOUNDATION, *GHAZALI ON THE PRINCIPLES OF
ISLAMIC SPIRITUALITY: SELECTIONS FROM* THE FORTY FOUNDATIONS OF RELIGION—
ANNOTATED & EXPLAINED, P. 11)

50   How could it be otherwise? If God is all that is and all that is happening, then all that happens is God's will. But do not imagine that
things happen according to a plan. God is infinite possibility actualizing
as everything and its opposite. When good happens, it isn't a reward;
when bad happens, it isn't a punishment; it is simply good happening
and bad happening because the situation requires something to happen and you then decide to label that something good or bad. When
things happen to you, resist spinning a story about why they happen.
Resist the temptation to see yourself as hero or villain, saint or sinner,
God's beloved or God's betrayer. Just see yourself as you are: God
being you as only you can be in this moment.

51   God is just, but do not imagine God's justice to mirror your sense of
right and wrong. God's justice is the same for all: everything befalls
everyone over time. The timing differs for each of us, and it may
appear that some are winners and others losers. But in the end the
same fate awaits us all.

God wills all existent things, directing all that occurs.
Nothing transpires in the physical or spiritual worlds,
whether it be little or much, small or large,
good or bad, beneficial or harmful,
belief or disbelief, knowledge or ignorance,
victory or loss, increase or decrease,
obedience or disobedience,
except by divine decree, destining, wisdom, and willing.[50]
For whatever God wills is, and whatever God does not will
is not.

(AL-GHAZALI, BOOK 1: THE FIFTH FOUNDATION, *GHAZALI ON THE PRINCIPLES OF
ISLAMIC SPIRITUALITY: SELECTIONS FROM* THE FORTY FOUNDATIONS OF RELIGION—
ANNOTATED & EXPLAINED, P. 21)

There is nothing in existence other than God,
except that it is created by God's action,
flowing from God's justice in the best,
most perfect, complete, and just way.[51]

(AL-GHAZALI, BOOK 1: THE EIGHTH FOUNDATION, *GHAZALI ON THE PRINCIPLES
OF ISLAMIC SPIRITUALITY: SELECTIONS FROM* THE FORTY FOUNDATIONS
OF RELIGION—ANNOTATED & EXPLAINED, P. 29)

52 There is only one universe, and there is only one administrator, and you flow from these the way an oak tree "flows" from an acorn, and an apple "flows" from an apple tree.

53 You are not immortal. You—the "you" you take yourself to be when you forget the "you" you really are—are dying from the moment of your birth. There is no escaping the passing of time. The question is how will you use the time you have? If you use the time wisely, you spend time scattering the clouds that mask the truth. When the sky is clear, you will know that all is God. Then when the clouds return—and they always return—you can simply enjoy them, knowing that they, too, are God.

You must now at last perceive
of what universe you are a part,
and of what administrator of the universe
your existence flows from,[52]
and that a limit of time is fixed for you,
which if you do not use for clearing away
the clouds from your mind,
time will go and you will go,
and it will never return.[53]

(MARCUS AURELIUS, THE MEDITATIONS OF MARCUS AURELIUS:
SELECTIONS ANNOTATED & EXPLAINED, P. 141)

54 Jesus's metaphor of light arising from itself is the nondual metaphor of the sun and its rays. The sun produces light from itself. God, the Absolute with whom there is no second, is the ultimate source and substance of all reality. You arise from God, in God.

55 Just as the sun is revealed through its rays, so God is revealed through you. Whatever you do, for good or for ill, reveals an aspect of God, for there is nothing other than God. God is not good or evil; God is the reality that makes good and evil possible. The actualization of either is up to you. When you act justly, kindly, and humbly, you reveal the goodness God contains. When you act unjustly, cruelly, and self-ishly, you reveal the wickedness God contains. "I create good and I create evil, I, the Eternal One, do all these things" (Isaiah 45:7), and the Eternal One does them through the choices you make about the actions you take.

56 Though the rays of sunlight are nothing but the sun, they cannot claim to be the sun itself. Hence Jesus speaks of us as the children of the Father, the offspring of the Source. Do not play God; only know that God is playing you.

57 What is the sign of your divinity? Your actions—"By their fruits you shall know them" (Matthew 7:16). And what are your actions? Your doing and your non-doing, your movement and your rest.

Do not romanticize doing and non-doing. They are nothing but the everyday and the ordinary. As explained by Martin Buber in *The Way of Man according to the Teachings of Hasidism*, "It is here where we have been placed, exactly here and nowhere else [that the truth of your existence] may be found.... Here is what I encounter day after day. Here I meet my daily demands. Only here is my essential task. Here is the fulfillment of my existence that is available to me" (p. 32).

Jesus said:
If they ask you,
"Where are you from?"
reply to them,
"We have come from the place
where light is produced from itself.[54]
It came and revealed itself in their image."[55]
If they ask you,
"Are you it?"
reply to them,
"We are its Children.
We are chosen ones of the living Father."[56]
If they ask you,
"What is the sign within you of your Father?"
reply to them,
"It is movement. It is rest."[57]
(GOSPEL OF THOMAS 50, *THE GOSPEL OF THOMAS: ANNOTATED & EXPLAINED*, P. 65)

58 Salome senses there is something more to Jesus than appears on the surface. Jesus visits her like any other man and shares a meal with her like any other traveler, but there is something about him that nags at her. You too sense this something more when in the presence of one who lives the likeness of God in the ordinariness of everyday actions.

59 What Jesus reveals to Salome is cryptic: he comes from that which is not other than he is. He doesn't say, "I have come from God," or "I am the Son of God," for to put it this way would separate Jesus from the rest of us. Jesus is a mirror, not a measuring stick. He reflects your true nature back to you that you might see yourself as he sees you: a manifestation of God.

60 If Jesus is the only child of the One, then wholeness is impossible. If Jesus is only the child of God, then you are right to worship him rather than to put on the Mind of Christ and become him (1 Corinthians 2:13–16). Salome wants to follow Jesus; Jesus wants Salome to wake up. You wake up when you realize that what is true of Jesus is true of you as well: "I and the Father are One" (John 10:30).

61 What is a whole heart? A heart that accepts all emotions: the pleasant and the unpleasant, the good and helpful, as well as the selfish and hurtful. Such a heart knows its own shadow, its own dark secrets, and because it knows them it is free from acting on them. Such a heart can love both neighbor (Leviticus 19:18) and stranger (Leviticus 19:34), for nothing and no one is alien to it.

62 What is a whole breath? One that is not frantic with fear but calm and tranquil. Such a heart and such a breath belong to those who know that they "come into being from One who is the same." And knowing this, they love the One as the many and serve the many with all they have and who they are.

Salome asked Jesus:
Who are you, man?
As though coming from someone,
you have come onto my couch and eaten from my table.[58]
Jesus replied:
I am he who comes into being from one who is the same.[59]
Some of the things of my Father have been given to me.
[Salome said:] I am your disciple.
Therefore I say that if one is unified
one will be filled with light,
but if one is divided one will be filled with darkness.[60]
(GOSPEL OF THOMAS 61, *THE GOSPEL OF THOMAS: ANNOTATED & EXPLAINED*, P. 81)

You shall love the Ineffable One, your God,
with a whole heart,[61]
a whole breath,
and with all you have and are.[62]
(DEUTERONOMY 6:5)

63 God is both form and formlessness, both what is and what isn't, both what you can perceive and what cannot be perceived by anyone. God is all, and God is nothing. And because this is so, there are many ways to experience and understand the Divine. For some, the formless is best: the tao that can be named is not the eternal Tao, so stop naming and take comfort in silence. For others, the form is best whether it be a physical image such as a crucifix, an icon, or a statue, or a mental image such as a creed or theology. The issue is not which path to awakening you prefer, but what qualities your path cultivates in you. If your way leads you to compassion and justice, your way is sound. If it leads you to cruelty and selfishness, it is not.

64 If God is all, God can be met in all ways. For some, God is a kindly grandmother; for others, God is a stern schoolmaster. The god you imagine is the god you need at the moment of imagining. Do not fall into the trap of assuming that your god is God, for as the Muslims say, *la ilaha il Allah*, there is no god but God, and this God is, as Ramakrishna says, beyond final description. Do not judge the form of another's worship; note only how the worship forms the other.

65 Whatever form you ascribe to God, know that it is insufficient. The Hindus have a phrase, *neti, neti*, "not this, not that," meaning that just as the ocean is not the wave and yet the wave is nothing but the ocean, so God is not your ideas about God or images of God, even as they are nothing but God.

66 The world is a mirror reflecting the infinite faces of the Divine. When seeing the faces of the world, know that you are seeing God's face. In meditation you no longer look into the mirror, but look out from it knowing that you are all these faces as well.

God with form is as real as God without form.
Do you know what the describing of God
as formless only is like?[63]
It is like playing only a monotone on a flute,
though it has seven holes.
But on the same instrument another plays different melodies.
Likewise, in how many ways the believers in a Personal
God enjoy the Divine!
They enjoy God through many different attitudes:
the serene attitude, the attitude of a servant,
a friend, a mother, a husband, or a lover.[64]
The nature of Brahman cannot be described.
About It one remains silent.
Who can explain the Infinite in words?
However high a bird may soar,
there are regions higher still.[65]

(RAMAKRISHNA, *SELECTIONS FROM THE GOSPEL OF SRI RAMAKRISHNA:*
ANNOTATED & EXPLAINED, P. 141)

God Himself
has become the universe and all its living beings....
I would see God in meditation ...
and I would see the same God
when my mind came back to the outer world.
When looking at this side of the mirror
I would see Him alone,
and when looking on the reverse side I saw the same God.[66]

(RAMAKRISHNA, *SELECTIONS FROM THE GOSPEL OF SRI RAMAKRISHNA:*
ANNOTATED & EXPLAINED, P. 161)

67 God cannot be one thing or the other, but only one thing and the other, and always in equal proportion. A pitcher of water and a thimble of water differ only in how much water they contain, but the water itself is the same in both. Do not imagine God is somewhere or some when. God is everywhere and every when: even here, even now.

68 Shankara is speaking from the perspective of the Whole rather than the realization of the part. From the perspective of the ocean, there is nothing but ocean: each wave is nothing but the ocean waving.

69 There is no second in truth, only in your imagination. When you give yourself over to ideas that divide the One from the other—ideas of Chosenness and unchosenness, salvation and damnation, class and caste—you create a false dualism that leads you into a zero-sum game of winners and losers that exhausts you with the phantoms of prize and perdition.

70 "God" and "soul" are both mental constructs, concepts in your mind. There is something greater, the Tao that cannot be named, the God unshackled by theologies, the One without second. It is This that is your true ground and nature. It is This in which you arise, from which you come, to which you belong, and to which you return.

The more God is in all things,
the more God is outside them.
The more God is within,
the more without.[67]
(MEISTER ECKHART, CITED IN ALDOUS HUXLEY, *PERENNIAL PHILOSOPHY*, P. 2)

Brahman is pure existence, pure consciousness, eternal bliss,
beyond action, one without a second.
In Brahman there is no diversity whatsoever.
Brahman is the innermost consciousness,
filled full of endless bliss, infinite, omnipresent,
one without second.
In Brahman there is no diversity.
Brahman cannot be avoided, since it is everywhere.
Brahman cannot be grasped, since it is transcendent.
It cannot be contained, since it contains all things,
It is one without a second.
In Brahman there is no diversity whatsoever....
Brahman is reality itself....[68]
(SHANKARA, *CREST-JEWEL OF DISCRIMINATION*, PP. 110–111)

Behold but One in all things;
it is the second that leads you astray.[69]
(KABIR, CITED IN ALDOUS HUXLEY, *PERENNIAL PHILOSOPHY*, P. 10)

The Ground of God and the Ground of the Soul
are one and the same.[70]
(MEISTER ECKHART, CITED IN ALDOUS HUXLEY, *PERENNIAL PHILOSOPHY*, P. 12)

71 The lover separated from the Beloved is no longer a lover but a longer, and longing for intimacy blinds you to the real divine intimacy that is your everyday reality.

72 When you hunt for God, you pretend that God is other than you and other than where you are. The hunting itself creates the distance between hunter and hunted. The more you seek God, the further God recedes. This is the paradox of organized religion: it promises an intimacy with God but offers an idea of God that, like the horizon, seems to back away from you with every step you take toward it.

73 When the Hebrew prophet Elijah sought God in the tornado, God was not in the tornado. When he sought God in the earthquake, God was not in the earthquake. When he sought God in the fire, God was not in the fire. God is not *in* anything; God is everything. But when Elijah stopped looking for God in anything, the presence of God was known to him as the fragile sound of stillness (1 Kings 19:11–12).

74 If the gate is great, meaning wide, and there are no obstacles to entering it, why do you hesitate? In his masterful parable "Before the Law," Franz Kafka tells of a man who grows old and dies by the gate. At the gate stands a powerful guard who, the man imagined, was stationed there to guard the gate and keep him from passing through it. The man spent his life seeking permission to enter the gate. None was ever granted. With his last breaths the man asks why, after all these decades, no one else has ever come seeking entrance through the gate. The guard tells him that this gate was his alone and that no permission was needed to enter. All that was required was the act of entering itself. The gatekeeper was there to maintain the gate and not to keep him out. The man misunderstood what he saw and was too afraid to enter. Your gate too is open. Do not seek permission to enter; simply pass through it.

The Beloved is all in all; the lover merely veils Him;
The Beloved is all that lives, the lover a dead thing.[71]
(RUMI, CITED IN ALDOUS HUXLEY, *PERENNIAL PHILOSOPHY*, P. 12)

One Nature, perfect and pervading, circulates in all natures.
One Reality, all-comprehensive,
contains within itself all realities....
Like space it knows no boundaries,
Yet it is even here, within us,
ever retaining its serenity and fullness.
It is only when you hunt for it that you lose it;[72]
You cannot take hold of it, but equally you cannot get rid of
it,
And while you do neither, it goes on its own way.
You remain silent and it speaks; you speak and it is dumb;[73]
The great gate of charity is wide open,
with no obstacles before it.[74]
(YUNG-CHIA TA-SHIH, CITED IN ALDOUS HUXLEY, *PERENNIAL PHILOSOPHY*, P. 9)

God is ... One without second,
the Whole without parts.
(MUNDAKA UPANISHAD 3.1.8)

Hear O Israel:
YHVH is Elohim. YHVH is one.
(DEUTERONOMY 6:4)

I am YHVH. There is nothing else.
(ISAIAH 45:5)

75 God is the One and Only, and everything is a part of This. God has no face and yet is every face. God has no qualities and yet is every quality. When you know you are God, when you know God is you, when you know you are everything, and when you know everything is you, then you understand the nature of God's unity. Then you know you come from here, that you belong here, and indeed that you are here.

76 A more standard translation of the Buddhist Heart Sutra uses nouns rather than gerunds: "Form is emptiness. Emptiness is form." But this is misleading. When does form become emptiness, and when does emptiness become form? How does one thing turn into its opposite? Look at this shape:

$$)$$

Is it convex or concave? It is both, depending on which side of the shape you rest your attention. But can something be both convex and concave? Aren't these opposites? Yes and yes. The opposites are part of a singular reality, hence forming does not differ from emptying and emptying does not differ from forming.

God is one, hidden in all beings, all-pervading,
the Self within all selves,
watching over all doing,
dwelling in all being,
the witness, the perceiver,
the single one, free from all qualities.[75]

(SVETASVATARA UPANISHAD 6.11)

Forming is emptying, and emptying is forming;[76]
emptying does not differ from forming;
forming does not differ from emptying;
whatever is forming, that is emptying;
whatever is emptying, that is forming.
The same is true of emotions, perceptions,
compulsions, and consciousness.

(HEART SUTRA)

77 Everything is alive and in flux. Everything is emptying and forming and emptying again. All this activity is the activity of God. It is what God is, for God is what is.

78 Wherever you look, wherever you go, it is God. Whatever you do, whatever you say, it is God. If you act kindly and speak compassionately, it is God. If you act cruelly and speak harshly, it is God. There is no escaping this. God is all there is, and not just what you imagine should be.

This is the heart and challenge of *Advaita*, or nondual teaching. God isn't good or bad; God is the play of good and bad. Think of a magnet and its two poles, one positive, the other negative. Try and remove the negative in order to have a positive-only magnet and you will fail. Learn the true nature of the magnet and its polarity, and you can do wonderful things with it.

Is the magnet something other than its poles? Or is "magnet" the name we give to that unity of positive and negative energies? If you cannot separate the poles from the magnet, why speak of the magnet at all?

Now apply this to "God." "God" is what we call the nondual reality that holds all opposites in a greater unity. The word "God" is not God. It is a grammatical ghost: a necessary fiction for a reality we cannot name. There is no problem with this as long as we know what we are doing. But when we forget that the name is not the reality, we begin to worship the name, to organize into camps around our different names, and ultimately to go to war with the understanding that this is what God wants, for how else can we prove which name is the true name unless we slaughter those who speak the false name? This is the insanity of religion.

Emptying upon emptying!
Emptying upon emptying!
Everything is emptying.[77]
(ECCLESIASTES 1:2, *ECCLESIASTES: ANNOTATED & EXPLAINED*, P. 3)

The Infinite is
below, above, behind, before, to the right, to the left.
I am all this.
This Infinite is the Self.
The Self is below, above, behind, before,
to the right, to the left.
I am all this.
(CHANDOGYA UPANISHAD 2.23–25)

Where can I find You,
and where can I not find You?
Above—only You;
Below—only You;
To the east—only You;
To the west—only You;
To the south—only You;
To the north—only You;
If it is good—it is You;
If it is not—also You;
It is You; It is only You.[78]
(*DUDELE*, RABBI LEVI YITZCHAK OF BERDICHEV)

79 We imagine God to be pristine. We imagine God to be above the mundane, beyond the physical, something that is pure spirit, something formless only. But the reality of God is much larger. God is spirit and matter, the ordinary and the extraordinary, the One and the many, and That which holds them all is something greater still.

Chuang-tzu isn't afraid of this "greater still." He calls it Tao and has no need to protect it from itself by detaching it from the Whole that it is. So, God is the most majestic mountain and the deepest canyon. God is the most brilliant human mind and the most clouded. God is the saint and the sociopath. God is the finest meal and the manure into which it transforms. It cannot be other than this, for God is all this.

Master Eastwall asked Chuang-tzu,
"What we call Tao, where is it?"
"There is no place where it is not."
"Can you be more specific?"
"It's in ants and crickets."
"How can it be so low?"
"It's in grass and weeds."
"But that's even lower!"
"It's in tiles and shards."
"Really, so very low?"
"It's in urine and feces."[79]
Master Eastwall did not respond.
Chuang-tzu said,
"Your questions do not get to the heart of the matter."
(CHUANG-TZU, CHAPTER 22, *CHUANG-TZU: THE TAO OF PERFECT HAPPINESS—
ANNOTATED & EXPLAINED*, P. 133)

80   Sheol is the place of the dead. In biblical times the ancient Hebrews believed that at death all people went to Sheol, and stayed there until the end-times, when bodies would be resurrected and lives judged. Do not imagine that God is heaven only. God is Sheol as well.

81   Darkness and light represent all opposites. God is all of this, and sees it all as Self. Darkness and light are the same to God in that they are both manifestations of God. This is not the same as saying darkness is light and light is darkness. That makes no sense. Knowing that a magnet is both positive and negative is not to pretend that there is no difference between positive and negative. Nondualism is not monism. Monism reduces all things to the same thing, erasing all diversity and difference. Nondualism celebrates difference and affirms diversity. It simply refuses to see this diversity as anything other than the greater unity of a singular Reality.

Where can I escape from Your spirit?
Where can I flee from Your presence?
If I ascend to heaven, You are there.
If I descend into Sheol, You are there.[80]
If I take wing at dawn and come to rest
on the western horizon,
Even there Your hand will guide me;
Your right hand will hold me close.
If I say, "Darkness will conceal me,
and night will hide me from You,"
Dark is not dark for You;
night is as bright as day;
darkness and light are the same.[81]

(PSALM 139:7–12, *THE DIVINE FEMININE IN BIBLICAL WISDOM LITERATURE:
SELECTIONS ANNOTATED & EXPLAINED*, P. 61)

82 This contemporary poem is the mantra of nondualism. Knowing this from the inside, experiencing it as true, is what it is to be awake to God. Acting from it leads you to compassion, justice, and humility.

83 Can this really be so? Can God be it, regardless of what the "it" is? Is everything a manifestation and emanation of the One Thing? This is the question you have to ask yourself. The quality of your life depends upon your answer (and there are only two answers, "yes" and "no"). If you say "no," you will imagine a world in which God is somewhere else and dedicate yourself to a search without a satisfactory conclusion. If you say "yes," you will imagine a world in which God is everywhere, and finding replaces searching at each moment. Both are imaginary worlds, however. About the real world, the world of God not as an object to be sought or found, but as the infinite and eternal Subject, you can say nothing.

This is It
and I am It
and You are It
and so is That
and He is It
and She is It
and It is It
and That is That

O it is This
and it is Thus
and it is Them
and it is Us
and it is Now
and Here It is
and Here We are
so This is It[82]

(JAMES BROUGHTON, *PACKING UP FOR PARADISE: SELECTED POEMS 1946–1966*)

There is really nothing in the world
other than God
and God's emanated powers which are a unity.
Other than that, nothing exists.
Although it seems that there are other things,
everything is really God and the divine emanations.[83]

(RABBI MESHULLAM FEIBUSH HELLER OF ZBARAZH, CITED IN RAMI SHAPIRO,
AMAZING CHESED: LIVING A GRACE-FILLED JUDAISM, P. 7)

84 The message of the wise is the same: God is all. This teaching is universal, arising in all cultures. It is perennial, arising at all times. Yet it is so difficult for us to grasp. This is why you need to hear the message again and again. These are seeds spilled upon the field of egoic mind. Given enough seed and enough time, at least one will take root. Like Jesus's mustard seed (Matthew 13:31), it will take over the field of mind and free your ego from playing God, that you at last might know that it is God who is playing you.

85 What is it to be free? It is to be home. It is to recognize the entire world as home and all beings as family. Nonbeing doesn't mean the absence of being, for that would be just another duality. Nonbeing is the source of being the way the deep and waveless ocean is the source of all waves. Nonbeing is the substance of being the way the deep and waveless ocean receives all waves at the end of their run. Being one with nonbeing is being one with being as well. Nothing is alien—nothing apart from, and everything a part of—this is the reality to which the wise awake.

The absolute reality of God,
while extending beyond the conceptual borders of "existence,"
also fills the entire expanse of existence as we know it.
There is no space possible for any other existences
or realities we may identify—
the objects of our physical universe,
the metaphysical truths we contemplate,
our very selves ... do not exist in their own reality;
they exist only as an extension of divine energy....[84]
(RABBI MENACHEM MENDEL SCHNEERSON, *TOWARD A MEANINGFUL LIFE*, P. 215)

The whole earth is full of God's glory.

(ISAIAH 6:3)

It emerges without origin;
it passes without opening.
It is real but without firm location;
it is extensive but without clear measure.
Emerging yet without clear opening, it is real.
Being real but without a firm location refers to space.
Being extensive but without a clear measure refers to time.
It lives and dies, emerges and passes, yet one cannot see its form.
This is why we call it the gate to heaven.
As such it is nonbeing—the myriad things emerge from it.
Being cannot create being;
it must come from a state before, which is nonbeing.
It is in oneness with nonbeing that the sage is at home.[85]
(CHUANG-TZU, CHAPTER 23, *CHUANG-TZU: THE TAO OF PERFECT HAPPINESS—
SELECTIONS ANNOTATED & EXPLAINED*, P. 119)

86 What is it like to see the world as God sees it? It is to see absolute beauty. But do not imagine this absolute beauty to be the same as relative beauty, the beauty that is in opposition to ugliness. It is something else entirely.

To see the world as God sees it, to see the absolute beauty of a sunset and a sinkhole, to see the absolute beauty of a newborn infant and a charred corpse is to stand in awe, as awe. You stand in awe when you stand free from the conditioning of the relative self, the judging self, the labeling self. Free from conditioning you can see what is as it is: God. You see the awesome and the awful, and you experience them both as absolute beauty, as equal manifestations of the One who is without second.

God is present in all things, great and small.
God's power is manifest in all events, great and small.
Look at the animals roaming the forest:
God's spirit dwells within them.
Look at the birds flying across the sky:
God's spirit dwells within them.
Look at the tiny insects crawling in the grass:
God's spirit dwells within them.
Look at the fish in the river and sea:
God's spirit dwells within them.
There is no creature on earth in whom God is absent.
Travel across the ocean to the most distant land,
and you will find God's spirit in the creatures there.
Climb up the highest mountain,
and you will find God's spirit among
the creatures who live at the summit....
Look too at the great trees of the forest;
look at the wild flowers and the grass in the fields;
look even at your crops.
God's spirit is present within all plants as well.
The presence of God's spirit in all living beings
is what makes them beautiful;
and if we look with God's eyes,
nothing on the earth is ugly.[86]

(PELAGIUS, A LETTER TO AN ELDERLY FRIEND, *CELTIC CHRISTIAN SPIRITUALITY:*
ESSENTIAL WRITINGS—ANNOTATED & EXPLAINED, P. 43)

Where Am I Going? ☐

Our topic here is death: where are you going when you die? As with the previous questions, this question, too, has two basic answers: somewhere and nowhere. I hope you notice the similarity here with the last question, *Where did I come from?* The similarity results from the fact that what you believe happens to you when you die tells us nothing about what really happens when you die and everything about who you imagine yourself to be while alive.

If, for example, you answered the previous questions *Who am I?* and *Where did I come from?* saying, "I'm somebody who came from somewhere other than here," then your answer to this third question is most likely "I'm going somewhere other than here as well." On the other hand, if you answered our first two questions saying, "I'm nobody from nowhere," your answer to *Where am I going?* is probably "nowhere" as well; after all, if you think you're nobody and you came from nowhere, then you may also think there is nowhere to go and no one to go to there.

The Death of Somebody

Most people who believe they are somebody also believe they are somebody other than and separate from all the other somebodies in the universe and the Somebody who created all these somebodies. The somebody they believe themselves to be isn't the physical body but a separate spirit body—call it "soul" if you like—that lives on after the body dies. This soul may or may not look like you; it may or may not be gendered; it may or may not have a religion—people differ on these things—but however this soul differs from the physical "you" you see when you look at yourself in a mirror, it is still you, and its fate is tied to how you act and what you believe while inhabiting the body reflected in the mirror.

"How could it be otherwise?" a pastor friend of mine told me one day over lunch. "If the fate of the soul isn't connected to the decisions we make on earth, then there is no connection between our eternal soul and our temporal self."

"Help me understand this," I said. "The soul enters a body at conception and then leaves that body at death, right?"

"That's what we believe, yes."

"OK, but why is the soul forced to pay for the sins of the body after the body dies?"

"That's because it isn't the body that commits the sins, or rather the body is simply the vehicle through which sin is done; it is the soul that sins."

"So the soul is really my personality, the 'me' I take myself to be when I do this or that or believe one thing or another. So genetics has nothing to do with my personality."

"Genetics will shape your body, and that will influence the soul's choices while it is in that body. The same can be said of the family and culture into which the body is born and through which the soul engages the world—all these will influence the soul. But the essential things, the moral choices you make, and the decision whether or not to accept Jesus Christ as your Lord and Savior, for example, these are purely soul decisions."

"Which is why the soul is punished or rewarded after the body dies."

"Right."

"So help me understand in what way the soul is me. My body is that of a white male. It has certain likes and dislikes determined by both nature and nurture, but none of this is the soul, the real me. When I die and go to my fate …"

"Heaven if you accept Christ, hell if you don't. We need to be honest about that."

"OK, I appreciate that. But when I die and, let's assume I remain a Jew all my life and never accept Jesus as my Lord and Savior, I go to hell, I will suffer there as me, right? I mean, the body is gone but the soul that refused to accept Jesus is still self-identifying as such, still has a sense of 'me' and a memory that knows why I'm suffering."

"Of course. What is the point of punishment if the person being punished doesn't know why the punishment is being meted out? The same is true of heaven. When I die I will, praise God, go to heaven, where I will be reunited with my parents, for example."

"This is where I get confused," I said. "The soul isn't the body, but it will recognize its parents and be recognized by them? Does your soul look like you that your parents will recognize you? And since you will recognize them as your parents, I presume the soul has all its memories of being raised by these parents even though it existed prior to these parents conceiving the body the soul entered."

"That's my point. That's why heaven is such a joy. All your memories are intact. So is your personality. You are the 'you' they remember. That's why they are happy to be reunited with you."

"Then how is the soul different from ego?"

"Well, it isn't really. You could say your soul is your ego."

I'll Be Back

I was recently in New Delhi where I shared the dais with many spiritual teachers, including His Holiness the Dalai Lama, as we celebrated the 150th anniversary of the birth of Swami Vivekananda. During a private conversation with several Hindu swamis, I brought up the notion of reincarnation.

One swami explained it this way: "Just as you would get rid of old clothes that no longer function as they should and buy new ones, so you drop this body and take on a new one in a new life."

"Which means that there is a true me, an eternal soul, that moves from body to body, right?" I asked.

"Yes. The 'you' you appear to be in this body is not really you at all. You come back over and over until you realize the true nature of the self and achieve *moksha*, liberation from physical rebirth, and then move on to higher, more spiritual realms of incarnation."

"So my personality dies when my body dies."

"Yes. The ego is a product of the brain, and when the brain dies, the ego goes with it. But you are not this ego. You are Atman, the eternal soul, moving from life to life until at last you have purified yourself of negative karma and cease to physically reincarnate at all. Then you become one with Brahman, God."

"But what about the teaching that Atman, the soul, is really Brahman right now?" I asked. "I always think of Atman as a wave arising in the divine ocean. The wave isn't other than the ocean, God, just not all of the ocean or God."

"False teaching," he said. "Don't think of a wave arising in the ocean; think of a river flowing into the ocean. The river is never the ocean, but it pours into the ocean, where it ceases to be a river. Atman is the flowing river that, over many lifetimes, comes closer and closer to the ocean and eventually empties into it. At that point Atman becomes Brahman, but not before."

"Well," a second swami said hesitatingly, "that is the dualistic view: God is always other than the created world. But there is the *Advaita* view, the nondual view, that God is the world, and that while reincarnation is real, it isn't 'you' who returns, but God. This is like your wave and ocean metaphor. Nothing is other than the ocean, and no wave dies and returns. Rather the ocean keeps waving."

This debate between dualism and nondualism is an ancient one in Hinduism, and while I would have liked to have heard the swamis settle the matter once and for all, I was called away and never got to hear how this conversation ended.

The thing to note, however, is that the dualism of the first swami was temporary, while the dualism of my pastor friend is permanent. While the two swamis differ as to when Atman and Brahman, soul and God, are one, they still agree that sooner or later they become one, while the pastor believed that the soul in heaven will dwell near God but never dwell as God.

The position offered by the perennial wisdom, and supported by the texts we explored in the previous chapters, is that of the nondual swami: you are God in extension, a wave of God, and not a river flowing into God. You may or may not accept this position of course, and I would never seek to convince you to do so. But for me it is self-evident.

I began meditating when I was sixteen, almost fifty years ago. Over the years I have devoted time and energy to learning (though sadly never mastering!) a variety of meditative practices: Jewish, Christian, Hindu, Buddhist, Sufi, and Sikh. My experience with all of them has been the same: my sense of separate self—my ego, or soul if you like—is surrendered to an egoless awareness that leaves me (once my meditation session ends and "I" return) with an unshakeable sense that, as one of rabbis put it to me, *Alles iz Gott*—all is God.

Knot This, Knot That

While I enjoy listening to adults wrestle with the question *Where I am going?* I am saddened that most often they settle on some version of "I'm somebody who came from somewhere, and who is going somewhere, and the 'me' that was and will be is somehow the recognizable 'me' I am here and now." The notion that the ego transcends the body seems so narcissistic to me. I understand why you might not like the idea that the "you" you cherish comes to an end, but I cannot shake the conviction that this is indeed what happens. The answer isn't to cling to the ego all the more strongly, but to begin to loosen our grasp and see if there is something more to us than meets the eye.

That's why I like exploring these ideas with children. They are less invested in eternity, and while they too may assume they are who they think they are, they are often more open than adults when it comes to seeing things differently.

When I share the perennial wisdom on death with fifth and sixth graders, for example, I often do so with pieces of rope. I hand each child a foot-long strand of rope and ask them to tie a knot in their piece of rope. We then discuss the relationship between the knot and the rope. The knot is simply the rope in a specific form. It is in no way other than or different from the rope.

I then ask them to tie a second knot. Comparing the two knots it is clear that each knot has its own uniqueness, its own place on the rope, its own degree of tightness, its own shape, yet both knots are not other than the single stand of rope.

I then ask them to name their knots. One knot is called "me" and represents the child who holds that particular piece of rope. The second knot is named after someone they love who has died—a grandparent or a pet—or, if death has not yet touched this child's life, someone who is considerably older who will, we hope, die much sooner than this child. I then ask them to untie their second knot.

The discussion now turns to the impact the missing knot has on the rope. Sure, the rope appears a bit longer, but it really isn't any different than it was. There is no less rope with knots and no more rope without knots. The amount of rope is constant even if its length seems to change as we add or remove knots.

So knotting and unknotting the rope doesn't change the nature of the rope. It isn't anything other than rope regardless of the number of knots it has. When this is clear, I ask them where the knot goes when it is untied. Is the rope that was once the knot gone? How can it be that the rope is still there while the knot is not?

You can, I expect, see where this investigation is leading. The rope is constant; knots come and go. The extent to which you identify as a knot or with a knot, the untying of that knot is experienced as a loss, and that loss is expressed in grief. But what is really lost? Only the form is lost; the rope itself is still present.

I then explain that this is a metaphor for birth and death and for the relationship between ourselves, one another, and God. The rope is God, Reality itself. The knots are people, animals, things, indeed everything that composes the world, both seen and unseen. Birth is the tying of knots, and death the untying of knots. The rope—Reality itself—remains unchanged. You are a knot on the rope that is God.

"So is my grandma gone or not?" one little girl asked when I shared this exercise at a synagogue Sunday school.

"Well, this is a metaphor. Playing with the rope is like what happens to people when they die. So you tell me, where is grandma knot?"

"She's gone," the girl said waving her rope to show me that the knot labeled "grandma" was no longer there.

"And where is the rope that was grandma knot?"

"Wait," she said looking carefully at the rope, "the rope is still here. This is the part that was my grandma knot, but the knot is gone, but the rope is right here."

"So grandma was the knot, and the knot was the rope, and the knot is gone, but the rope is still here."

"Yes."

"So is grandma gone or not?"

"Both!" another girl shouted.

"Both?"

"Sure. Look, the knot was the rope, and the rope was the knot, so grandma was both knot and rope, and so while grandma knot is gone, grandma rope is still here. Is that right?"

"Let's look together. Please say this again, and everyone look to your rope to see if what she says is true."

The little girl repeated her insight slowly and everyone looked to see if what she said was true, and in the end they all agreed.

"But I still miss my grandma," the little girl said.

"Of course you do. Why wouldn't you? You loved grandma knot. You loved her shape, her smell, her jokes ..."

"Her cookies!"

"Her cookies. So of course you miss all of that. There was no one just like grandma knot, and the knot is untied and she is gone. So you are sad, and may cry, and have lots of memories about her that make you happy and sad at the same time."

"Yeah," a couple of kids said softly.

"But the rope is still there. Your connection to her is still there because you are both the same rope."

I am never certain how much of this sinks in, but I invite the children to take the rope home and do the exercise with their parents and see what they have to say. If nothing else, playing with knots and rope introduces the perennial wisdom notion of nondual reality: we are all knots on a single rope.

Unlike the scenarios of heaven and hell and even reincarnation, each of which imagines a "you" separate from God, in the perennial wisdom there is no separate "you," there is only God. The knot is nothing but the rope. When the knot is untied, there is nothing but the rope. Nothing is gained; nothing is lost. All is rope.

So where do you go when you die? Nowhere. There is no "you" separate from the rope to come from somewhere and move on somewhere. There is no after-rope fate that can befall the untied knot, because the knot doesn't exist separate from the rope. When you die, you don't go anywhere, because there is nowhere to go. All there is is rope.

Near-Death Experience

Whenever I present this idea to adults, someone always brings up the experience of people who can remember past lives or people who have had near-death experiences. Are these people deluded? If they aren't deluded, doesn't this support the dualism of conventional Judaism, Christianity, and Islam that says the personality survives the death of the body and goes on to have further disembodied experiences?

I have seriously investigated the near-death phenomenon, and I'm not inclined to dismiss either near-death experiences or past-life recollections. What I question is what they mean.

First of all, the near-death experience is just that: near death, and not death itself. Few people have actually died, stayed dead for days, and then returned to life. We have stories of Elijah and Elisha who each raised a little boy from the dead (1 Kings 17:17–24; 2 Kings 4:17–37, respectively), and Jesus resurrects a widow's son (Luke 7:13–15), Jarius's daughter (Matthew 9:25), and Lazarus (John 11:43–44), but none of these people report having near-death experiences. Jesus himself upon returning to earth after his death seems completely disinterested in talking about what happens after you die. So while near-death experiences may tell us what happens as we die, what happens when we are dead is still a matter of speculation and faith.

Based on the dozens of reports I have read, the classic near-death encounter is decidedly egocentric. The "dead" person separates from her body, floats to the ceiling, observes her corpse, and then floats along a tunnel, sometimes lined with loved ones recognized and unrecognized, only to confront a light with which she wishes to unite but that sends her back into her body to complete her task on earth. Throughout all of this, she remains the person she thought she was while alive. While she no longer carries the bodily form, she in no way has lost her sense of self. The disembodied soul is not other than the once embodied ego.

I am more than willing to accept that as the body dies, the ego experiences some type of journey. Nor do I deny that the dying ego feels the presence of loved ones who welcome the dying person. This may well be how our brain copes with the fact of its own dying.

What I object to isn't the experience of the dying person, but the assumption that near death is the same as death. What I suggest is that the near-death experience isn't complete. The near-death-experiencing self draws near to the light but never merges with it. If the death is permanent and the person doesn't return, I believe the self is stripped of all elements of selfhood and becomes the light. This fits both of the metaphors offered earlier by the two swamis I spoke with in India: just as the wave returning to the ocean loses its form as it does so, and just as the river flowing into the ocean becomes the ocean and is no longer the river, so the self merges with Self, the singular "I" that is the Divine.

While both metaphors can be used here, they do differ, and to be clear, I prefer the wave-ocean metaphor to the river-ocean metaphor. The difference is that the unity of river and ocean happens only at that point in time and space where the river flows into the ocean, whereas the unity of wave and ocean is always the case and is independent of time and place. The river becomes the ocean; the wave is the ocean. While the differences may not seem all that great to you, it is the wave-ocean metaphor that is most in line with perennial wisdom as I understand it.

Whose Life Is It, Anyway?

Near-death experiences are one thing, but what about people—sometimes little children—who can remember past lives? What about people who can clearly recall places they have never been to or speak languages they do not know? Are they frauds? Not necessarily. While each case must be examined on its own merits, even if some cases seem true, they need not undo the nonduality at the heart of perennial wisdom.

If we are all part of the same ocean (the same rope), we all have access to the same reality, the same divine consciousness. If that consciousness includes every experience of every knot or wave, and if we are made of the same stuff as these long untied knots and surrendered waves, could it not be that we are recalling their lives and experiences and simply mistaking them for our own?

Several years ago I attended a fascinating lecture at Vanderbilt University on the nature of the egoic self. The speaker, a visiting experimental psychologist, told us of one series of experiments he ran that mirrored an oft-repeated bit on Drew Carry's television show *Who's Line Is It Anyway?*

In both the television show and the lab test, one person stands with her hands clasped behind her back, while another person slips her arms under the arms of the first person so that the second person's arms take the place of the first person's arms.

In the science experiment, both people are wearing white lab coats so that the arms of the second person look like the arms of the first person. Person number two, whose arms are free, then completes a series of actions involving person number one. In the comedy skit, the point is to be as silly possible, and the first person is never asked to describe what is happening. The whole thing is done for laughs. But in the lab test things are a bit different.

As the arms of the second person reach out and lift an object on a table placed before the first person, the first person is asked why she chose to lift the object. Remember, she didn't choose anything, and she didn't reach out and grab anything. Yet time after time person number one would tell a story explaining why "her" arms did what they did. She claimed responsibility for what was going on even though she had no control over the other's arms at all, and she created a story that allowed her to maintain the notion that she willed herself to do whatever the other person was actually doing.

So strong is the ego's need to maintain the illusion of control that it will forget the obvious and claim another's hands, arms, and actions as its own. This may be exactly what is going on in so-called past-life memories. The ego may pick up memories of others and claim them as its own—the longing of the ego for immortality is that strong. Just as the mind of the subject in the lab experiment takes ownership over the doings of another, the ego may take ownership of the experiences and memories of others who lived before she was born.

Again, none of this can be proved, and I am not trying to convince you that what I am saying is true. What I am saying is this: the egoic you is real, precious, unique, and temporary. It is a manifestation of a singular reality—call it God, Allah, Tao, or the rest—but it tends to forget this and imagines itself to be apart from God rather than a part of God.

As the great twentieth-century Indian sage Ramana Maharshi was dying, his students crowded around him begging him not to go. His response was pure perennial wisdom: "Where could I go?" The aim of spiritual practice is to remember who you really are, and when you do, the answer to the question *Where am I going?* is "nowhere."

1 The origin of all that happens includes the end of all that happens. Birthing and dying are part of the unending living that is God, the singular source and substance of all reality.

2 Because God is all there is, everything there is *is* God. When we separate light from dark and good from evil, we create a false world of competing opposites rather than embrace the reality of interdependent polarities.

3 The "Me" in this text is Krishna, one of Hinduism's names for the singular reality that is all things. You cannot escape dying; indeed, you are dying right now. But you can die well. Dying well means dying with the wisdom that you are not a separate being on your way to eternal reward or punishment, nor are you a migrating soul that will take off one body and put on another. These are both egoic illusions that maintain a sense of separate self even when no such self exists outside the body. Dying well is dying knowing who you are: God manifest. When you die as God, you die into God. This dying is *sat-chit-ananda*, the awakening to pure being, consciousness, and bliss.

4 Not only is there a life span for seeming individuals, but there is also a life span for life itself. Suns die and become black holes, devouring the worlds they once illumined. Whole galaxies collapse and die. Like you, their collapse and death are part of the ebb and flow of the Divine. Nature is God manifesting in and as time and space. All things return to the One, and then the One spins out new things. There is no end to the One who is both birthing and dying, and yet in and of itself it is birthless and deathless.

5 Just as the ocean cannot be reduced to its waves, so the Absolute is not reduced to the relative. God is all that is happening, and all that surpasses what is happening. God is completely engaged in you as you, for there is nothing but God. Knowing you are both the part and the whole allows you to play your part without fear or hesitation, knowing that you are the part you play and yet so much more.

I am all-devouring Death;
I am the Origin of all that shall happen.[1]
(BHAGAVAD GITA 10:34, *BHAGAVAD GITA: ANNOTATED & EXPLAINED*, P. 85)

I create light. I fashion darkness.
I make good, and I make evil.
I the Unnameable Is'ing do all this.[2]
(ISAIAH 45:7)

If at the time of death you think only of Me,
and thinking thus leave the body and go forth,
assuredly you will know Me.
On whatever sphere of being your mind may be intent
at the time of death,
thither you will go.
Therefore meditate always on Me ...
if your mind and your reason be fixed on Me,
to Me shall you surely come.[3]
(BHAGAVAD GITA 8:5–7, *BHAGAVAD GITA: ANNOTATED & EXPLAINED*, P. 65)

All beings ... return at the close of every cosmic cycle
into the realm of Nature, which is a part of Me,
and at the beginning of the next I send them forth again.
With the help of Nature, again and again
I pour forth the whole multitude of beings....[4]
But these acts of Mine do not bind Me.
I remain outside and unattached.[5]
(BHAGAVAD GITA 9:7–9, *BHAGAVAD GITA: ANNOTATED & EXPLAINED*, P. 71)

6 From the perspective of perennial wisdom, Krishna isn't talking about reincarnation but recycling. Think of this in terms of the ocean and its waves. Each wave must "die" and return to the ocean, and no one wave is waved a second time. Yet that which waves, that which each wave is—the ocean itself—waves unceasingly.

7 There are two kinds of grief corresponding to the egoic self and the divine Self, the wave and the ocean. When you experience the death of a loved one from the place of the limited self, you naturally grieve the loss of the beloved. There is neither shame nor harm in this. When you experience the death of a loved one from the place of the unlimited Self, you experience no loss and so no grief. You can only lose that which is other than you, and there is no other when you know God as all.

It is impenetrable;
It can be neither drowned nor scorched nor dried.
It is Eternal, All-pervading, Unchanging,
Immovable, and Most Ancient.
It is named the Unmanifest, the Unthinkable, the Immutable.
Wherefore, knowing the Spirit as such,
you have no cause to grieve.
Even if you think of it as constantly being born,
constantly dying;
even then ... you still have no cause to grieve.
For death is as sure for that which is born
as birth is for that which is dead.[6]
Therefore grieve not for what is inevitable.
The end and beginning of beings are unknown.
We see only the intervening formations.
Then what cause is there for grief?[7]

(BHAGAVAD GITA 2:24–28, *BHAGAVAD GITA: ANNOTATED & EXPLAINED*, P. 15)

8   Notice that the sage isn't without desires, she just doesn't cling to them. The sage isn't free from suffering, he just isn't ruffled by suffering. The sage isn't without enjoyment, she just isn't ensnared by enjoyment. To be without desire, without suffering, without joy is to be dead, but the sage is the most alive among us: experiencing the fullness of life without seeking to hold on to any of it.

9   To attain perfection is to be open to all things and their opposite. The sage doesn't avoid good and evil, only accepts them both equally. This is Job's response to the death of his children and the loss of his businesses and health: "Shall we not accept the bad as well as the good from God?" (Job 2:10). Knowing yourself to be what Is, you have no need to resist what is. Without resistance, there is acceptance. With acceptance, there is tranquility. From tranquility, you can engage whatever you meet with grace, compassion, and love.

When you have given up the desires of your heart
and are satisfied with the Self alone,
be sure that you have reached the highest state.

The sage, whose mind is unruffled in suffering,
whose desire is not roused by enjoyment,
who is without attachment, anger, or fear—
take this one to be standing at that lofty level.[8]

Those who, wherever they go, are attached to no person
and to no place by ties of flesh;
who accept good and evil alike,
neither welcoming the one nor shrinking from the other—
take them to be merged in the Infinite.
Those who can withdraw their senses
from the attraction of their objects,
as the tortoise draws his limbs within his shell—
take it that these have attained Perfection.[9]

(BHAGAVAD GITA 2:55–58, *BHAGAVAD GITA: ANNOTATED & EXPLAINED*, P. 21)

10 The self-controlled are not oblivious to the senses, only free from being buffeted by them. It isn't experiencing the world that is the problem, it is trying to avoid what you don't like and hold on to what you do like that is the problem. Stay open to everything without fixating on anything and you will attain peace.

11 Right discrimination is the ability to see Reality as it is, both form and formlessness. To see form as formless and formless as form requires meditation, the ability to look deeply into everything and to discover the One Thing that is all things. Just as reading a travel guide about Rome is not the same as walking the streets of Rome, so reading a book about meditation is not the same as actually meditating. Just as walking the streets of Rome on your own can be pleasant, walking with one well acquainted with the city can be richer still. You may begin to meditate with the guidance of a book, but seek out a teacher who is familiar with the places meditation will take you. But, just as you would not turn your life over to your tour guide, do not turn your life over to your guru. If your teacher needs your devotion rather than just your attention, find another teacher.

12 Again, don't imagine that meditation and resting in the Self will erase pleasure and pain. On the contrary: it will make you all the more sensitive to both. Sensitive to pain, you will avoid causing pain to others. Sensitive to pleasure, you will bring pleasure to others. But neither pleasure nor pain will disturb you. You know both. You accept both. You move on.

But the self-controlled soul,
who moves among sense objects free
from either attachment or repulsion,
wins eternal peace.[10]
Having attained peace,
it becomes free from misery;
for when the mind gains peace,
right discrimination follows.
Right discrimination is not for one who cannot concentrate.
Without concentration, there cannot be meditation;
one who cannot meditate must not expect peace;
and without peace, how can anyone expect happiness?[11]
(BHAGAVAD GITA 2:64–66, BHAGAVAD GITA: ANNOTATED & EXPLAINED, P. 23)

The wise attain Eternity when,
freed from pride and delusion,
they have conquered their love for the things of sense;
when, renouncing desire and fixing their gaze on the Self,
they have ceased to be tossed to and fro
by the opposing sensations, like pleasure and pain.[12]
(BHAGAVAD GITA 15:5, BHAGAVAD GITA: ANNOTATED & EXPLAINED, P. 119)

13 The Beloved is the greater Self in which the lesser self rests. It is not other than you, yet you insist on pretending you are other than it. Seeking that which you already are, you attach to whatever holds the projections you toss about. But nothing satisfies, because everything is counterfeit. The Real is not in your projections.

14 The Divine isn't passive. It allows the self to forget the Self, for this is the nature of self and must be honored. Yet the Self never tires of stirring you from your slumber, of awakening you from your dreams of love to be embraced by the reality of the Beloved.

15 Saint Augustine is speaking of the moment just prior to awakening. The Beloved is so close yet still other. His choice of words reflects the experience of the prophet Isaiah, "I will scream like a woman in labor, I will pant and I will gasp" (Isaiah 42:14). Embracing the Beloved is like birthing a child, only the child you are birthing is your true Self. There is an erotic quality to Augustine's words because there is an erotic quality to the embrace of the Beloved. One's entire body is alive with Life; there is an orgasmic moment at the awakening of the oceanic consciousness. Putting on the Mind of Christ, awakening to the Divine within and without is—as the Hindus put it, *sat-chit-ananda*—pure being, pure consciousness, pure bliss.

Late have I loved you,
Beauty so ancient and so new,
late have I loved you!
Lo, you were within, but I outside, seeking there for you,
and upon the shapely things you have made
I rushed headlong, I misshapen.
You were with me, but I was not with you.[13]
They held me back far from you,
those things that would have no being were they not in
you.
You called, shouted, broke through my deafness;
you flared, blazed, banished my blindness;
you lavished your fragrance,[14]
I gasped, and now I pant for you;
I tasted you, and I hunger and thirst;
you touched me, and I burned for your peace.[15]

(SAINT AUGUSTINE, *CONFESSIONS* X.27.38, *SAINT AUGUSTINE OF HIPPO:*
SELECTIONS FROM CONFESSIONS AND OTHER ESSENTIAL WRITINGS—
ANNOTATED & EXPLAINED, P. 79)

16 In God, all things are the One Thing. This is the truest you, your truest Self. All of you is embraced by the Beloved as the Beloved.

17 These moments of bliss may be fleeting and intermittent. Enjoy them when they come, and do not race after them when they go. But know that they are transforming you in ways you cannot imagine. The awakening to God in God as God is, from the perspective of the self, the birth of the new, and the new cannot be known before its time.

18 The Kingdom of Heaven is the world you experience when you have moved through duality to nonduality. This doesn't mean you can't tell the inside of a house from the outside, or a woman from a man, only that you know there is no inside without outside, no feminine without masculine. When you know that everything goes with everything else, and act in harmony with it all, then the Kingdom of Heaven is manifest in you and as you and through you.

19 When you set out on your journey for Self-realization, you are like one frantically searching for your glasses, never realizing they are on top of your head. You are looking for God when God is you. This is like trying to bite your teeth with your teeth. But in time you will discover the truth, and this will astonish you. So convinced were you that God is this or that image in your mind, you are shocked to discover that God is that which cannot be imaged. But once you realize this, Self will embrace self, and you will reign over yourself, over your desires, over your delusions. Because you are no longer driven by these, you are at peace and find rest.

Nowhere amid all these things
that I survey under your guidance
do I find a safe haven for my soul except in you;
only there are the scattered elements of my being collected,
so that no part of me may escape from you.[16]
From time to time you lead me
into an inward experience quite unlike any other,
a sweetness beyond understanding.
If ever it is brought to fullness in me,
my life will not be what it is now,
though what it will be I cannot tell.[17]
(SAINT AUGUSTINE, *CONFESSIONS* X.40.65, *SAINT AUGUSTINE OF HIPPO:
SELECTIONS FROM CONFESSIONS AND OTHER ESSENTIAL WRITINGS—
ANNOTATED & EXPLAINED*, P. 79)

When the Lord was asked when the kingdom would come,
he said,
"When the two will be one,
and the inner as the outer
and the male with the female, neither male nor female."[18]
(THE GOSPEL OF THE EGYPTIANS IN CLEMENT OF ALEXANDRIA, *STROMATA*
3.13.92, *THE LOST SAYINGS OF JESUS: TEACHINGS FROM ANCIENT CHRISTIAN, JEWISH,
GNOSTIC AND ISLAMIC SOURCES—ANNOTATED & EXPLAINED*, P. 49)

Seeker! Do not stop searching until you find,
and when you find you will be astonished,
and when you are astonished, you will reign,
and once you reign you will find rest.[19]
(THE GOSPEL OF THE HEBREWS IN CLEMENT OF ALEXANDRIA, *STROMATA*
5.14.96, *THE LOST SAYINGS OF JESUS: TEACHINGS FROM ANCIENT CHRISTIAN, JEWISH,
GNOSTIC AND ISLAMIC SOURCES—ANNOTATED & EXPLAINED*, P. 63)

20 The disciples are asking about the afterlife and Jesus asks them—you among them—to concern themselves with this life: the place you can reach. That place is the place of knowing that God is everything, that God is you. That place is the place of knowing that going and coming is the way of life and that when you die you simply return to what you are: the Divine Life birthing and dying eternally.

21 So much theology is wrapped up in a judging God saving some and condemning others. In this way we frighten ourselves into conforming to one religion or another, each religion promising salvation from the wrathful God of its own imagining. But Muhammad reveals a different vision, a vision of God who desires only to forgive.

Asking for forgiveness requires that you recognize your errors. Recognizing your errors as errors means that you have also recognized the way of righteousness. Recognizing the way of righteousness is humbling. Being humbled, the lesser self is engulfed in the greater Self the way the light of a single candle is engulfed by the light of the sun.

They said to him, "What is the place we are going to?"
The Lord said, "Stand in the place you can reach."[20]

*(DIALOGUE OF THE SAVIOR 77–78, THE LOST SAYINGS OF JESUS:
TEACHINGS FROM ANCIENT CHRISTIAN, JEWISH, GNOSTIC AND ISLAMIC SOURCES—
ANNOTATED & EXPLAINED, P. 85)*

O humans, so long as you call upon Me and ask of Me,
I shall forgive you for what you have done,
and I shall not mind.
O humans, were your sins to reach the clouds of the sky
and were you then to ask forgiveness of Me,
I would forgive you.
O humans, were you to come to Me
with sins nearly as great as the earth,
and were you then to face Me, I would bring you forgiveness nearly as great.[21]

*(MUHAMMAD, THE QUR'AN AND SAYINGS OF PROPHET MUHAMMAD:
SELECTIONS ANNOTATED & EXPLAINED, P. 15)*

22 Resurrection is not the return of your body, but the awakening from spiritual sleep. You are not other than That which is all. But you have forgotten. You are asleep to the truth of yourself and all life. But you can be taught, and unless you resist the teaching by clinging to your sense of separateness from the Whole, you will find the truth. It may come early or late, in the fullness of your life or in the moment of your death, but truth will come, and the truth will set you free (John 8:32). Being free is the ultimate resurrection.

23 How you envision the moment of death tells you much of what you value during your years of life. Muhammad spells out what matters in this life through the questions he imagines are asked of you at death: Did you use your life in service to the living? Did you pursue wisdom and use it for the benefit of others? Did you earn your money honestly in a manner that caused no suffering to others? Did you share your wealth—great or small—with those in need? Did you honor the gift of physical incarnation, caring for your body and seeing that your actions were for the good? These are the things that matter.

O humanity, if you are in doubt about the resurrection,
remember that We created you from dust, then from a
drop,
then from a clot, then from a lump of flesh,
formed and unformed, in order to edify you.
And We keep in the womb those who We wish, up to a
designated term;
then We bring you out as infants, and enable you to reach
your maturity:
but some of you will pass away,
and some of you will be kept here until the age of senility,
such that they know nothing of what they knew before.
And you see the earth lifeless,
but then We shower water on it,
and it stirs and swells and produces every beautiful species.[22]
(QUR'AN 22:5, *THE QUR'AN AND SAYINGS OF PROPHET MUHAMMAD:
SELECTIONS ANNOTATED & EXPLAINED*, P. 67)

The servants of God will remain standing
on the Day of Requital
till they are questioned about their life on earth
and how they spent it,
and about their knowledge and how they utilized it,
and their wealth and how they acquired it
and in what did they spend it,
and about their bodies and how they used them.[23]
(MUHAMMAD, *THE QUR'AN AND SAYINGS OF PROPHET MUHAMMAD:
SELECTIONS ANNOTATED & EXPLAINED*, P. 75)

24 The spiritual quest is not at the expense of ordinary life; indeed, it makes no sense outside of it. The spiritual quest is the quest for awakening that you might engage life—this life—with grace, compassion, justice, and wisdom. So make time for learning, for family, and for work, and never lose hope that you can awaken here and now.

25 Other rabbis added a fifth question to the four mentioned above: did you take delight in being alive? Legitimate pleasure is not the enemy of spirituality; illicit pleasure is the enemy of spirituality. Legitimate pleasure delights the senses and causes no harm to another or yourself. An illicit pleasure is one gained at the expense of another or at the cost of your own authenticity. Embrace the former; reject the latter.

26 There are those who value faith over deeds, and those who value deeds over faith, each confident that they hold the keys to life in the world to come. But it is not a matter of "either/or," but of "and." It is not a matter of faith *or* works, but of faith *and* works.

There are those—in Hinduism they are called karma yogis—who seek union with God through selfless service to others. Do they lack faith? No. Their faith is in knowing that by serving others they serve God, and by serving selflessly they will awaken to the Self.

There are others—in Hinduism they are called bhakti yogis—who seek union with God through devotion to God. Do they lack works? No. Their devotion to God reveals the One manifest as the many, and their devotions embrace the entire world.

Whatever your spiritual path may be, if it fails to lead you to the realization that faith and works are two sides of a single coin, it is not yet a complete spiritual path.

When you die and meet God four questions will be asked of you:
Did you make time for learning wisdom?
Did you devote sufficient energy to your family?
Did you conduct your business with integrity?
Did you always maintain hope?[24]

(TALMUD, *SHABBAT* 31A)

[When you die and meet God,
this question will be asked of you:]
Did you enjoy all legitimate pleasures that came your way?[25]

(TALMUD, *KIDDUSHIN* 4:12)

Those who have faith and do righteous deeds,
they are the best of creatures.

(QUR'AN 98:7–8, *THE QUR'AN AND SAYINGS OF PROPHET MUHAMMAD:
SELECTIONS ANNOTATED & EXPLAINED*, P. 87)

Of what value are those who say they have faith
but do not have works?
Can faith save them?
If a brother or sister is naked, destitute, and hungry,
and you say to them,
"Go in peace, be warmed and filled,"
but you do not also clothe and feed them,
what good does it do?
Therefore faith alone,
unaccompanied by righteous deeds,
is dead.[26]

(EPISTLE OF JAMES 2:14–26)

27 Everything returns. The wave returns to the ocean, the ocean returns to waving. The end of your life is a return to the Source of your life, but it is not an end to living. Know who you are now and your return will be effortless and blessed. Cling to the illusion of separateness and your return will be marked by fierce resistance and struggle. Know who you are and return now even as you live, and your dying will be, as the Jewish mystics taught, as effortless as pulling a hair from a glass of milk.

28 When you turn your body inside out, will you find your Self within it? No. The Self isn't within the body, it permeates the body; it is the body and so much more. You are not body and soul, but a single entity, one and undivided. You are a knot on a strand of rope. Yes, the body grows old and dies; the knot grows slack and is in time unknotted. But the knot is the rope, and the rope remains. You cannot find the rope in the knot, but only as the knot.

Attain the ultimate emptiness
Hold on to the truest tranquility
The myriad things are all active
I therefore watch their return
Everything flourishes; each returns to its root
Returning to the root is called tranquility
Tranquility is called returning to one's nature
Returning to one's nature is called constancy
Knowing constancy is called clarity
Not knowing constancy, one recklessly causes trouble
Knowing constancy is acceptance
Acceptance is impartiality
Impartiality is sovereign
Sovereign is Heaven
Heaven is Tao
Tao is eternal
The self is no more, without danger[27]

(TAO TE CHING, CHAPTER 16, *TAO TE CHING: ANNOTATED & EXPLAINED*, P. 33)

Turn the body inside out,
and see what kind of thing it is;
and when it has grown old,
what kind of thing it becomes,
and when it is diseased.[28]

(MARCUS AURELIUS, THE *MEDITATIONS OF MARCUS AURELIUS:*
SELECTIONS ANNOTATED & EXPLAINED, P. 101)

29 Death is as natural to life as birth. While some deaths are more welcome than others, and some deaths more horrifying than others, death
itself is natural. Do not fear death; only seek to die well and wisely by
living wisely and well. Yet even this is no guarantee; living comes with
none. When a person dies, grieve. When a person dies tragically—
grieve and then do what you can to minimize such tragedies in the
future.

30 You are dying. How long the process will take is unknown, but you
are dying nonetheless. The question isn't when will you die, but how
will you live? The key is to become simple. To become simple is to realize that while life is complex, living is not complicated. Make time for
quiet and solitude. Treat everyone with respect. Know that wisdom
and justice go hand in hand.

31 Nothing falls out of the universe. No wave falls out of the ocean.
Everything returns to its source, and the source recycles everything.
Everything is in the process of flux. Do not imagine that God is outside
the universe; only know that God is greater than the universe. Do not
imagine that God changes; only know that God is change.

Death is such as germination is—a mystery of nature,
a composition out of the same elements,
and decomposition into the same;
and altogether not a thing of which
anyone should be ashamed,
for it is not contrary to the nature of a reasonable animal,
and not contrary to the reason of our constitution.[29]

(MARCUS AURELIUS, THE MEDITATIONS OF MARCUS AURELIUS:
SELECTIONS ANNOTATED & EXPLAINED, P. 103)

You will soon die, and you are not yet simple,
not free from disturbances,
nor without suspicion of being hurt by external things,
nor kindly disposed towards all;
nor do you yet place wisdom only in acting justly.[30]

(MARCUS AURELIUS, THE MEDITATIONS OF MARCUS AURELIUS:
SELECTIONS ANNOTATED & EXPLAINED, P. 105)

That which has died falls not out of the universe.
If it stays here, it also changes here,
and is dissolved into its proper parts,
which are elements of the universe and of yourself.
And these too change, and they murmur not.[31]

(MARCUS AURELIUS, THE MEDITATIONS OF MARCUS AURELIUS:
SELECTIONS ANNOTATED & EXPLAINED, P. 105)

32 Death is not a punishment, nor does it lead to punishment. Reward and punishment after death assumes there is a "you" that survives the return. This is simply your egoic self insisting that it cannot die, even if eternal life means eternal torment. But such thinking is in error. There is no "you" separate from the One, just as there is no wave separate from the ocean. When you die, you are still what you were and are: God.

Do not despise death, but be well content with it,
since this too is one of those things which nature wills.
For such as it is to be young and to grow old,
and to increase and to reach maturity,
and to have teeth and beard and gray hairs,
and to beget, and to be pregnant and to bring forth,
and all the other natural operations which
the seasons of your life bring,
such also is dissolution.
This, then, is consistent with the character
of a contemplative human being,
to be neither careless nor impatient
nor contemptuous
with respect to death,
but to wait for it as one of the operations of nature.[32]

(MARCUS AURELIUS, THE MEDITATIONS OF MARCUS AURELIUS:
SELECTIONS ANNOTATED & EXPLAINED, P. 109)

33 Is there such a thing as a death out of proper time? There are deaths we view as tragic. When a child dies, we sense that this life was cheated of living. When an elderly person dies, we grieve but also take heart in a long life now ended. But death is a result of circumstance—death can only come at its proper time, even if that time is soon after birth. This is not predestination but simply the nature of nature. When the circumstances of maintaining life cease, so does the life that was maintained. This is not meant to comfort the bereaved, but only to state the facts.

34 So is a premature death not useful? If fate is not in play, if a murdered child would, had she lived, grown up to be a person whose deeds were of benefit to others, how many of those others will now suffer because of her premature death? All death is natural, but some deaths rob the living of a life most precious.

35 The cross in first-century-CE Roman-occupied Jewish Palestine meant only one thing: death. Taking up your cross and following Jesus was not a disembodied act of faith, but a political act of nonviolent resistance. Jesus calls you to confront the evils of your day, knowing that doing so may cost you your life. If you are going to die, make your death matter by making your life matter: die in service to the living.

Any one activity whatever it may be,
when it has ceased at its proper time,
suffers no evil because it has ceased;
nor does the one who has done this act,
suffer any evil for this reason that the act has ceased.
In like manner then the whole which consists of all the acts,
which is our life,
if it ceases at its proper time,
suffers no evil for this reason that it has ceased;
nor has the one who has terminated this series at the proper
time,
been ill dealt with.[33]
But the proper time and the limit nature fixes,
sometimes as in old age the peculiar nature of man,
are determined by the universal nature
and in a way that maintains the whole universe
ever young and perfect.
And everything that is useful to the universal
is always good and in season.[34]

(MARCUS AURELIUS, THE MEDITATIONS OF MARCUS AURELIUS:
SELECTIONS ANNOTATED & EXPLAINED, P. 205)

Take up your cross and follow me.[35]

(GOSPEL ACCORDING TO MATTHEW 16:24)

36 Jesus is offering not simply what your eyes have not seen, but what your eyes cannot see; not simply what your ears have not heard, but what your ears cannot hear; not simply what your hands have not held and your mind has not conceived, but that which your hands cannot hold and your mind cannot conceive. What is that? Your eyes cannot see themselves, your ears cannot hear themselves, your hand cannot touch itself, your mind cannot conceive itself. Jesus is offering not something outside of yourself, but your very Self itself.

37 To drink from Jesus's mouth is to drink in the wisdom he shares, allowing it to nourish your self and awaken you to Self. The fog of ego that blinds you to your true nature will dissipate and you will know what was hidden from you: you, your Self. And when you awake to who you already are, you become like Jesus, for this is who Jesus is: the awakened Self, one who knows God as all and who acts godly toward all.

38 Everyone longs to know what happens after death because every-one is deluded into thinking that something happens after death. But what happens to the rope when the knot is untied? What happens to the ocean when the wave returns? Nothing. Of course, this way of understanding is anathema to the egoic self so desirous of eternal life as itself. The ego insists on personal immortality and clings to this notion desperately. This clinging to ignorance is the source of much unnecessary suffering.

39 Jesus, like so many great Jewish teachers, answers a question with a question. Have you found the Beginning? It is the same as the ending. You arise in God as God, and you return to God as God.

40 The self dies. The knot when untied is gone. The wave returned to the sea is no longer a wave, but it was and is so much more. The Self is God, the knot is the rope, and the wave is the sea, and these do not die. There is no escape from death when the "you" is the egoic self. There is no death at all when the "you" is the divine Self.

Jesus said: I will give you that
which eyes have not seen,
ears have not heard,
hands did not touch,
and minds have not conceived.[36]

(GOSPEL OF THOMAS 17, *THE GOSPEL OF THOMAS: ANNOTATED & EXPLAINED*, P. 23)

Jesus said: He who drinks from my mouth
will become like I am,
and I will become he.
And the hidden things will be revealed to him.[37]

(GOSPEL OF THOMAS 108, *THE GOSPEL OF THOMAS:
ANNOTATED & EXPLAINED*, P. 131)

The disciples asked Jesus:
Tell us about our end. What will it be?[38]
Jesus replied:
Have you found the Beginning so that you
now seek the end?[39]
The place of the Beginning will be the place of the end.
Blessed is anyone who will stand up in the Beginning
and thereby know the end and never die.[40]

(GOSPEL OF THOMAS 18, *THE GOSPEL OF THOMAS: ANNOTATED & EXPLAINED*, P. 25)

41 The Kingdom of God is not elsewhere than here. It is not in heaven
or in some foreign land. It is not in one religion or another, or one
political philosophy or another. You don't have to travel somewhere to
find it or take yet another class to learn of it. It is within you. It is you,
when you know the "you" you truly are.

Because the Kingdom is you, the Self, the Atman that is Brahman, the eternal "I" that is your very "I," it cannot be seen. It cannot
become an object. It is the eternal Subject. The Kingdom is not a static
thing to be found, but a dynamic way to be lived. Know who you
are—God—and live as you are—godly.

Jesus said:
If your leaders say to you,
"Look! The Kingdom is in the sky!"
then the birds will be there before you are.
If they say that the Kingdom is in the sea,
then the fish will be there before you are.
Rather, the Kingdom is within you and it is outside of you.
(GOSPEL OF THOMAS 3A, *THE GOSPEL OF THOMAS: ANNOTATED & EXPLAINED*, P. 5)

Surely this teaching which I give you this day
Is not baffling or out of reach.
It is not in the sky, that you should say,
"Who among us can fly into the heavens and retrieve it for
us?"
Nor is it beyond the sea, that you should say,
"Who among us can cross the oceans and retrieve it for us?"
Know the teaching is very close to you,
In your mouth and in your heart—live it![41]
(DEUTERONOMY 30:11–14)

O God, when you are closer to me than my jugular vein,
how can I call out to you saying "O, O"
because the address of "O" is used
for those who are at a distance.
(RUMI, *MESNEVI*, CITED IN *FUNDAMENTALS OF RUMI'S THOUGHT:
A MEVLEVI SUFI PERSPECTIVE*, P. 264)

42   The Beloved and the Kingdom of God, which is the state of knowing
the Beloved, are not other than you, or elsewhere than here, or some
time other than now. This is the central message of perennial wisdom:
tat tvam asi, you are That, as the Hindu sages put it in Sanskrit. As
long as you are looking for God, you cannot find God, because God is
the one who is looking.

I am not talking of a reunion with the Beloved
since I have never been away from the Beloved.

(UNNAMED SUFI POET CITED IN *FUNDAMENTALS OF RUMI'S THOUGHT:
A MEVLEVI SUFI PERSPECTIVE*, P. 264)

Jesus was asked, "When will the Kingdom of God come?"
He answered, "The coming of the Kingdom of God
cannot be observed.
People will not say, 'Look! Here it is!' or 'Look! There it is!'
For the Kingdom of God is within you."[42]

(GOSPEL ACCORDING TO LUKE 17:20–21)

His disciples asked him:
When is the Kingdom coming?
He replied: It is not coming in an easily observable manner.
People will not be saying, "Look, it's over here"
or "Look, it's over there."
Rather, the Kingdom of the Father is already
spread out on the earth,
and people aren't aware of it.

(GOSPEL OF THOMAS 113, *THE GOSPEL OF THOMAS:
ANNOTATED & EXPLAINED*, P. 137)

43 How could you observe the Kingdom? How could you recognize it? It isn't something you have seen before, that you might say, "Oh, there it is." The Kingdom isn't an object to be seen, but a way of seeing in and of itself. When you see God in all things and all things in God (regardless of the name you use to point toward the Tao that cannot be named), you are in the Kingdom; indeed, you are the Kingdom. There is no waiting for the Kingdom of God; there is only living the way of godliness here and now—living it not as a tactic to earn some reward, but living it because, knowing who you are, you can live no other way.

44 Look deeply into the faces of the mother suckling her child and of the child suckling, and you will see a moment of complete surrender: the mother surrendering to the child, and the child surrendering to the mother. Compare this to people in a restaurant feeding themselves or trying to get their young children to eat or behave or at least stop disturbing the diners around them. What is the difference? The lack of surrender. The Kingdom manifests when you are surrendered to Self. This is a gift you cannot give yourself, but it is one for which you can prepare yourself to receive. The purpose of spiritual practice—meditation, prayer, chanting, yoga, tai chi—is to prepare you to receive the gift of awakening, the milk of the Mother, when it is time.

45 The self thinks in literal terms and misunderstands the sages, who most often teach in parables and paradox.

46 In other words, when you reconcile all opposites and know that each goes with the other, then you will see the Kingdom and be the Kingdom.

47 That is when you realize that you are the Kingdom and therefore cannot see, grasp, walk, or imagine it as other than the One that is you. It is then you shall discover that you have already entered into that state of nondual consciousness that is the Kingdom of God.

His disciples asked him:
When will the dead rest?
When will the new world arrive?
He replied:
That which you are waiting for has come,
but you don't recognize it.[43]
(GOSPEL OF THOMAS 51, *THE GOSPEL OF THOMAS: ANNOTATED & EXPLAINED*, P. 67)

Jesus saw infants being suckled.
He said to his disciples:
These infants taking milk are like
those who enter the Kingdom.[44]
His disciples asked him:
If we are infants will we enter the Kingdom?[45]
Jesus responded:
When you make the two into one,
and when you make the inside like the outside
and the outside like the inside,
and the upper like the lower,
and thus make the male and the female the same,
so that the male isn't male and the female isn't female.[46]
When you make an eye to replace an eye,
and a hand to replace a hand,
and a foot to replace a foot,
and an image to replace an image,
then you will enter the Kingdom.[47]
(GOSPEL OF THOMAS 22, *THE GOSPEL OF THOMAS: ANNOTATED & EXPLAINED*, P. 33)

48 The self must be emptied of itself that the Self might know itself.

49 When you are stripped of ego, the narrow mind—the self prone to alienation, selfishness, and exploitation—then you will see Jesus as he really is, and as you really are: God manifest.

50 When you can dance joyously without the covering of ego, experiencing and expressing the sheer delight of being alive as the living One, you will know the Kingdom of Heaven.

51 Then you will see yourself mirrored in Christ consciousness, reflected in the face of God, as a face of God, and you will not be afraid. You are always reflected in the face of God, but when the ego looks into that mirror and sees its true Self, it is frightened, imagining that the true Self exists only at the expense of the ego's existence. This isn't so. When the ego is empty and humble, you realize that it too is a face of God. The knot is no less the rope for being a knot. The wave is no less the ocean for being waved. The self when awake is no less itself, just so much more than itself: the Self.

52 There is only one way to know with certainty that what these teachers teach is true: experience it for yourself. Books can remind you of what your Self knows but your self has forgotten. Reasoning can help you discern which books and which teachers lead you to compassion, and which only seek to enlist you in their service. But in the end, you have to prove or disprove the Truth for yourself. This is what makes the spiritually independent, spiritually independent.

Unless you change and become as little children,
you cannot enter the Kingdom of Heaven.
Whomever becomes as humble as a tiny child,
This one is the greatest in the Kingdom of Heaven.[48]

(GOSPEL ACCORDING TO MATTHEW 18:3–4)

His disciples asked him:
When will you appear to us?
When will we see you?
Jesus replied:
When you strip naked without shame[49]
and trample your clothing underfoot
just as little children do,[50]
then you will look at the son of the living one
without being afraid.[51]

(GOSPEL OF THOMAS 37, *THE GOSPEL OF THOMAS: ANNOTATED & EXPLAINED*, P. 49)

How are you to know for certain
that you are liberated from the bondage of ignorance
and have realized the Atman, which is absolute existence,
pure consciousness and abiding bliss?
The words of the scriptures,
your own power of reasoning
and the teachings of your master
should all help to convince you—
but the only absolute proof is
direct and immediate experience, within your own soul.[52]

(SHANKARA, *CREST-JEWEL OF DISCRIMINATION*, P. 112)

53 Free from the illusion of this and that, you are now free to play in the fields of this and that. Knowing you are God doesn't lift you out of the world but brings you more deeply into the world. It is said of the second-century sage Rabbi Samuel Yarhina'ah that the streets of heaven were as bright to him as the streets of his own town (Talmud, *Berachot* 58b). But as Martin Buber tells us in *The Way of Man according to the Teachings of Hasidism*, "It is a greater thing if the streets of your native town are as bright to you as the paths of heaven. For it is here, where you stand, that you should try to make shine the light of the hidden divine life" (p. 38, adapted).

54 This is where you are "going." Whether you realize your truest Self during your lifetime or at the moment of your death, the discovery is the same: *tat tvam asi*, you are That.

55 These are the four basic postures available to humans: you can sit, walk, lie down, or stand up. Shankara is telling you that in all you do, know the You you are. When you walk, ask yourself, "Who is walking?" and notice that one who observes the walking isn't herself walking. When you sit or lie down, ask yourself, "Who is sitting, who is lying down?" and notice that the one who knows you are sitting or lying down isn't doing either. This is the knower that cannot be known; this is the pure Subject that cannot know itself as object. This is the One in which knower, knowing, and known are one.

Nothing binds me to this world.
I no longer identify myself
with the physical body or the mind.
I am one with the Atman, the undying.
I am the Atman....
I am absolute reality, eternal goodness....
I am neither this object nor that.
I am That which makes all objects manifest....
I am Reality, without beginning, without equal.
I have no part in the illusion of "I" and "You,"
"this" and "that."[53]

(SHANKARA, *CREST-JEWEL OF DISCRIMINATION*, P. 115)

I dwell within all beings as Atman,
the pure consciousness,
the ground of all phenomena, internal and external.
I am both the enjoyer and that which is enjoyed.
In my days of ignorance,
I used to think of these as being separate from myself.
Now I know that I am All.[54]

(SHANKARA, *CREST-JEWEL OF DISCRIMINATION*, P. 115)

No matter what you are doing—
walking, standing, sitting or lying down,
the illumined seer whose delight is the Atman
lives in joy and freedom.[55]

(SHANKARA, *CREST-JEWEL OF DISCRIMINATION*, P. 120)

56 Moses offers a similar teaching. Again referencing the four basic postures—sitting, walking, lying down, and standing up—Moses teaches you to recite the wisdom that he has imparted to you: *YHVH Eloheinu, YHVH Echad*—Reality is God, Reality is one. Knowing this, you know that when you sit, God sits; when you walk, God walks; when you lie down, God lies down; when you stand up, God stands up; because, again, you are That. If this teaching seems to be the opposite of the previous teaching, remember there are no opposites, only polarities in a singular Reality.

57 Death is your koan, the puzzle that will ultimately crack open the narrow mind of self and awaken you to the spacious mind of Self. When working with any koan, any parable offered by the sages of perennial wisdom, "turn Her, and turn Her, for everything is in Her. Reflect on Her and grow old and gray with Her. Don't turn from Her, for nothing is better than Her" (*Pirke Avot* 5:26). Turning the koan of death means witnessing the passing away of self moment by moment, and then noticing that the One who witnesses does not pass away. Rest in That even as you climb the ladder as the other.

58 Ceaseless prayer is the recitation of a text, or word—a mantra, if you like—throughout your waking day. Working with a mantra, like working with a koan, is a simple and yet powerful way to awaken your self to the Self. In the tradition of the Desert Mothers and Fathers, many Orthodox Christians ceaselessly pray the Jesus Prayer: "Jesus Christ have mercy on me."

59 Abba Benjamin is drawing from Saint Paul: "And we urge you, beloved, to admonish the idlers, encourage the faint-hearted, help the weak, be patient with all of them. See that none of you repays evil for evil, but always seeks to do good to one another and to all. Rejoice always, pray without ceasing, and give thanks in all circumstances, for this is the will of God in Christ Jesus in you" (1 Thessalonians 5:14–18, NRSV).

Take to heart this wisdom with which I give you this day.
Impart it upon your children.
Recite them when you sit at home
and when you walk on your way,
when you lie down and when you stand up.[56]

(DEUTERONOMY 6:6–7)

[Amma Sarah] also said,
"I put my foot out to ascend the ladder,
and I place death before my eyes before going up it."[57]

(AMMA SARAH, DESERT FATHERS AND MOTHERS: EARLY CHRISTIAN
WISDOM SAYINGS—ANNOTATED & EXPLAINED, P. 77)

As he was dying,
Abba Benjamin said to his sons,
"If you observe the following, you can be saved:
'Be joyful at all times,
pray without ceasing,[58]
and give thanks for all things.'"[59]

(ABBA BENJAMIN, DESERT FATHERS AND MOTHERS: EARLY CHRISTIAN
WISDOM SAYINGS—ANNOTATED & EXPLAINED, P. 125)

60 Balance that is out of kilter is not balance. This is the double bind of spiritual practice: you are trying to become that which you already are and, in so doing, pit one sense of self against another, albeit a higher or holier sense of Self. The war that you wage is with yourself. The self that seeks to change itself is the self that needs changing. The self that seeks to surrender itself is the self that must be surrendered. This spiritual work and inner warfare, if you engage in it, may lead to awakening as you at last realize the foolishness of your quest. But there is an easier way: realize that balance and imbalance are both part of Reality's dance.

When Chuang-tzu was close to death,
his disciples wanted to prepare for a sumptuous burial.
Chuang-tzu said, "I take heaven and earth
for my inner and outer coffins,
the sun and the moon for my jade disks,
the stars and constellations for my pearls and beads,
and the myriad things for my parting gifts.
The furnishings for my funeral are already prepared;
what is there to add?"
"But we are afraid the crows
and vultures will eat you, Master!"
"Above ground I will be eaten by crows and vultures;
below ground I will be eaten by worms and ants.
How partisan to take from one group to give to the other!
If you use imbalance to achieve balance,
your balance will be out of kilter.
If you use speculation to establish solid thinking,
your thinking will be specious.
Bright guys are mere servants of things;
only spirit people can think it all through.
It has always been true that bright guys
cannot hold a candle to spirit people—
they are fools who rely only on what their senses tell them
and immerse themselves in the human realm.
All their efforts are wasted—what a shame!"[60]

(CHUANG-TZU, CHAPTER 32, *CHUANG-TZU: THE TAO OF PERFECT HAPPINESS—
SELECTIONS ANNOTATED & EXPLAINED*, P. 45)

61 The penultimate spiritual achievement is that reached by Yen Hui. This is why he is always "getting there" and never "being there." The "there" at which Yen Hui arrives is the state of Witness. He can observe his body and not be his body. He can watch his emotions and desires, and not identify with them. He can see the workings of his mind, and yet not be attached to them. He is getting there.

Being "there" is one step beyond. When you are free from your body, you are free to inhabit the body without fear that you will be trapped in the appetites of the body. When you are free from emotions, you are free to feel all emotions, knowing you will not be trapped in one or the other. When you are free from thoughts, you are free to think widely and creatively without fear of becoming trapped in cleverness. When resting in the Nothing, you are free to play with everything.

62 Confucius praises Yen Hui for having gotten as far as he did. Then he lays a trap for him that he hopes will push him one step beyond. The trap is the trap of the teacher. Those who rest in oblivion alone have nothing to teach, for they have become as nothing themselves. To take up the mantle of teacher you have to shift from being empty to constantly emptying, from being superior to constantly humbling yourself. The teacher who is constantly emptying can fill another with wisdom and yet not become filled with pride. In this, form and emptiness are both honored, and the true arrival is realized.

Yen Hui said, "I'm getting there!"
Confucius asked, "How so?"
"I am oblivious about benevolence and righteousness."
"That's great. But not quite it."
The next day he was back again.
"I'm getting there!"
"How so?"
"I am oblivious about rites and music."
"That's great. But not quite it."
The next day he was back again.
"I'm getting there!"
"How so?"
"I can sit in oblivion!"
Confucius was startled: "What do you mean,
'sit in oblivion'?"
"I let my limbs and physical structure fall away,
do away with perception and intellect,
separate myself from body-form,
and let go of all knowledge,
thus joining Great Pervasion.
This is what I mean by 'sitting in oblivion.'"[61]
"Joined with Tao, you have no more likes within.
Transformed in Tao, you have no more guidelines without.
You have indeed become a worthy man!
May I ask to become your follower?"[62]

(CHUANG-TZU, CHAPTER 6, *CHUANG-TZU: THE TAO OF PERFECT HAPPINESS—*
SELECTIONS ANNOTATED & EXPLAINED, P. 111)

63 This is the poem of the awakened sage. This is the realization toward which you are moving, and which you will realize at this moment or the next moment or the last moment. Everything has its place, its purpose, and its time. Everything is ripening and falling away. The lesser self is no less vital than the greater Self. Nothing is discarded and nothing is kept. Everything is allowed to come in its time and to depart in its time. You are never closer or farther away from "now," and "now" is the only time in which realization can happen.

Everything in this world has its moment,
a season of ripening and falling away:
Moments of birthing and moments of dying;
moments of planting and moments of reaping.
Moments of killing and moments of healing;
moments of demolition and moments of building.
Moments of weeping and moments of laughing;
moments of mourning and moments of dancing.
Moments of scattering stones and
moments of gathering stones;
moments of embracing and moments of distance.
Moments of seeking and moments of losing;
moments of clinging and moments of releasing.
Moments of tearing and moments of mending;
moments of silence and moments of talking.
Moments of loving and moments of hating;
moments of warring and moments of peacemaking.[63]

(ECCLESIASTES 3:1–10, *ECCLESIASTES: ANNOTATED & EXPLAINED*, PP. 27–28)

How Shall I Live? ☐

If you believe heaven is an option for you, you will, assuming you are a rational person, choose to live in a manner that will earn you entrance to heaven when you die. Or, if you believe it isn't actions but beliefs that get you into heaven, you will do your best to hold to those beliefs throughout your life, or at least at the moment of your death.

There isn't anything unusual or wrong with this. It's merely common sense. If I want to get into Harvard, I will work hard to get the grades and build a resume that will motivate Harvard's admissions committee to let me in. The difference between Harvard and heaven is that while you can contact Harvard and get a pretty clear sense of what the admissions folks are looking for, there is no clear understanding of what it is that will get you into heaven. Of course this is not for lack of trying. Every religion that posits a heaven has its own entrance exam. The problem is you have no idea as to which one is the right one.

The Odds of Gods

I was born and raised as a Jew. While it is true that for all I know my Southern Baptist friends have the actual key to heaven, namely accepting Jesus as my Lord and Savior and being baptized into the Southern Baptist version of Christianity, but if they do, there is no way I'm going to reach for it. My Jewish conditioning is just too strong. In a sense I would rather risk eternal damnation than break a covenant with God to which my parents insist I'm bound, even though it was made thousands of years before I was born. I'm one of God's chosen, but according to Saint Paul and most of my Christian neighbors, unless I accept Jesus as Christ, the only thing I'm chosen for is hellfire.

There are millions upon millions of Christians who believe this way. Can they all be deluded? If I were to judge the correctness of belief by the numbers of believers, the twelve million Jews in the world hardly stack up against two billion plus Christians.

But even if I thought this way, which Christianity would I join? Some of them are mutually exclusive and hold that only they are the true Christians destined for heaven. As Jesus himself says, "Not everyone who cries 'Lord, Lord' gets to enter the Kingdom of Heaven" (Matthew 7:21). So how do I choose?

Add to the competing Christianities the competing claims of over a billion and a half Muslims and eight hundred million Hindus. Perhaps one of their religions or sects is the true faith. I can't prove which if any are false, and I can't discern which if any might be true, so what am I to do if I want to get into heaven?

There are basically only three options open to me. First, I can dismiss religion altogether. Atheism at least has the decency to be consistent and simple in its message: God is a delusion, and religion a con, so avoid both at all costs. Fair enough, but can they prove this? No, they can't. The atheist can no more prove that there is no God than my local swami can prove Krishna is God. So opting for atheism is no more logical than opting for any of the competing faiths to which we humans adhere.

The second option, a variation on the first, is to just pick a religion and hope for the best. This is a version of Pascal's Wager. The French philosopher Blaise Pascal (1623–1662) also admitted that there was no way to prove or disprove the existence of God. He reasoned, however, that if there is no God and yet you choose to believe in God, you haven't lost anything. This is like believing in unicorns: it does no harm as long as you don't hear voices of the Great Unicorn telling you to murder those unicorn deniers in your neighborhood.

On the other hand, if there is a God and you choose not to believe in God, this could go badly for you, and you might end up in hell for all eternity. So Pascal argued that it is in your best interest to opt for belief, because the cost of unbelief could potentially be catastrophic.

As a Catholic, Pascal, when he thought of "God," thought of only one: the Holy Trinity (God the Father, God the Son, and God the Holy Spirit) professed in the Nicene Creed. It never occurred to him that he might choose the Jewish YHVH or the Muslim Allah, let alone the Hindu's Kali or Shiva. The problem with Pascal's Wager is that it isn't just a matter of choosing a God—you have to choose the right God. And, because we have no objective way of determining which God is the right God, having to choose one God among others is no less risky than choosing no God at all.

Add to this the notion that if there is a God, and you happen to choose that God instead of a false God, chances are that God is going to know your profession of faith is simply a hedge against eternal damnation and not an authentic expression of love and devotion. If I were this God, I would be angrier at the person playing the odds in a cosmic crapshoot than at the person who sincerely opted for atheism.

Which brings me to our third option: refusing to play. This is the way explored in the texts found in this chapter. The assumption of perennial wisdom is that no god is God and that all names fall short of the absolute Reality that can't be named. Free from the need to figure out which god is God and which religion is the true religion, we are free to see for ourselves what might constitute the right way to live.

Being spiritually independent doesn't mean we lack a road map to right behavior. On the contrary, we are free to examine all maps to see where each leads us, and if any roads overlap or converge, thus hinting at a common truth, that just might be the right way for all of us. But, without a fixed God or revelation, how would we know if we are moving in the right direction?

Without God, All Things Are Permitted?

First let's look at the notion that God is a reliable guide to right and righteous behavior. In Dostoevsky's novel *The Brothers Karamazov* (1880),

Ivan Karamazov says that without God, all things are permitted (part 4, book 11, chapter 4). The idea is simple enough: without God to tell us what is right, and without the promise of punishment for doing what is wrong, we humans would be at a loss to determine the former, and without restraint when it comes to doing the latter. So ingrained is this idea in some people that I regularly have students in my classes tell me that if it wasn't for their fear of going to hell, they would give in to every demonic desire that occurred to them.

When I push back a bit on this, they double down on their own innate wickedness. I still doubt they are as evil as they have been taught to believe they are, but I am impressed by how deep their conviction goes and how well indoctrinated these students are in the wickedness of humanity and the wrath of God.

Once it is clear that they are serious, I take another tack and ask them what it is that God requires of them. Never in all my years of teaching has any of these students quoted the prophet Micah: "You know, O humans, what God requires: do justly, love mercy, and walk humbly with your God" (Micah 6:8). Instead, they immediately begin to rage against a series of "anti-Christian" agendas—liberalism, feminism, secularism, and civil rights for homosexuals—all of which God opposes.

I often bring up Jesus's teaching in the Gospel according to Matthew that we are to clothe the naked, feed the hungry, care for the ill, and visit the imprisoned (Matthew 25), and many of them think I'm misquoting Jesus, which I assuredly am not. "It sounds like socialism to me," more than a few students have told me. When I show them that it is Jesus and not Karl Marx who said this, echoing centuries of Hebrew prophets before him, they just reiterate their argument as if I—and more importantly Jesus—had said nothing at all. My point isn't to pick a partisan fight, but to say that God can be used to sanction any moral stance one wishes to hold.

During a passionate and largely liberal discussion among clergy about the horrors of genocide, especially those sanctioned by Allah, the God of Islam, I raised the genocides sanctioned by YHVH, the God of the

Hebrews. In the book of Deuteronomy, the Hebrews are told to slaughter every man, woman, and child of the Amorites (Deuteronomy 2:33–35) and to do the same to the inhabitants of the kingdom of Og (Deuteronomy 3:4–7). In the book of Joshua, we are told that when the walls of Jericho fell, God told the Hebrews to massacre not only all the human inhabitants of the city but their livestock as well (Joshua 6:21). If God sanctions these acts of brutality, why could God not sanction others?

"No, no, no," one pastor told me, with others nodding in agreement, "God had to erase these evil people from the earth because they were polluting the human race spiritually and even genetically. The Hebrew people were a tool for a very justified and necessary end."

"Do you think the people of Jericho, Og, and the Amorite kingdom saw themselves as evil?" I asked.

"Probably not," he replied. "But they were, and that's why God had to eradicate them."

"If they didn't know they were evil," I asked, "and yet God knew and used the Hebrews to cleanse the world of their evil, how do we know we aren't evil, and God, Allah, isn't using Muslims to cleanse the world of the plague of Western culture?"

While I changed no minds on that panel, I did force the argument to devolve into the bedrock of religious relativism: "God would never order the destruction of God's church, and besides, Allah isn't God."

"And how do we know Allah isn't God?"

"Because God has a Son, Jesus Christ, and Allah does not."

There is no arguing with that position, and the only option is to start a rousing chorus of "Is too; is not; is too; is not." Is it at all surprising that the rise of the spiritually independent is happening at an ever more rapid pace?

With God, All Things Are Permitted

While seeing through the silliness of such religious debate doesn't yet offer us a path toward righteousness, it does place responsibility for finding that path on us rather than God. Dostoevsky's Ivan is wrong when he says, "Without God all things are permitted." It is truer to say the opposite: *with* God all things are permitted.

Just this morning, in a conversation with a nationally renowned Imam, I was told, "Allah sanctions none of the violence done in His Name. On the contrary, people are misusing the Name of God to excuse their own quest for power. In this they are polluting the very essence of Islam."

When it comes to the "essence of Islam" I yield to my friend the Imam. But when it comes to God, I both agree and disagree with him. My understanding of God is not drawn from holy books, but from my own experiences with contemplative practice. For me, God is reality, and while reality includes good and evil, it sanctions neither. So in this sense I agree with the Imam. But, Allah (like Krishna, YHVH, the Trinity) are images of God reflecting the biases of those poets, prophets, priests, and theologians who create them. And because these gods made in our image, they reflect our biases and excuse and even sanction both the best and the worst of what we humans are capable.

It is God who sanctions genocide, whereas left to our own devices few of us would opt to participate in one.

> When YHVH your God brings you to the land that you are about to enter and possess, and He dislodges many nations before you—the Hittites, Girgashites, Amorites, Canaanites, Perizzites, Hivites, and Jebusites, seven nations much larger than you—and YHVH your God delivers them to you and you defeat them, you must doom them to destruction: grant them no terms and give them no quarter.... Instead, this is what you shall do to them: you shall tear down their altars, smash their pillars, cut down their sacred posts, and consign their images to the fire. For you are a people consecrated to YHVH your God: of all the peoples on earth YHVH your God chose you to be His treasured people.
>
> (DEUTERONOMY 7:1–6, JPS)

It is God who willed the First Crusade (1096–1099), at least according to Pope Urban II, and had God's will not been backed up by the church's promise that participation in the Crusade would earn one atonement for all worldly sin, most people would have merely shrugged and stayed home.

It is God who orders us to kill infidels, "to slay them wherever you find them and drive them out of the places they drove you out of, for persecution is worse than slaughter" (Qur'an 2:191). It is God who plants the idea that martyrdom is good for the soul, whereas most of us, left to our own devices, would prefer a more benign "live and let live" attitude. With God, all manner of madness is permitted, indeed commanded and sanctioned. But without God, we are forced to think these things through for ourselves.

But let's be careful here. I'm not saying that atrocities don't occur without God. Look at Hitler's Germany, Stalin's Russia, Pol Pot's Cambodia, and Kim Jong-un's North Korea. But were these really God-free horrors, or did Nazism, Stalinism, and Communism not become gods in and of themselves? In this context, "God" refers to any idea to which people are willing to surrender their will, their reason, their freedom, and often their lives (though it is preferable to surrender the lives of others in the name of your God than your own life in service to your God).

What I am saying is that all theologies and ideologies are of human origin. The gods produced in these systems are gods that can be named and not the Eternal God beyond naming. This doesn't mean there is no God, only that whatever this God may be, it cannot be named, owned, or monopolized by any group to sanction its own ends and excuse whatever means it uses to achieve those ends.

Those of us who are spiritually independent are not without ideas about God, but we, in sync with the prophet Micah, walk humbly with our ideas of God, knowing with Lao Tzu that any God that can be named is not the Eternal God.

Perennial Compass

If it is true that "with God, all things are permitted," how then do we spiritually independent types decide what is right and wrong? We return to our philosophical principles: we are all manifestations of a singular Reality and, as such, are intrinsically called to love both neighbor and self.

The principle is not rocket science: treating others justly and with compassion is good, while treating them unjustly and cruelly is bad. Of course we can argue over exactly what is just and kind in any given situation, but it is justice and kindness rather than obedience to an idea of God that motivates us. We can argue passionately about justice and kindness, and the end of our argument will always be a more nuanced understanding of these ideas. In short, the spiritually independent place values over theology. We are not the first to do so.

In the story of Sodom, God informs Abraham of God's intent to slaughter all the people of Sodom. Abraham's response is hardly one of acquiescence: "Far be it from You to do such a thing, to bring death upon the innocent as well as the guilty!... Shall not the Judge of all the earth deal justly?" (Genesis 18:25, JPS). God and Abraham then bargain over what it will take to save Sodom, and eventually they settle on ten righteous people: if ten righteous people can be found in Sodom, God will spare the city. While it is true that these ten people cannot be found, and God does what God intended to do from the beginning, it is also true that it is the role of the spiritually independent to stand up to the gods of the world's religions and demand justice, even as we continue our struggle to define just what justice may be.

If you listen to the great sages and mystics of perennial wisdom in the pages that follow, you will find a moral compass whose needle always points toward justice and compassion. You will still have to apply the compass to every situation you encounter, and specifics are still yours to work out, but you are not left without direction—it's called the Golden Rule:

In all things, do to others what you would have others do to you;
for this is the Law and the Prophets.

(CHRISTIANITY, MATTHEW 7:12)

Do not do to others what you do not want done to yourself.

(CONFUCIANISM, CONFUCIUS, ANALECTS 15:23)

Do nothing to others that you yourself would find hurtful.

(BUDDHISM, BUDDHA, UDANA-VARGA 5,1)

This is the sum of duty: do not do to others that if done to you
would cause you suffering.

(HINDUISM, MAHABHARATA 5, 1517)

Treat all creatures in the world as you would like to be treated.

(JAINISM, MAHAVIRA, SUTRAKRITANGA 1.11.33)

No one of you is a believer until you desire for others that which
you desire for yourself.

(ISLAM, MUHAMMAD, HADITH)

What is hateful to you, do not do to another. That is the entire
Teaching; all the rest is commentary.

(JUDAISM, HILLEL, TALMUD, SHABBAT 31A)

Regard your neighbor's gain as your gain, and your neighbor's loss
as your loss.

(TAOISM, TAI SHANG KAN YIN P'IEN)

Do not do to others whatever is injurious to yourself.

(ZOROASTRIANISM, SHAYAST-NA-SHAYAST 13.29)

Lay not on any soul a load that you would not wish to be laid upon
you, and desire not for anyone the things you would not desire for
yourself.

(BAHÁ'Í, BAHÁ'U'LLÁH, GLEANINGS)

The texts that speak to the question *How shall I live?* compose the longest section of *Perennial Wisdom for the Spiritually Independent.* The
reason for this is simple: answering the question *How shall I live?* is the
core quest of the spiritually independent, and it is where the wisdom of

the world's religions tends to free itself from competing theologies and institutions and focus on just what it takes to live well for the benefit of self and other. While I would not suggest you take Pascal's Wager and bet on one god or another, I would not hesitate to suggest you follow the ethical guidance offered in this chapter.

1 While you will come to see that pleasure isn't the foundation of a life well lived, there is no need to deny yourself pleasure altogether. The wise live the middle way, the way of moderation. Pleasure is not your enemy; pain is not your friend. Cultivate and cling to neither; simply enjoy what is pleasurable and suffer through what is not.

2 Since nothing lasts, making any one thing essential to your goal is a trap. You are like a person seeking to fill a bucket with water, never realizing that there are cracks in the bottom that allow the water to run out. You can devote yourself to pleasure, but you will never escape its opposite.

3 The task of the sage is to learn what is true and how best to find it, and then to teach this to others. A teacher who knows only what is written in books and has not tested these things in life is an ineffectual teacher. A learner who takes what is taught and doesn't test it out in life is an ineffectual learner.

4 Light is superior to darkness when you're trying to navigate a darkened room. If you are trying to sleep, however, darkness is superior to light. Don't worry about superior or inferior. Simply take up the tool best suited for the task at hand.

5 What are you given to do? Don't imagine it need be something world-changing, some singular task that is yours alone. Rather, see what each moment is calling you to do: feed your child, walk your dog, save a person from friendless despair. Whatever it is you are called to do, if it leads to justice and compassion, do it with joy, knowing that you are here to do and not simply to be.

6 Eat, drink, work ... this is your life. Don't ask for something more or different; rather, realize that you are the way God plants gardens each spring, cuts grass each summer, rakes leaves each autumn, and clears the sidewalk of snow each winter. When you know this, nothing is mundane: "Behold! How wonderous! How marvelous! I chop wood! I carry water!" (Zen proverb).

I yielded to every desire
my eyes made known to me;
I denied myself nothing.
No pleasure was taboo.
And, in truth, my heart rejoiced in it all,[1]
and this joy was the reward for all my accumulation.
Yet when I measured this joy
against the quality of my deeds
and the energy spent in doing them,[2]
there was no doubt that this, too, was absurd,
a useless panting,
yielding nothing of lasting value.
Having tested pleasure,
I turned to folly and madness.
Perhaps these would surpass wisdom.
For this is the task of the sage,
to do all that can be done
that those who follow
might learn from their example.[3]
And I discerned that wisdom is superior to folly
the way light is superior to darkness.[4]

(ECCLESIASTES 2:10–13, ECCLESIASTES: ANNOTATED & EXPLAINED, P. 17)

So I concluded that
there is nothing better for you
than to find joy in what you are given to do,
for doing is your lot.[5]
And none can see what the future holds.[6]

(ECCLESIASTES 3:22, ECCLESIASTES: ANNOTATED & EXPLAINED, P. 37)

7 Anxiety arises when you wish things to be other than they are or when you imagine they could be other than they are. Things are the way they are because at the moment they cannot be other than they are. Embrace the moment without hesitation—the good and the bad—and joy will arise and anxiety will fade.

8 It takes very little to bring joy to the wise: sufficient food and drink; clean clothes; combed hair; a beloved friend, partner, or spouse; and a willingness to do whatever good you can do without reservation.

So what is worthwhile?
Simply to eat and drink
and find pleasure in your daily tasks.
This is the life-way you are given.
Take pleasure in whatever you receive,
no matter how much or how little;
accept what is and learn to enjoy it;
this is the gift reality offers.
In this way you will not fall prey to anxiety,
for you will be filled with joy.[7]

(ECCLESIASTES 5:17–19, *ECCLESIASTES. ANNOTATED & EXPLAINED*, P. 53)

So here is my guidance
and the right path:
eat your bread with joy, and drink your wine with gladness;
let your clothes be white, and let your head never lack for
oil;
find a beloved with whom to share your life—
no matter how long or short.
This is what makes your life and your labor worthwhile.
Whatever falls into your hand to do, do it without
hesitation.[8]
For in the grave there is neither doing, nor reason,
nor knowledge, nor wisdom.

(ECCLESIASTES 9:7–10, *ECCLESIASTES: ANNOTATED & EXPLAINED*, P. 85)

9 There is much wisdom in scripture, but you have to tease it out, and there are always those who manipulate scripture for their own ends. Test everything against reason and righteousness. What is true will always lead you toward compassion and justice. What is false will always lead you to the exploitation of person and planet in service to self and selfishness.

10 Don't imagine that the passion people have for the opinions they hold says anything about the quality of the opinions themselves.

11 Do not seek to find the right teaching, but seek to know the truth for yourself.

12 Karma yoga awakens you to the union (yoga) of the-One-as-many through service to the many-as-the-One. If you practice the way of service, do so selflessly, seeking no benefit or reward other than the opportunity to serve. In this way your actions are always for the benefit of the other, and resting in that, you are free from worrying about results.

13 Spirituality isn't about the cessation of doing, but the cessation of doing for selfish reasons. Do what is right to maintain yourself in good health. Do what is right to help others do the same. Just don't imagine you are in control of the results.

14 How can you tame the mind? If you go after it with a stick, you only cause more agitation. The mind is like a puppy jumping from this to that and back again. Give the puppy something to chew on, and she will settle down. With regard to the mind, the something to chew on is a text repeated in Passage Meditation, and a mantra or koan designed to open the self to Self when turned over and over in the mind.

As one can drink water from any side of a full tank,
so the skilled theologians can wrest from any scripture
that which will serve their purpose....[9]
When your reason has crossed the entanglements of illusion,
then shall you become indifferent both
to the philosophies you have heard
and to those you may yet hear.[10]
When the intellect, unbewildered by
the multiplicity of holy scripts,
stands unperturbed in blissful contemplation of the Infinite,
then have you attained spirituality.[11]

(BHAGAVAD GITA 1:46–53, *BHAGAVAD GITA: ANNOTATED & EXPLAINED*, P. 19)

All honor to those whose minds control their senses;
For they are thereby beginning to practice Karma Yoga,
the Path of Right Action,
keeping themselves always unattached.[12]
Do your duty as prescribed;
for action for duty's sake is superior to inaction.
Even the maintenance of the body would be impossible
if one remained inactive.[13]

(BHAGAVAD GITA 3:7–8, *BHAGAVAD GITA: ANNOTATED & EXPLAINED*, P. 25)

It is good to tame the mind,
which is flighty and difficult to restrain,
rushing wherever it will.
A tamed mind brings happiness.[14]

(DHAMMAPADA 3:1–2, *DHAMMAPADA: ANNOTATED & EXPLAINED*, P. 13)

15 The wording here can be misleading. Self-abnegation is not self-deprivation. The self, the ego, is a necessary aspect of your larger Self. As the ancient Jewish sages taught, without the capacity for self you couldn't fall in love, raise a family, or run a business (*Midrash Rabbah* 9:7). The problem isn't that you have a self, it is that you allow the self to fall into the trap of selfishness. You can avoid that trap by doing what you do for the sake of God and the benefit of others. In this way you are nourished, but never at the expense of others. In this way you are honored without being elevated to playing God, knowing instead it is God who is playing you.

16 There is no one way to Truth, only your way. There is no one magic name for God that will get God's attention. You can pray to Christ or Krishna, to Allah or YHVH. The name isn't the thing, and it is the quality of your prayer, not the name you pray to, that awakens you. There may be a path best suited to you, but if someone tells you there is only one way to Truth, you can be certain that they don't know the Truth.

17 Wait, don't you want to be remembered? Don't you want someone to know what it is you have done for them or the world? If so, you are acting for self rather than Self, for ego rather than God. But there is more to this teaching than simply a reminder to avoid self-aggrandizement. Think of a seasoned camper who, when she leaves the forest, takes everything she brought with her back home, leaving the forest as she found it. What do others think when they stumble on a campsite abandoned and yet littered with garbage? Yes, they know someone was there. But the knowing brings no honor to the previous camper and no joy to the next one.

Many have merged their existence in Mine,
being freed from desire, fear, and anger,
filled always with Me,
and purified by the illuminating flame of self-abnegation.[15]
Howsoever people try to worship Me,
so do I welcome them.
By whatever path they travel,
it leads to Me at last.[16]

(BHAGAVAD GITA 4:10–11, *BHAGAVAD GITA: ANNOTATED & EXPLAINED*, P. 35)

One who is without attachment, free,
the mind centered in wisdom,
actions, being done as a sacrifice,
leaves no trace behind.[17]

(BHAGAVAD GITA 4:23, *BHAGAVAD GITA: ANNOTATED & EXPLAINED*, P. 37)

18 Spirituality is something you do. Someone who is spiritual is engaged in practices—service, devotion, study, meditation—that help cultivate the sense of union with God in God that is your true nature. But these practices should be moderate and not extreme. Teachers who ask you to do the impossible rather than the merely difficult are setting you up to fail in order to make their claims to success all the more seductive to you. The unhappiness that results will be renamed "ego" and "resistance," and you will be told to surrender even more—more money, more time, more devotion, more everything—with the promise that when you have given everything to the guru, the guru will give you God. This is a situation to be avoided. If your teacher makes you miserable, find another teacher.

19 Is the mind ever completely controlled? Perhaps there are some who can do so, but this isn't the only way to find spiritual fulfillment. The very notion of control places you at war with yourself. Don't imagine control this way. Rather than seeking to control your thoughts, seek only to watch them. As you watch them, ask yourself, "Who is watching them?" There is a greater you free from these thoughts. This is the Self that needs neither to control nor to be controlled. This is spacious mind that makes room for all thoughts—good and bad, rational and crazy—without allowing any thought to trigger an action that is detrimental to yourself or others.

Thus keeping your mind always in communion with me,
and with your thoughts subdued,
you shall attain that Peace which is Mine
and which will lead you to liberation at last.
Meditation is not for one who eats too much,
nor for one who eats not at all:
nor for one who is overmuch addicted to sleep,
nor for one who is always awake.
But for one who regulates food and recreation,
who is balanced in action, in sleep and in waking,
it shall dispel all unhappiness.[18]
When the mind, completely controlled,
is centered in the Self
and free from all earthly desires,
then is a person truly spiritual.[19]
(BHAGAVAD GITA 6:15–18, *BHAGAVAD GITA: ANNOTATED & EXPLAINED*, P. 51)

20 These are the signs of the spiritual person: compassion, selflessness, humility, equanimity, forgiveness, grounded, and reasonable. Being spiritual is doing spiritual and not just feeling spiritual. The spiritual life is a life that serves self and other as equal manifestations of the One who is all.

21 Krishna is not saying you don't have these impulses; of course you do. Krishna is saying that they need not control your behavior.

22 Because you are pure, there is no clouding of the self that blinds you to the Self. You know the smaller self to be a manifestation of the larger Self, and you make room for whatever arises in the smaller self. Indifference doesn't mean uncaring; indifference means that you are not asking the world to be different than it is and are confident that you can cultivate justice and compassion no matter how it is.

23 When you see all opposites as complementarities, you no longer imagine a world of fronts without backs or good without evil. You are ready to engage with love whatever you encounter. This is the gift that spiritual practice gives.

One who is incapable of hatred toward any being,
who is kind and compassionate, free from selfishness,
without pride, equable in pleasure and in pain, and forgiving,
Always contented, self-centered, self-controlled, resolute,
with mind and reason dedicated to Me,
such a devotee of Mine is My beloved.
One who does not harm the world,
and whom the world cannot harm,[20]
who is not carried away by any impulse of joy, anger, or fear,
such a one is My beloved.[21]
One who expects nothing,
who is pure, watchful, indifferent,[22] unruffled,
and who renounces all initiative,
such a one is My beloved.
One who is beyond joy and hate,
who neither laments nor desires,
to whom good and evil fortunes are the same,
such a one is My beloved.
One to whom friend and foe are alike,
who welcomes equally honor and dishonor,
heat and cold, pleasure and pain, who is enamored of nothing,
who is indifferent to praise and censure,
who enjoys silence,
who is contented with every fate,
who has no fixed abode,
who is steadfast in mind and filled with devotion,
such a one is My beloved.[23]

(BHAGAVAD GITA 12:13–19, *BHAGAVAD GITA: ANNOTATED & EXPLAINED*, P. 101)

24 If you cannot be honest with yourself, with whom can you be honest? If you cannot bear to hear the truth about yourself from your Self, how can you listen to it from another? Just look without shame and see what is. Don't change it, just observe. The act of seeing is enough to bring you freedom. Knowing that you are capable of evil allows you to be watchful against the evil you might do and frees you from having to project your capacity for evil on to others.

25 That one is your truest Self, the you that knows God is all. This greater you has only compassion for the lesser you, and when this greater you tests your smaller you, it isn't to find you lacking, but to help you grow.

26 This can be tricky. There are tests you can devise that can too easily be passed and thus give you a false sense of divinity that allows you to play God rather than to cultivate the true humility that comes when you know God is playing you. On the other hand, there are tests so difficult that they cannot be passed at all and thus lead you to a despair that takes you off the path altogether. Find the right test, the one that allows you to be your self even as you are surrendered to your Self.

27 There is no arriving on your spiritual journey. There is only this step and the next. Awakening to God in, with, and as you and all beings isn't the end of the journey, just another turn in the road. Keep walking. There may be nothing new to learn, but there is always some new good to do.

Forge ahead, my brothers and sisters;
always examine yourselves without self-deception,
without flattery, without buttering yourselves up.
After all, there's nobody inside you
before whom you need feel ashamed,
or whom you need to impress.[24]
There is someone there,
but one who is pleased with humility;
let that one test you.[25]
And you, too, test yourself.[26]
Always be dissatisfied with what you are,
if you want to arrive at what you are not yet.
Because wherever you are satisfied with yourself,
there you have stuck.
If, though, you say, "That's enough, that's the lot,"
then you've even perished.
Always add some more,
always keep on walking,
always forge ahead.
Don't stop on the road,
don't turn round and go back,
don't wander off the road.[27]

(SAINT AUGUSTINE, SERMON 169.18, *SAINT AUGUSTINE OF HIPPO:*
SELECTIONS FROM CONFESSIONS *AND OTHER ESSENTIAL WRITINGS—*
ANNOTATED & EXPLAINED, P. 5)

28 If there is one prayer that might occupy you throughout your life, it is this, the Prayer of Saint Francis of Assisi:

> *Lord, make me an instrument of your peace.*
> *Where there is hatred, let me sow love;*
> *where there is injury, pardon;*
> *where there is doubt, faith;*
> *where there is despair, hope;*
> *where there is darkness, light;*
> *and where there is sadness, joy.*
>
> *O Divine Master, grant that I may not so much seek*
> *to be consoled as to console;*
> *to be understood as to understand;*
> *to be loved as to love.*
> *For it is in giving that we receive;*
> *it is in pardoning that we are pardoned;*
> *and it is in dying that we are born to eternal life. Amen.*

29 In the book of Genesis, Abraham is called by God to be a "blessing to all the families of the earth" (12:3). You are called to be the same, to live so that all the families of the earth—human and otherwise—are enriched by you. You know you are walking the path of spirit when your family expands and all beings become your brothers and sisters.

Ask God that you may love one another.[28]
You should love all people, even your enemies,
not because they are your brother or sister,
but so that they may become your brother or sister,
so that you may always be aflame with such love,
whether toward one who has become your brother or sister,
or toward your enemies,
so that by loving them
they may become your brothers and sisters.[29]
(SAINT AUGUSTINE, HOMILIES OF THE FIRST EPISTLE OF JOHN, 10.7,
*SAINT AUGUSTINE OF HIPPO: SELECTIONS FROM CONFESSIONS AND OTHER ESSENTIAL
WRITINGS—ANNOTATED & EXPLAINED, P. 97*)

30 Friendship is often an unsung key to the spiritual life. While the texts presented here are about friendship with others, we can extend this to friendship with animals as well. And, as Albert Einstein told us in an interview in the *New York Times* (March 13, 1940), even with the universe itself:

> I think the most important question facing humanity is, "Is the universe a friendly place?" This is the first and most basic question all people must answer for themselves.
>
> For if we decide that the universe is an unfriendly place, then we will use our technology, our scientific discoveries and our natural resources to achieve safety and power by creating bigger walls to keep out the unfriendliness and bigger weapons to destroy all that which is unfriendly, and I believe that we are getting to a place where technology is powerful enough that we may either completely isolate or destroy ourselves as well in this process.
>
> If we decide that the universe is neither friendly nor unfriendly and that God is essentially "playing dice with the universe," then we are simply victims to the random toss of the dice and our lives have no real purpose or meaning.
>
> But if we decide that the universe is a friendly place, then we will use our technology, our scientific discoveries and our natural resources to create tools and models for understanding that universe. Because power and safety will come through understanding its workings and its motives.[1]

Without a friend,
nothing in the world seems friendly.
Friendship should not be bounded by narrow limits,
for it embraces all to whom we owe affection and love,
though it is inclined more eagerly toward some
and more hesitantly toward others.
It, however, extends even to enemies,
for whom we are also commanded to pray.
Thus, there is no one in the human race
to whom we do not owe love,
even if not out of mutual love,
at least on account of our sharing in a common nature.[30]

(SAINT AUGUSTINE, LETTER 130.2.4; 13, *SAINT AUGUSTINE OF HIPPO:*
SELECTIONS FROM CONFESSIONS *AND OTHER ESSENTIAL WRITINGS—*
ANNOTATED & EXPLAINED, P. 103)

31 Here friendship is linked to compassion, shared (*com*) suffering (*passion*). When you look at those whom for whatever reason you call "my enemy," know that what is causing them to hurt you is also in you. The capacities for cruelty are no more or less in one than in the other. Every saint houses a sinner, and every sinner houses a saint. So look with compassion upon everyone, for there is no one who is not your Self.

32 Where Saint Augustine reminds you of the theoretical aspect of friendship, the author of Ecclesiastes focuses on the practical side: friends can help us weather the tough times and celebrate the good times. While it is true that spiritual practice must be done by yourself, it isn't true that it must be done by yourself alone. Finding friends with whom to share the journey can make sticking with that journey all the more likely and pleasant.

Friendship begins with married partner and children,
and from there moves on to strangers.
But if we consider that we all have
one father and one mother [Adam and Eve],
who will be a stranger?
Every human being is neighbor to every other human being.
Ask nature; is he unknown? He's human.
Is she an enemy? She's human.
Is he a foe? He's human.
Is she a friend? Let her stay a friend.
Is he an enemy? Let him become a friend.[31]

(SAINT AUGUSTINE, SERMON 299 D.1, *SAINT AUGUSTINE OF HIPPO:*
SELECTIONS FROM CONFESSIONS AND OTHER ESSENTIAL WRITINGS—
ANNOTATED & EXPLAINED, P. 103)

Working with a partner is better than working alone,
and together you earn a greater reward.
And if you should fall, your friend can lift you up.
How sad to fall alone with none to raise you!
And at night in bed, you can warm one another,
for how does one who sleeps alone stay warm?
And when alone you may be overpowered;
two can withstand an attacker,
and a three-ply cord is not easily severed.[32]

(ECCLESIASTES 4:9–12, *ECCLESIASTES: ANNOTATED AND EXPLAINED, P. 41–43)*

33 To renounce is to free yourself from things, but this is not the same as ceasing to use things. The Self-realized person is free to have and to use without being had and used.

34 The cross is the sign of the oppressor. The oppressors are those who fear free women and men, knowing that one who is free cannot be controlled. To take up the cross of Christ is to die with him at the hands of the fearful and then to rise up again as if to say, "Even your fear cannot erase my freedom."

35 To become worthy of Jesus is to realize that you too are the son and daughter of God.

36 Good and evil are no less natural to the world than light and dark, birth and death, hope and horror. As God says, "Behold I place before you life and death, blessing and curse, now choose living that you and your child may live" (Deuteronomy 30:19). All reality is placed before you, the good and the bad. Choosing life is to choose to live with all of this, but not necessarily to be the bearer of it. You cannot escape the good, but you can choose to be a channel for goodness. You cannot escape evil, but you can choose not to be a channel for evil.

A person without a soul friend
is like a body without a head.
(SAINT BRIGID OF KILDARE, *CELTIC CHRISTIAN SPIRITUALITY: ESSENTIAL WRITINGS—
ANNOTATED & EXPLAINED*, P. 105)

Whoever does not renounce all that they have,[33]
does not take up their cross and follow me,[34]
is not worthy of me.[35]
(*LIBER GRADUUM* 3.5, *THE LOST SAYINGS OF JESUS: TEACHINGS FROM ANCIENT
CHRISTIAN, JEWISH, GNOSTIC AND ISLAMIC SOURCES—ANNOTATED & EXPLAINED*, P. 33)

Never be happy, except when
you look upon your brother with love.
(GOSPEL OF THE HEBREWS IN ORIGEN, COMMENTARY ON JOHN 2.12, *THE LOST
SAYINGS OF JESUS: TEACHINGS FROM ANCIENT CHRISTIAN, JEWISH, GNOSTIC AND
ISLAMIC SOURCES—ANNOTATED & EXPLAINED*, P. 63)

It is necessary that good things will come,
and blessed is the one through whom they come.
And it is also necessary that evil things come,
but woe to those through whom they come.[36]
(PSEUDO-CLEMENTINE HOMILIES 12.29, *THE LOST SAYINGS OF JESUS:
TEACHINGS FROM ANCIENT CHRISTIAN, JEWISH, GNOSTIC AND ISLAMIC SOURCES—
ANNOTATED & EXPLAINED*, P. 65)

37 The "word" is Logos, Wisdom, the Tao that is the nature and flow of all things. To attend to the Tao is to become wise, to know life and to love her. Yet even when you listen to Logos, there is still the inner oppressor, that voice also heard, that denies the wisdom of what you hear. Seeking to silence the inner critic only reinforces it. Making room for it defuses it. Listen to whatever is heard; pay heed only to what is true.

38 If you want a quick and accurate barometer of your spiritual maturity, listen to the quality of your speech. Are you respectful or rude? Are you willing to listen or eager to interrupt and speak? Are your words compassionate and self-deprecating, or are they cutting and hurtful? Are you wise or merely clever? The words of your mouth will reveal the quality of your heart.

39 Be both trusting and trustworthy. Act in a way that makes none suspicious of your motives. "Let your 'yes' be 'yes,' and your 'no' be 'no'; anything else comes from evil" (Matthew 5:37). Or, simpler still: say what you mean and do what you say.

40 Gossip is among the most evil aspects of speech. Before you speak, ask yourself this: "Is what I am about to say true?" If it isn't true, don't say it. If it is true, ask yourself a second question, "Is what I am about to say kind?" If it is both true and kind, say it. If it is true but unkind, ask yourself a third question, "Is what I am about to say necessary for the welfare of self and others?" If it is, then say it as gently as you can. If it isn't for the good, even if true, don't say it.

41 Words of your mouth are words spoken aloud. Meditation of your heart is the inner dialogue of the mind. Both should reflect the compassion that comes with knowing the One who is all.

Listen to the word,
understand knowledge,
love life,
and no one will persecute you or oppress you,
other than you yourselves.[37]

(APOCRYPHON OF JAMES 6.24–26, *THE LOST SAYINGS OF JESUS:*
TEACHINGS FROM ANCIENT CHRISTIAN, JEWISH, GNOSTIC AND ISLAMIC SOURCES—
ANNOTATED & EXPLAINED, P. 97)

O you who believe,
people should not mock other people,
for these may be better than they are.
And women should not mock other women,
for these may be better than they are.
And do not ridicule each other,
or call each other by insulting nicknames.
Evil is the name of impiety after achieving faith;
and they who do not refrain are wrongdoers.[38]
O you who believe,
avoid suspicion, for some suspicion is sin,[39]
and do not spy on each other,
and do not defame each other in their absence.[40]

(QUR'AN 49:11–12, *THE QUR'AN AND SAYINGS OF PROPHET MUHAMMAD:*
SELECTIONS ANNOTATED & EXPLAINED, P. 109)

May the words of my mouth and
the meditations of my heart
be pleasing to you, O Ineffable One.[41]

(PSALM 19:14)

42 All the great saints, prophets, and sages take on the same task: helping you become godly. Any teaching that leads to cruelty rather than compassion is false. Any god that leads to genocide and murder in this life and/or torture and cruelty in the next is false.

43 You cannot control the results of your actions, but the intent is up to you. If you intend good, and evil comes from it, you are credited with the intent. But if you intend good and evil *always* comes of it, your intention is a lie. You are not responsible for the results of your actions, but look to the fruits nonetheless, for sometimes they reveal the quality of the seeds that gave them birth.

44 Not being able to control the result of your action doesn't free you from trying to discern in advance the benefit or suffering your action might cause. Focusing on intent doesn't free you from forethought. Saying "But I didn't mean for that to happen" doesn't excuse you from the obligation to carefully consider what might happen.

The Prophet was asked,
"Which Muslim has the perfect faith?"
He answered, "One who possesses the best moral character."
I have not been sent except to perfect noble character.[42]
The reward of deeds depends upon the intentions,
and you will get the reward
according to what you intended....[43]
Keep God in mind wherever you are;
follow a wrong with a right that offsets it;
and treat people courteously.
Should you wish to act, ponder well the consequences.
If good, carry on; if not, desist.[44]

(MUHAMMAD, *THE QUR'AN AND SAYINGS OF PROPHET MUHAMMAD:*
SELECTIONS ANNOTATED & EXPLAINED, P.119)

O you who believe!
Persevere, excel in patience, and be constant.
Be conscious of God so that you may be successful.

(QUR'AN 3:200, *THE QUR'AN AND SAYINGS OF PROPHET MUHAMMAD:*
SELECTIONS ANNOTATED & EXPLAINED, P.127)

45 Not contending isn't the same as being passive. Not contending means not confronting evil with evil. This is precisely what Jesus taught when he said, "But I say unto you, don't resist evil. If someone strikes you on the right cheek, offer the other cheek as well" (Mathew 5:39).

In Jesus's time it was legal for Roman soldiers to dismiss any Jew as subhuman by slapping his or her face with the back of the hand. Because the vast majority of people are right-handed, this meant slapping them on the right cheek, just as Jesus said. Slapping a person with one's palm on the left cheek was a sign of anger between equals. When Jesus says, "Resist not evil," and then goes on to say you are to offer your left cheek to the oppressor who just struck your right cheek, he is daring you to challenge the oppressor to treat you as an equal. This is not an act of passivity; it is a bold act of nonviolent resistance. The followers of perennial wisdom aren't violent, but neither are they submissive.

46 The world you encounter is shaped by the beliefs you hold. If Tao is your guide, you are supple, yielding, and quietly powerful. If virtue is your guide, you are virtuous. The same is true of negative qualities. Build your life around fear of loss, and loss will haunt you. The quality of your life is simply the result of the quality of your living.

47 If you cannot trust another, your untrusting nature makes you untrustworthy as well. Everything returns to you. Cause others to fear you, and you will become as fearful as you are fearsome. Cause others to hate you, and you will become as hate-filled as you are hated. If you wish to be loved, be loving. If you wish to be trusted, be trusting. Everything echoes the quality of your own life.

Yield and remain whole
Bend and remain straight
Be low and become filled
Be worn out and become renewed
Have little and receive
Have much and be confused
Therefore the sages hold to the one as an example for the world
Without flaunting themselves—and so are seen clearly
Without presuming themselves—and so are distinguished
Without praising themselves—and so have merit
Without boasting about themselves—and so are lasting
Because they do not contend,
the world cannot contend with them[45]
What the ancients called "the one who yields and remains whole"
Were they speaking empty words?
Sincerity becoming whole, and returning to oneself
(TAO TE CHING, CHAPTER 22, *TAO TE CHING: ANNOTATED & EXPLAINED*, P. 45)

Thus those who follow the Tao are with the Tao
Those who follow virtue are with virtue
Those who follow loss are with loss
Those who are with the Tao, the Tao is also pleased to have them
Those who are with virtue, virtue is also pleased to have them
Those who are with loss, loss is also pleased to have them[46]
Those who do not trust sufficiently, others have no trust in them[47]
(TAO TE CHING, CHAPTER 23, *TAO TE CHING: ANNOTATED & EXPLAINED*, P. 47)

48 The way of perennial wisdom honors both self and other, and the Self who is both self and other. The work of the spiritually independent is both inner and outer, but it is the inner work that brings your deepest wisdom alive.

49 Psalm 119:22.

50 Proverbs 16:32.

51 Psalm 128:2.

52 1 Samuel 2:30.

Those who understand others are intelligent
Those who understand themselves are enlightened
Those who overcome others have strength
Those who overcome themselves are powerful[48]
(TAO TE CHING, CHAPTER 33, *TAO TE CHING: ANNOTATED & EXPLAINED*, P. 67)

Ben Zoma teaches,
Who is wise?
One who learns from everyone, for it says,
"From all my teachers I grew wise."[49]
Who is strong?
One who subdues oneself, for it says,
"Patience is better than strength,
and self-control is superior to controlling armies."[50]
Who is rich?
One who loves what is, for it says,
"Praise and contentment belong
to those who eat from their own labor."[51]
You are praised in this world,
and content in the World to Come.
Who is honored?
One who honors others, for it says,
"Those who honor Me are honored;
and those who scorn Me are degraded."[52]
(*PIRKE AVOT* 4:1, *ETHICS OF THE SAGES*. PIRKE AVOT—
ANNOTATED & EXPLAINED, P. 61)

53 Life is complex, but not complicated. Life is complex in that everything is connected to everything else, and to act here is to set in motion effects over there that you cannot foresee. Thus you should act lightly and only when the timing is right. Life appears complicated only when you seek to impose your will on the effects.

54 Buckminster Fuller, the American architect, inventor, and futurist (1895–1983), used to talk about trim tabbing. A trim tab is a small rudder that is used to turn the main rudder of a large ship. Before the invention of hydraulics, the pressure of the sea on the main rudder made it impossible to turn the rudder directly. Instead, you turned the trim tab, which shifted the pressure and allowed the main rudder to turn. The work of the wise is to turn trim tabs: to learn to apply the least amount of pressure to attain the maximum amount of good.

Act without action
Manage without meddling
Taste without tasting
Great, small, many, few
Respond to hatred with virtue
Plan difficult tasks through the simplest tasks[53]
Achieve large tasks through the smallest tasks
The difficult tasks of the world
Must be handled through the simple tasks
The large tasks of the world
Must be handled through the small tasks
Therefore, sages never attempt great deeds all through life
Thus they can achieve greatness[54]
One who makes promises lightly must deserve little trust
One who sees many easy tasks
must encounter much difficulty
Therefore, sages regard things as difficult
So they never encounter difficulties all through life
(Tao Te Ching, chapter 63, *Tao Te Ching: Annotated & Explained*, p. 127)

55 It is important to note that Maimonides isn't asking you to be without emotions and desires. Even anger has its place. Stripping away feelings that arise of their own accord places you in a state of perpetual
war with yourself, a war you cannot win. Rather than seek to perfect
yourself by erasing anything negative, realize your perfection in this
moment—perfect as whole and not perfection as some imbalanced
ideal. You have feelings; feel them. Just don't let them dictate your
actions. You have thoughts; think them. Just don't let them drive you
to extremes. The wise allow things to be as they are so that they can
better engage with them in service to God and godliness.

56 This is "smiling practice." Cultivate a face that is open and welcoming. Notice when your face is tight, your jaw tense, your eyes nar-
rowed and straining, your nostrils flared, and then relax these by
taking a few slow, soft breaths. As your face relaxes, your body relaxes,
your heart opens to what is, and your mind sees how to navigate the
most troubled waters in peace.

The upright way is the middle point in all character traits,
equidistant from both extremes.
Therefore, our early sages commanded
that you examine your character traits constantly,
and evaluate them and direct them to the middle road
so you will be physically sound.[55]
Do not be choleric and quick to anger,
nor like a dead person who lacks feelings.
Rather, you should be in the middle,
not becoming angry except for a serious matter.
Likewise, do not lust after anything
except those things that you need for your basic sustenance ...
as it is stated, "A righteous person eats
to satisfy his soul" (Proverbs 13:25).
A person should not engage in work
except to attain that which is needed
for immediate sustenance, as it is stated,
"A little is good for the righteous" (Psalm 37:16).
A person should not be overly stingy or profligate with money;
rather, you should give charity according to your ability
and give loans appropriately to those who need [to borrow].
One should not laugh excessively or be silly,
nor be overly sad and mournful.
A person should maintain a constant spirit
of happiness and pleasantness,
with a kind countenance.[56]

57 It is better to be wise than pious. The pious focus on perfecting the self by following rules. This focus on self is not spiritual but narcissistic. Have compassion on yourself and you will have compassion on others. Know that there is no "straight" path and that all paths weave this way and that. Do not judge yourself against an arbitrary standard; this only leads to endless self-obsession. Simply accept yourself as you are and bring compassion to bear in all you do.

So it is with the other character traits.

This is the way of the sages.

(MAIMONIDES, *MISHNEH TORAH*, LAWS RELATING TO MORAL AND ETHICAL CHARACTER 1:4, *MAIMONIDES—ESSENTIAL TEACHINGS ON JEWISH FAITH AND ETHICS: THE BOOK OF KNOWLEDGE AND THE THIRTEEN PRINCIPLES OF FAITH— ANNOTATED & EXPLAINED*, P. 45)

Those whose character traits are in the middle

are called wise.

Those who are exceedingly exacting with themselves,

veering a bit one way or the other from the middle path,

are called pious.

For example,

those who distance themselves to the last degree

away from haughtiness,

so that they are very meek, are called pious;

and this is the quality of piety.

If they followed the middle path so that they are humble,

they are called wise;

and this is the quality of wisdom.

And so it is with the other traits....[57]

(MAIMONIDES, *MISHNEH TORAH*, LAWS RELATING TO MORAL AND ETHICAL CHARACTER 1:5, *MAIMONIDES—ESSENTIAL TEACHINGS ON JEWISH FAITH AND ETHICS: THE BOOK OF KNOWLEDGE AND THE THIRTEEN PRINCIPLES OF FAITH— ANNOTATED & EXPLAINED*, P. 47)

58 How can one be holy as God is holy? By acting godly. Acting godly is not a matter of "whipping oneself into shape," but a matter of freeing the self from ignorance and allowing your self to be embraced by the Self. Then you will act godly because it is your nature to be godly.

We are commanded to walk on the middle paths,
which are good and upright, as it is stated,
"And you shall walk in God's ways" (Deuteronomy 28:9).
Here is how [our sages] explained this commandment:
just as God is called gracious,
so you should be gracious;
just as God is called compassionate,
so you should be compassionate;
just as God is called holy, so you should be holy.
Our prophets described God with such adjectives as for-
bearing, filled with kindness, righteous and upright,
pure, mighty and strong, and so forth,
to teach that these are good and upright qualities
that a person must adopt,
emulating God as much as possible.[58]
(Maimonides, Mishneh Torah, Laws Relating to Moral and Ethical
Character 1:6, Maimonides—Essential Teachings on Jewish Faith and Ethics:
The Book of Knowledge and the Thirteen Principles of Faith—
Annotated & Explained, p. 49)

59 Do not imagine you can withstand the influence of others. So seek out those that hold compassion and justice as the norm and in this way find yourself nurtured from without as well as from within.

60 Given the influence of your environment, Maimonides urges you to avoid the wicked even if you must live alone in a cave. This is, of course, hyperbole. Things are rarely so stark. Rather than flee to a cave, cultivate good friends who share the values of justice and compassion and with whom you can help one another live life well and wisely.

It is human nature to be influenced by the attitudes
and behaviors of one's neighbors and friends
and to follow the mores of society.
Therefore, a person should cling to the righteous
and always live among sages so as
to learn from their actions.[59]
Distance yourself from the wicked who walk in darkness,
so as not to learn from their ways.
If you live in a realm that had bad moral traits
and where the people did not walk in the upright path,
you should move to a place
whose residents are righteous and good.
If all the lands of which you are aware have corrupt
societies,
or if you are unable to move to a good land ...
then dwell alone.
If the people around you are wicked sinners
who do not let you dwell among them
unless you blend in and behave according to their bad
mores,
then exile yourself to caves, thorny fields, or deserts
rather than following the ways of the sinners.[60]

(MAIMONIDES, MISHNEH TORAH, LAWS RELATING TO MORAL AND ETHICAL
CHARACTER 6:1, MAIMONIDES—ESSENTIAL TEACHINGS ON JEWISH FAITH AND ETHICS:
THE BOOK OF KNOWLEDGE AND THE THIRTEEN PRINCIPLES OF FAITH—
ANNOTATED & EXPLAINED, P. 65)

61 If you need a bumper-sticker summation of the way of the spirit, this would be it.

62 Do nothing that, if revealed, would cause damage and suffering to yourself or others.

63 There are those who seek death as the only exit from the suffering and evil of this world. They mortify their flesh, starve their hearts, and seek to free the soul by murdering the body. While pretending to be wise, such people are overly proud of their own ignorance.

There are those who flee from death, drowning out the very thought of their mortality with ceaseless pursuit of distraction. Rushing from pleasure to pleasure, they claim to be happy when in fact they are merely exhausted.

One who lives a balanced life, avoiding the extremes of asceticism and hedonism, this one has the opportunity to grow wise and live well.

If it is not right, do not do it:
if it is not true, do not say it.[61]
(MARCUS AURELIUS, THE MEDITATIONS OF MARCUS AURELIUS:
SELECTIONS ANNOTATED & EXPLAINED, P. 57)

Never value anything as profitable to yourself
which shall compel you to break your promise,
to lose your self-respect,
to hate any person,
to suspect, to curse, to act the hypocrite,
to desire anything which needs walls and curtains:[62]
for the person who has preferred to everything intelligence
and spirit and the worship of its excellence,
acts no tragic part, does not groan,
will not need either solitude or much company;
and, what is chief of all, will live without either pursuing or
flying from death.[63]
(MARCUS AURELIUS, THE MEDITATIONS OF MARCUS AURELIUS:
SELECTIONS ANNOTATED & EXPLAINED, P. 59)

64 Philosophy means the love (*philo*) of wisdom (*sophia*). Wisdom, *Chochmah* (in Hebrew), *Prajna* (in Sanskrit), Tao (in Chinese), Logos (in Greek) is the capacity to see the grain in wood and to cut with it; to sense the current in the ocean and to swim with it; to map the orbits of the stars and to navigate by them; to understand the workings of the body and to act in harmony with them.

65 You are a manifestation of the Source the way a wave is the manifestation of an ocean. The wave is precious but fleeting. The ocean is deep and enduring. Play the wave you are today, yet rest in the ocean that is forever.

66 You are the elements that compose you at this moment, and these are always changing. Your cells are constantly dying and birthing, and there is nothing of "you" today that existed a mere seven years ago. Nothing but the name you call your self and the stories you use to define your self. These are you, but not all of you. You are both the named and the Nameless. Both the storied and the unstoried; both self and Self; both the relative and the Absolute.

67 Evil arises when you go against your nature. Knowing your self to be the Self, you naturally engage life with compassion and justice. Not knowing your self to be the Self, you naturally engage life with fear and hesitation. Not knowing who you are prevents you from acting naturally. The potential for evil is part of the Whole that is God, but the actualization of evil manifests only when you forget you are God.

What then is that which is able to conduct a human being?
It is one thing and only one, philosophy.[64]
But this consists in keeping the spirit within
free from violence and unharmed,
superior to pains and pleasures,
doing nothing without purpose or falsely or with hypocrisy,
or feeling the need of another's doing or not doing anything;
and besides, accepting all that happens,
and all that is allotted,
as coming from thence, wherever it is,
from whence you yourself came;[65]
and, finally, waiting for death with a cheerful mind,
as being nothing else than a dissolution of the elements
of which every living being is compounded.
But if there is no harm to the elements themselves
in each continually changing into another,
why should a human being have any apprehension
about the change and dissolution of all the elements?[66]
For these things are according to nature,
and nothing is evil which is according to nature.[67]

(MARCUS AURELIUS, THE MEDITATIONS OF MARCUS AURELIUS:
SELECTIONS ANNOTATED & EXPLAINED, P. 137)

68 There is no need to escape from everyday life. If you are in a relationship, know the other is God, and devote yourself to her or his welfare. If you are a parent, know your children to be God, and devote yourself to their welfare. If you are a daughter or son, know your parents are God, and devote yourself to their welfare. And never forget that you, too, are God, and devote yourself to your welfare as well.

69 Nothing belongs to you. While you may use whatever comes into your hands for the welfare of self and others, do not imagine that you own or control what comes. If you cling to what is, your hands will be clenched around the past and unable to welcome or engage with the present.

How ought we to live in the world?
Do all your duties, but keep your mind on God.
Live with all—with spouse and children, father and
mother—and serve them.[68]
Treat them as if they were very dear to you,
but know in your heart of hearts that
they do not belong to you.[69]

(RAMAKRISHNA, *SELECTIONS FROM THE GOSPEL OF SRI RAMAKRISHNA:
ANNOTATED & EXPLAINED*, P. 11)

70 Repeating a name of God, chanting a mantra, is one of the simplest and yet most powerful techniques for realizing who you are. Find a name that speaks to you and repeat it throughout the day.

71 While the spiritually independent are not apt to surrender themselves to a teacher or tradition, it is often useful to open yourself to the teachings of trusted teachers and spiritual guides. The rule of thumb is this: if the teacher is more interested in his power than your progress, leave; if she is more interested in her answers than your questions, leave; but if she is more devoted to you than she expects you to be devoted to her, stay—at least for a while.

72 See everything as an opportunity to be of service to God manifest as everything and everyone.

73 Dedicate a quiet corner of your home for meditation. Set it apart with a rug, if you can, and place a few items in this space that remind you of your intention to awaken to Self.

74 Walking outside the constructs of humanity, both physical and intellectual, allows the self to be surrendered to the Self.

75 As the Hindu sage Shankara put it, "The world is illusory. Only God is real. God is the world." Don't forget the third sentence. Spirituality isn't escaping from the world, but seeing it as it truly is: a manifestation of God.

How, sir, may I fix my mind on God?
Repeat God's name and sing God's glories,[70]
and now and then visit God's devotees and holy ones.[71]
The mind cannot dwell on God
if it is immersed day and night in worldliness,
in worldly duties and responsibilities;
it is most necessary to go into solitude now and then
and think of God.
To fix the mind on God is very difficult, in the beginning,
unless one practices meditation in solitude....
There are three ways of meditating:
think of God while doing your duties,[72]
or meditate on God in a secluded corner of your house,[73]
or contemplate God in a wood.[74]
And you should always discriminate between
the Real and the unreal:
God alone is real, the Eternal Substance;
all else is unreal, that is, impermanent.
By discriminating thus,
one should shake off impermanent objects from the mind.[75]

(RAMAKRISHNA, *SELECTIONS FROM THE GOSPEL OF SRI RAMAKRISHNA:*
ANNOTATED & EXPLAINED, P. 11)

76 It's not so much that you "make" yourself clean, since the Self is always clean. It is more a matter of reminding yourself that you are clean. Each morning the observant Jew recites, "My God, the soul you breathe into me is pure." Your truest nature, the Self, the breath of God that is your consciousness, is pure, unstained, transparent. What is stained is the narrow mind, the mind clouded by isms and ideologies that fill it with dread of what isn't (hell, for example) and a longing for what you already are (God). Cleanse this self by steeping it in Self, and the brew will be pure love.

77 The eye of the heart is the eye that sees the Divine as all things. You protect this by practicing the art of looking deeply into what is, to see the One who is what is.

78 The voice of the heart is the soothing voice of compassion that ends the confusion arising from ignorance, and the thunderous voice of justice that brings down the walls of oppression with the trumpets of truth. You protect this voice by cleansing your speech of gossip, cruelty, and falsehood.

79 The mind of the heart is the intellect free from ideological conditions, seeing what is as the Is. You protect this mind by remembering that the menu is never the meal and that the god that can be named is not the Eternal God.

80 Everything comes from God. Everything happens in God. Everything is God. Because this is so, anything you experience is a vehicle for awakening and used to end your imagined separation from God. All that is required is that you center yourself in silence and hear the voice of God in the fragile sound of stillness asking, "Why are you here?" (1 Kings 19:13). This is the penultimate meeting with God, for God is still the other and not yet the Self. In this place of meeting is the eternal question: What is your purpose in this moment? How can you work for the benefit of self and the world in this situation? What is it to embrace this moment with compassion and justice?

I must learn to love myself with detachment.
I must have no attitude toward myself that is destructive.
I must learn how to love myself that,
In my attitude toward my self,
I will be pleasing to the Creator....
Here in silence, I find the appropriate attitude
That makes me whole and clean
In my own sight and in the sight of the Creator.[76]
(HOWARD THURMAN, *BAPTIST WISDOM FOR CONTEMPLATIVE PRAYER*, P. 32)

Protect the eye of the heart for as long as you have it.[77]
Protect the voice of the heart for as long as you have it.[78]
Protect the mind of the heart for as long as you have it.[79]
You cannot continue long to live without it.
(HOWARD THURMAN, *BAPTIST WISDOM FOR CONTEMPLATIVE PRAYER*, P. 35)

This is a sure Rule:
That which comes from God, leads to God.
Listen, then, to the still, small Voice of your Beloved.[80]
(ANNE DUTTON, *BAPTIST WISDOM FOR CONTEMPLATIVE PRAYER*, P. 72)

81 Standing in God's presence is like a single candle struggling to illumine a vast hall suddenly finding its light bolstered by a roaring fire effortlessly lighting the great expanse. The candle still burns but no longer struggles. In this kind of encounter with God as other, you still burn, your light still shines, though it is lost in the greater light of God, and because it is, it need no longer struggle at all.

82 This is the awakening you are waiting for: knowing you are God there is no longer any need to struggle to control desire, thought, feelings, and the like. It is all God, the crazy and the rational, the cruel and the kind. You are now free to enjoy the drama without having to direct it or bring it to any set conclusion. Free to watch and not control, you are free to choose which thoughts and feelings with which to embody, allowing the others to dissolve for lack of engagement.

Silent in God's presence,
you can relax yourself completely.[81]
Rely only on God....
One can almost stand back, as it were,
and watch these thoughts as they burst out of your mind—
these rampageous, weakening,
strange and startling thoughts!
Let them come, waiting silently for each without worry,
without concern.
See how they appear and disappear
in the deep calm of God's presence.[82]
(ANNE DUTTON, BAPTIST WISDOM FOR CONTEMPLATIVE PRAYER, P. 114)

83 The Word is not yet Jesus, but Logos, Tao, *Chochmah*, *Sophia*, *Prajna*—the ordering principle of the world that brings forth all beings in the world.

84 It is Wisdom who sets the principles by which all things manifest and function. The Word become flesh is the world you can perceive with your senses and their technological extenders. All beings are equally divine, though few of us are willing to know this. Fewer still are those who live what they know. Jesus is one of these few and hence is called the begotten of God.

85 Jesus arose in God as God the way all of us do, but unlike most of us, Jesus came to realize who he is. His coming was natural, his awakening no less so. It is the way of wisdom to manifest the wise, and it is through them that you awaken to wisdom as well. The purpose of the Christ isn't to raise up followers. The purpose of the Christ is to awaken more Christs.

86 Rather than the vertical "coming down" and "rising up," a metaphor that implies a hierarchy lacking in the Divine, think in terms of "reaching out" and "drawing in." The wise reach out from the Source and bring you back to the Source.

87 There are two ways to become gods. The right way is to realize that God is playing you. The wrong way is to fool yourself into playing God.

88 The task of Jesus and all the realized saints and sages is the same: to awaken you to your true nature that you might participate fully in the nature of the world.

The Word[83] became flesh[84]
so that the flesh, that is, the human race,
should ascend to God by believing in the Word
through the flesh,
so that through the natural, only-begotten Son
many should be adopted as children.[85]
Not for his own sake did the Word become flesh,
but for our sake,
who could not be changed into the children of God
except by the flesh of the Word.
He came down alone but ascends with many.[86]
That which made of God a human being
makes gods of men and women.[87]
And dwelt among us, that is,
he took possession of our nature
so that he might make us participators in his own nature.[88]
(JOHN SCOTUS ERIUGENA, HOMILY ON THE PROLOGUE TO THE GOSPEL OF
JOHN, *CELTIC CHRISTIAN SPIRITUALITY: ESSENTIAL WRITINGS—
ANNOTATED & EXPLAINED*, P. 79)

89 This is a powerful mantra. Repeat it over and over again many times each day and you will begin to embody the words with understanding and action. Yet it is not as precise as it need be. Given the limitations of time and culture, the text speaks of God as "in" this and "in" that. But the truth is even more profound. Read not "in" but "is" and the deepest wisdom will blossom in you and as you:

God enfolds me,
God surrounds me,
[God permeates me]
[God is me]
God is my speaking,
God is my thinking.
God is my sleeping,
God is my waking,
God is my watching,
God is my hoping.
God is my life,
God is my lips,
God is my soul,
God is my heart.
God is my sufficing,
God is my slumber,
God is mine ever-living soul,
God is mine eternity.

God to enfold me,
God to surround me,
God in my speaking,
God in my thinking.
God in my sleeping,
God in my waking,
God in my watching,
God in my hoping.
God in my life,
God in my lips,
God in my soul,
God in my heart.
God in my sufficing,
God in my slumber,
God in mine ever-living soul,
God in mine eternity.[89]

(*THE CARMINA GADELICA, CELTIC CHRISTIAN SPIRITUALITY:
ESSENTIAL WRITINGS—ANNOTATED & EXPLAINED*, P. 93)

90 These thieves are the doubts that cloud your heart and mind with distortions.

91 Learn to watch your mind and see thoughts as they arise. Learn to watch your heart and see emotions as they arise. Learn to guard your tongue that the harsh words arising are never spoken. You cannot control thoughts or feelings, but speech and actions are a different matter.

92 Note that Saint Isaiah isn't telling you to put an end to evil thoughts: thoughts cannot be controlled, and evil thoughts are recognized as evil only after you have thought them. He isn't telling you to control your thoughts, but to observe them wisely, being undisturbed by the wildness of the mind, and unattached to the madness it sometimes spins.

93 No one is asking that you be a saint, only that you not become a sinner. One way to become a sinner is to first insist you must be a saint. Discovering that you cannot achieve sainthood, you abandon yourself to its opposite. Rather, accept the unity of positive and negative in thoughts and feelings, and seek only to align your actions with justice and compassion.

94 Over and again the wise warn you against excess: excess in righteousness and piety, and excess in selfishness and pomposity. Find the middle way that allows the mind and heart to function naturally, while binding the hand and tongue to the good.

If the remembrance of God dwells peaceably within you,
you will catch the thieves when they try to deprive you of it.[90]
Have an exact knowledge about the nature of thoughts ...[91]
[and] recognize these evil thoughts for what they are.[92]

(SAINT ISAIAH THE SOLITARY, PHILOKALIA: *THE EASTERN CHRISTIAN SPIRITUAL TEXTS—SELECTIONS ANNOTATED & EXPLAINED*, P. 31)

Turn from evil and do good;
Seek peace and pursue it.

(PSALM 34:14)

To brood on evil makes the heart brazen....[93]
Vigils, prayer, and patient acceptance ...
benefits the heart,
provided we do not [do them to] excess.[94]

(SAINT MARK THE ASCETIC, PHILOKALIA: *THE EASTERN CHRISTIAN SPIRITUAL TEXTS—SELECTIONS ANNOTATED & EXPLAINED*, P. 37)

95　Obsession is not the way. Obsessing with the mistakes you have made is only more narcissism: "Look at me, look at me! No one is as wicked as I am! No one fails more miserably in turning from evil than me! Look at me, look at me!"

96　You cannot change the nature of what has been done, only learn from it and turn to do differently.

If you have done ill and talk about it
and think about it all the time
do not cast the base thing you did out of your thoughts,
and whatever one thinks, therein one is,
your soul is wholly and utterly in what you think,
and so you dwell in baseness.[95]
You will certainly not be able to turn,
for your spirit will grow coarse and your heart stubborn,
and in addition to this you may be overcome by gloom.
What would you?
Rake the muck this way, rake the muck that way—
it will always be muck.
Have I sinned, or have I not sinned—
what does Heaven get out of it?
In the time I am brooding over it
I could be stringing pearls for the delight of Heaven.
That is why it is written: "Depart from evil and do good—
turn wholly away from evil, do not dwell upon it,
and do good.
You have done wrong? Then counteract it by doing right."[96]
(RABBI YITZCHAK MEIR, THE GERRER REBBE, CITED IN MARTIN BUBER, THE WAY
OF MAN ACCORDING TO THE TEACHING OF HASIDISM, PP. 30–33).

97 Ultimately you want to achieve an active stillness, a state of being that allows you the capacity to do all that needs doing without unnecessary effort, without coercion, and without the delusion of controlling results. In the meantime, be content with making time each day to cultivate stillness. Practice watching the mind and its madness and observing the heart and its passions without attachment or judgment.

98 Self-control is the control of behavior rather than thought and feelings. By the time you know you have thought a negative thought, the negative thought has already been thought, so what can you do about it? By the time you know you are feeling a negative emotion, the emotion has already been felt, so what can you do about it? Thoughts are only known after they are thought; feelings are only known after they are felt. This is not a failure on your part, but simply the nature of things. But this is not true of actions. Actions most often are chosen. Actions most often are based on and excused by thoughts and feelings. Watching thoughts and feelings without attachment allows you to choose to act without compulsion.

99 Silence is the state of quiet, nonjudgmental watching of mind and heart.

100 Humility is the natural result of accepting the fact that your thoughts and feelings are beyond your control.

Stillness is an undisturbed state of the intellect,
the calm of a free and joyful soul,... light,
an unsleeping watchfulness,...
untroubled repose in the midst of great hardship,
and, finally, solidarity and union with God.[97]
(NIKITAS STITHATOS, PHILOKALIA: *THE EASTERN CHRISTIAN SPIRITUAL TEXTS—
SELECTIONS ANNOTATED & EXPLAINED*, P. 183)

There are three virtues connected with stillness:...
self-control,[98] silence,[99] and self-reproach,
which is the same thing as humility.[100]
(SAINT GREGORY OF SINAI, PHILOKALIA: *THE EASTERN CHRISTIAN SPIRITUAL
TEXTS—SELECTIONS ANNOTATED & EXPLAINED*, P. 189)

101 You are holy as God is holy: your true nature is God's nature. Think of the self as the rose of the rose bush. It is the nature of the bush to blossom as the rose, yet the rose cannot blossom on its own. So it is the nature of God to blossom as the self, the nature of the Infinite to blossom as the finite, the nature of the One to blossom as the many, but the self, the finite, and the many cannot blossom on their own. Blossoming is not yours to control. It is the gift of grace arising naturally from the nature of God.

102 Notice that you are to be the image and likeness of God in verse 26 and yet are only the image in verse 27. Being the image of God is a given, being the likeness of God—acting godly—is up to you.

You shall be holy, for I, YHVH, am holy.[101]

(LEVITICUS 20:26)

God made us so that we might become
"partakers of the divine nature" (2 Peter 1:4)

(SAINT MAXIMOS THE CONFESSOR, PHILOKALIA: THE EASTERN CHRISTIAN
SPIRITUAL TEXTS—SELECTIONS ANNOTATED & EXPLAINED, P. 201)

Let us make humanity in our image, after our likeness....
And God made humanity in the divine image,
in the image of God were they made,
male and female God made them.[102]

(GENESIS 1:26–27)

103 You cannot grasp God by effort. The pump can be primed by your effort, but the gift of water is a gift of grace.

104 There is no division between you and God's glory, God's grace, for grace permeates nature as wetness permeates ocean and wave. Realizing the grace of God as God in and as all things is like the wave realizing the wetness in both ocean and wave. While this awakening takes one beyond the limited self of ego, this beyond is not separate from ego. On the contrary, it embraces ego in the greater unity of God.

[And yet] created things are not by nature
able to accomplish deification,
since they cannot grasp God....[103]
Grace irradiates nature with a supernatural light
and by the transcendence of its glory
raises nature above its natural limits.[104]
(SAINT MAXIMOS THE CONFESSOR, PHILOKALIA: *THE EASTERN CHRISTIAN
SPIRITUAL TEXTS—SELECTIONS ANNOTATED & EXPLAINED*, P. 203)

105 When you first step on the path of wisdom, the step you take is conscious, chosen, an act of will. You surrender your thoughts to God's thoughts, and your feelings to God's feelings, but the you doing the surrendering is still the you that must be surrendered. So this is not a true or full surrender, but simply an elevating of the self within the limits of self.

106 Taking this first step is like rolling down a hillside. You may have chosen the first tumble thinking you could control the fall, but soon you are rolling beyond your control, falling headlong into the Self, whose gift of wisdom is always a gift of grace.

107 The way of wisdom is not restricted to one person or another, one people or another, one religion or another. Everyone is welcome. Indeed, everyone is already on the path, though some walk more slowly than others.

108 God is not other than you. God is the Self that is you. Preferring God's will to your will is preferring your highest desires to your basest ones.

This is the beginning of our salvation;
by our free choice we abandon
our own wishes and thoughts
and do what God wishes and thinks.[105]
If we succeed in doing this [we become] what God
from the beginning
has wished us to be:...
gods by adoption through grace,...[106]
whether we are rich or poor,
married or unmarried,
in authority and free or under obedience
and in bondage ...[107]
people who preferred the knowledge of God and God's will
to their own thoughts and wishes.[108]

(SAINT PETER OF DAMASKOS, PHILOKALIA: *THE EASTERN CHRISTIAN SPIRITUAL TEXTS—SELECTIONS ANNOTATED & EXPLAINED*, P. 209)

109 The way of wisdom is the ordinary way without the selfishness that leads to needless quarrel, suffering, and violence.

110 The way of wisdom is the way of the everyday without the distractions of the extraneous.

111 The way of wisdom is simple: Say what you mean. Do what you say.

112 The way of wisdom is broad enough to make room for everyone, everyone except those who choose not to walk it.

A brother questioned Abba Hierax, saying,
"Give me a word. How can I be saved?"
The old man said to him,
"Sit in your cell, and if you are hungry, eat;
if you are thirsty, drink;
only do not speak evil of anyone, and you will be saved."[109]

(ABBA HIERAX, *DESERT FATHERS AND MOTHERS:*
EARLY CHRISTIAN WISDOM SAYINGS—ANNOTATED & EXPLAINED, P. 3)

Yuan once asked his master, Hui Hai,
"What is your practice?"
Hui Hai replied,
"When hungry, I eat; when tired, I sleep."
"Doesn't everyone do this?" Yuan asked.
"Yes, but not as I do.
When they eat they think of other things;
when they lay down to sleep they think of a thousand things.
That is how their practice differs from mine."[110]

(ZEN TEACHING)

Tzu-kung asked what constituted the Noble Person.
The Master said,
"The Noble Person acts before speaking
and afterwards speaks according to his actions."[111]
The Master said,
"The Noble Person is broad-minded and not prejudiced.
The petty person is prejudiced and not broad-minded."[112]

(CONFUCIUS, *ANALECTS* II:13, *CONFUCIUS, THE ANALECTS:*
THE PATH OF THE SAGE—SELECTIONS ANNOTATED & EXPLAINED, P. 23)

113 Near, but not yet there. While there is much you can do to walk the way of wisdom, the final steps are not yours to control. The self cannot meet the Self, it can only melt into the Self. The self cannot transcend itself, it can only be awakened to the transcendent that embraces it. The self cannot empty itself, it can only be emptied by the Self that sustains it. Do what you can, and trust that God will do the rest.

114 The asking is yours; the answer is God's. The seeking is yours; the finding is God's. The knocking is yours; the opening is God's. Again: the doing is yours, the result is God's.

115 The way of wisdom can only be walked in absolute wholeness. But this does not mean it can be walked without brokenness. If brokenness is the opposite of wholeness, then wholeness is not really whole. The whole must include the broken; the perfect must include the imperfect. To seek with a whole heart is to walk the way with self and Self, with your weaknesses and your strengths, your successes and your failures. Leave nothing of you behind, and all you have will find a safe place in the One you are.

116 This is the way of wisdom: justice, compassion, and humility. If your practice makes you more just, more kind, and more humble, it is authentic practice. If your faith makes you more just, more kind, and more humble, it is a sound faith. If your teacher helps you become more just, more kind, and more humble, your teacher is a good teacher. If your scriptures instruct you to become more just, more kind, and more humble, they are worth reading. This is the measure by which you judge your path: any road that leads away from justice, compassion, and humility is false; turn from it and walk another way.

Let us leave aside anger,
let us forsake pride,
let us overcome all bondage!
Let us overcome anger by love,
let us overcome evil by good,
let us overcome the greedy by generosity,
the liar by truth!
Speak the truth;
do not yield to anger;
give if you are asked, even if you give but a little.
By these three steps you will come near the gods.[113]

(DHAMMAPADA 221, *DHAMMAPADA: ANNOTATED & EXPLAINED*, P. 71)

"Ask and it will be granted you;
seek and you will find;
knock and the door will be opened to you."[114]

(MATTHEW 7:7)

When you seek Me, you will find Me,
providing you seek Me with a whole heart.[115]

(JEREMIAH 33:3, *THE HEBREW PROPHETS: SELECTIONS ANNOTATED & EXPLAINED*, P. 67)

God has told you what is good.
What does the One Who Is require of you?
Only to do justly
and to love kindness,
and to walk humbly with your God.[116]

(MICAH 6:8, *THE HEBREW PROPHETS: SELECTIONS ANNOTATED & EXPLAINED*, P. 73)

Why? □

I almost dropped the question *Why?* from the questions asked in this book, and the only reason I didn't is that it is asked of me over and over again. The reason I thought to drop it, however, is not because the question is illegitimate, but because it is distracting.

Asking *Who am I?* leads us to the realization that we are so much more than the smaller self can imagine, and as we come to see ourselves as the many faces of the singular Self, we are freed from the fear and anxiety the small self suffers and from the ignorance, arrogance, and violence that often come from that fear and anxiety.

Asking *Where did I come from?* awakens us to the interdependence of all the living in the singular process of the Life that is all life. And as we awaken to our shared origins, we realize our shared responsibility for person and planet.

Asking *Where am I going?* shows us that we arise in and return to our truest Self, that there is nothing to fear regarding death, and because we are free to die fearlessly, we are free to live courageously in service to universal justice and compassion.

Asking *How shall I live?* offers us a toolbox of practices for applying the wisdom gleaned from the previous questions to the everyday encounters that compose our ordinary lives. But what does asking *Why?* do for us? I'm not sure it does anything at all—or at least nothing essential. In fact, asking *Why?* might distract us from all that we have learned thus far.

Job and the Question *Why?*

In the book of Job, the protagonist, Job himself, demands to know why he suffers, why his children died, why his business and his health have failed.

His friends come to comfort him, but after a week of wise silence, sharing only their presence and his grief, they fall into the trap of answering the question *Why?* While each of Job's friends puts his own spin on the answer, their answers are basically the same: Job suffers because there is a flaw in Job's character. Job is being punished, and unless and until Job admits his sins, God will continue to punish him. If Job would only repent, God would then forgive Job his failings and restore his fortune, family, and health.

To his credit, Job will have none of it. He is innocent, and his suffering is undeserved. He demands that God explain the *why* of life's tragedies. Job's plight is universal, and his demand of God no less so. We all want to know why things are the way they are, and we all imagine that only God can answer this for us.

What Job doesn't know, but the reader does, is this: Job is simply collateral damage in a wager God made with Satan. During one of the periodic meetings between God and the angelic host, Satan reports on the doings of humanity on earth, and God brags about Job and Job's love for God. Sensing a need that can be exploited, Satan suggests to God that Job's love for God is contingent on God blessing Job with health, wealth, and a great family. To test this devilish notion, God empowers Satan to take away all Job has that God might at last know whether Job loves God or merely loves what God does for him.

While Job and his friends argue about sin and its connection to punishment, the reader of the book of Job knows that this is irrelevant to the truth: Job is being tortured (and his servants and children murdered) just to see whether Job will, as his wife urges him to do, curse God and die (Job 2:9). Job refuses both to confess to sins he didn't commit and to curse a God he doesn't blame, and he clings mightily to the hope that God will appear and make known to Job just why it is that he and by extension all the innocent suffer.

When God appears, however, the fact of God's satanic wager is dropped in favor of something far more profound. Rather than simply admit that Job suffers as a result of God's self-doubt regarding Job's love for God, God reveals to Job the fundamental wildness of reality that renders mute all questions of why things are the way they are.

God doesn't fall into the trap of answering Job's question. Rather, God shows Job the absurdity of even asking such a question. The liberation that Job seeks, the book of Job seems to be saying, isn't found in answering the question *Why?* but in dropping it altogether.

God, as I read the book of Job, seems to be saying to Job: "Look, the universe is wild and chaotic and wonderful and terrifying all at the same time. You can't pick and choose what happens to you, and in time all of it will happen to you: good and bad, blessing and curse, joy and sorrow. That's the way it is. Your task isn't to erase or avoid suffering, but to embrace it and make the most of it. The key to living well in the madness of reality is radical acceptance, not control and avoidance."

I think Job gets this and, in so doing, comes to a realization that is profoundly comforting. Unfortunately, most English translations of Job seem to miss this and end the book of Job with Job despising himself as nothing but dust and ash, as if God's aim was to reduce Job to a meaningless blip on the cosmic screen of life, when in fact the Hebrew suggests something so much greater.

Rather than despise himself as dust and ash, Job finds comfort in being dust and ash (Job 30:19), knowing that dust and ash are the very stuff of divine creation and creativity. Job isn't made small by God's revelation of the enormity and wildness of the universe, he is made large through the realization that he too is this enormity and wildness.

> Job's comfort at the end is in his mortality. The physical body is acknowledged as dust, the personal drama as delusion. It is as if the world we perceive through our senses, that whole gorgeous and terrible pageant, are the breath-thin surface of a bubble, and everything else, inside and outside, is pure radiance. Both suffering and joy come then like a brief reflection, and death like a pin.[1]
>
> (STEPHEN MITCHELL, *THE BOOK OF JOB* [SAN FRANCISCO: NORTH POINT PRESS, 1987], P. XXVIII)

What *is* is what matters, not why it is. Once you know who you are, where you came from, where you are going, and how you are to live, the question of why is beside the point. Yet the question never seems to go away.

Free Will

"When we talk about why the world is the way it is," a rabbi friend once told me, "we are really talking about suffering. Nobody asks *Why?* when things go well. They only ask *Why?* when things go badly. What we are really asking is, why am I suffering?"

"OK," I said, "how do you answer that?"

"The answer is this: we suffer because we have free will, we suffer because we are free to do things that come back to haunt us. Without free will, there would be no suffering. But without free will, there would be no point to living."

"What about natural disasters?" I asked. "What about someone whose home is taken away in a tornado or whose family is killed in a flood? Where is the free will in that?"

"You have to make a distinction between natural disasters, acts of God, and human evil."

I know lots of people say this, but why? What difference does it make if my family is killed in a car accident caused by a drunk driver or in a tornado? What difference does it make if my loved ones are killed in a landslide or at the hands of a psychopathic murderer?

I put this question to a Buddhist teacher of mine, who answered it this way: "There is no difference. The loss is the same. You may respond to the loss differently, of course. If your family is killed by a drunk driver, you might start an organization to end drunk driving, but if your family is killed in an avalanche, chances are you won't start an organization to stop avalanches. But the reality is the same: no family. Suffering is the nature of nature. There is no escaping it, only learning to live with it."

For a moment I was tempted to challenge this statement with the Buddha's teaching that suffering comes from desire and that desire can be extinguished, but I thought better of it. Like the author of the book of Job, I happen to agree with the notion that suffering is woven into the very fabric of nature and that there is nothing we can do or need do about it. All we can do and all we need do is learn to live wisely with it.

"Not at all," a young pastor told me when I was relating this story to her. "Suffering is optional. It is the result of sin." Clearly she hadn't read the book of Job, or at least hadn't read it the way I read it. "And sin is a necessary consequence of free will."

Again free will. What is so great about free will? What is so essential about suffering that we would be less well off without it?

"Have you read *The Shack* by William Paul Young?" she asked me, not waiting for my reply (I have read it). "In *The Shack* a dad whose eight-year-old daughter is found raped and murdered in an abandoned shack has a conversation with God about why God didn't stop this horror from happening. The answer is free will. God has to allow people to have free will, and that means allowing people to do horrible things; otherwise, life isn't worth living."

"But why?" I asked. "And whose free will is God protecting: the murdered little girl's or the murderer's? It certainly isn't the will of the little girl to be raped and murdered; the killer robs her of her free will, so if God is protecting free will, it must be the free will of the wicked and the powerful who can do what they want to those who cannot defend themselves against them."

"But you can't ask God to erase the free will of the wicked without also asking God to erase the free will of the good," the pastor said.

"OK, let's ask God to take away all free will."

"But that would be horrible!"

"Really? I don't see why this would be horrible at all. What if you woke up tomorrow morning with no free will, would you even know it was gone? No. You'd still think thoughts and have feelings, and act on them, but the thoughts you'd think and the feelings you'd feel would all be good and loving without a trace of selfishness or evil. You would be incapable of doing evil. What would be wrong with that?"

"But if you could only do good, what would be the purpose of hell?"

"Wait a second. Are you saying that the purpose of free will is to justify eternal damnation in the fires of hell?"

"I'm saying," she said, emphasizing each word with an edge to her voice that suggested I was hell-bound for sure, "that hell would be superfluous if sin were impossible."

"OK, so what is wrong with that?"

"The world is the way it is so that you will be forced to choose between good and evil, right belief and heresy, and then suffer the consequences for choosing incorrectly. God made heaven for the righteous and hell for the wicked, so there has to be righteous and wicked, and for there to be righteous and wicked there has to be free will. End of story." Well, at least the end of our conversation.

Suffering and Perennial Wisdom

For some people it always comes back to punishment and eternal damnation, but perennial wisdom doesn't posit such a God. Rather, it teaches that God is all, and being all means including everything and its opposite. To imagine that God could create a world without suffering is to imagine God could create a world with fronts and no backs, with ups and no downs, with ins and no outs. It can't be done because joy and suffering, no less than fronts and backs, go together. But this has nothing to do with God rewarding some and punishing others.

Everything goes with everything else. To have anything is to have everything. Hence the world cannot be other than it is, because there is nothing other for it to be.

Please don't confuse this view with that of the eighteenth-century German philosopher Gottfried Leibniz, who argued that this world is the best of all possible worlds. According to Leibniz, there are multiple options to any given situation, and God chooses the option that is most beneficial at the moment. So this world isn't the best world, but the best of all options available.

The perennial wisdom view isn't that this world is the best option God has, but that this world is the only option God has. Just as it is the nature of a sun to shine, so it is the nature of God to manifest the universe. This is what it is to be a sun; a sun that fails to shine isn't a sun but a collapsed star or black hole. This is what it is to be God; a God who fails to manifest in all as all isn't God.

This answer rarely satisfies. But from the perspective of perennial wisdom there is no other answer. God is not outside the world fashioning it to our benefit; God is the world manifesting the dynamic polarity of God in the seeming opposites that define human experience. Where most people imagine a God who could erase evil but chooses not to, the nondualist understands God as that greater unity embracing and transcending good and evil. Where those who imagine a good God have to explain why God allows for evil, the nondualist realizes Isaiah's God who creates light and dark, good and evil (Isaiah 45:7), and cannot do otherwise. In short, the world is the way it is because God is the way God is.

Lama? Kakha.

In modern Hebrew we have a saying, *Lama? Kakha,* "Why? Because." Not "because I said so," or "because God wills it," or "because it is your karma or fate or destiny," just *kakha,* "because." *Kakha* can also be translated as "just so." Things are just the way they are because they can't be other than the way they are. This is what the book of Job is trying to tell us. Job suffers because suffering is part of the divine play. You don't deserve it and you can't escape it; you can only accept it and move on.

Such an answer doesn't leave much room for further conversation, and that's the point. Discussing *Why?* is an endless conversation that tends to get more and more removed from the world. Once you understand who you are, where you came from, where you are going, and how you should live, the question *Why?* becomes somewhat irrelevant.

To avoid getting trapped in *Why?* and yet without ignoring those who continue to ask the question, I am offering only a few wisdom texts in this final section and ending with a simple litany of *Because* that comes from no one other than myself. I'm not asking you to stop asking *Why?* but I am asking that you put the question aside until you first realize the answers to the other four questions. When you do, I suspect you'll find asking the fifth question totally unnecessary.

1 Why are you here? Why do you have a sense of self that is alien to and alienated from the Self of which you are actually a part? Why, if all is One, do you have this sense of being other? Are you in this state to profit from it or are you here at a loss? Mary's question reflects the limited understanding of the smaller self. Jesus's reply seeks to lift her out of it: You are here to reveal the greatness of the Revealer. But do not imagine he is speaking of himself, the small self, Jesus. This would be narcissism at its highest. Jesus is speaking of the One who reveals All in all. He is speaking of the Infinite in and as the finite, the One as the many, and the Self as the self.

You aren't here to profit or to lose. You are here to become wise and live wisely. You are here to realize God and live godly.

Mary said,
"Lord, tell me why I have come to this place,
to profit from it or to lose?"
The Lord said,
"You have come to reveal the greatness of the revealer!"[1]

(DIALOGUE OF THE SAVIOR 62–63, THE LOST SAYINGS OF JESUS:
TEACHINGS FROM ANCIENT CHRISTIAN, JEWISH, GNOSTIC AND ISLAMIC SOURCES—
ANNOTATED & EXPLAINED, P. 81)

2 If it is true that God is all, including yourself, why can't you simply cease your struggles and find rest in this very moment? It is a good question, but it is rooted in a faulty premise. The false premise is that rest is a steady state you can attain when you realize that God is you. God is not one thing or another, one state or another. God is all things, and every state. God is rest, but also activity. To realize God is not to cease to do, but to cease to do needlessly.

Think in terms of a musical score. If there were no rests, the music would manifest as noise. If there were no notes, the music would not manifest at all. Notes and rest, playing and refraining from playing, are equal parts of the beauty that is music. The same can be said of reality as a whole. It is a dynamic chorus of sound and silence, notes and rests, doing and not doing, ons and offs. One is not superior to the other, and each needs the other. Both are aspects of God.

Awakening is resting at the moment when rest is optimal, and awakening is doing at the moment when doing is optimal. Awakening is knowing which moment is which.

3 The burden Jesus asks you to drop is the false notion that reality can be one thing or another when in fact reality is all things and the other. This leads to the further burden of trying to make reality other than it is so you can be other than you are. There is no need to be other than you are. Cease only to be less than you are. When you are all that you are, you will rest when resting is right, and you will act when acting is right. Then neither rest nor activity is a burden.

4 The small cannot unite with the great because it cannot be separated from the great. A wave cannot unite with the ocean because it is nothing other than the ocean. What Jesus wants us to abandon is the burden of faulty thinking that insists you are other than you are, less than you are. Faulty thinking cannot follow you into the truth of God as all. When you are free from faulty thinking, you will see the unity of self and Self, you will know all in God and God in all, and you will be free from the burden of rest and activity: free to act when necessary and rest when necessary.

Matthew said,
"Why can't we rest immediately?"[2]
The Lord said,
"You will when you give up these burdens!"[3]
Matthew said,
"How does the small unite itself with the great?"
The Lord said,
"When you abandon the things
that will not be able to follow you,
then you will have rest."[4]

(DIALOGUE OF THE SAVIOR 65–68, THE LOST SAYINGS OF JESUS:
TEACHINGS FROM ANCIENT CHRISTIAN, JEWISH, GNOSTIC AND ISLAMIC SOURCES—
ANNOTATED & EXPLAINED, P. 83)

5 You are here to realize that everything that happens happens because it must. Not that it should, but that it must. There is a difference. Saying something should happen is giving a moral value to that happening. Take, for example, the saying "May the best team win." The best team always wins. That's what winning means. That is what it means to be the best team on that day.

Saying something must happen, however, is not the same as saying that it should happen. Nothing should happen. Things just happen. In this way a Self-realized person does not become trapped in her thoughts and feelings and is thus free from the cleverness needed to mask evil as good, and selfishness as altruism. You are here to sober up. You are here to wake up. You are here to witness it all and to promote the compassion and justice that comes with Self-realization.

Wherefore, on every occasion you should say:
this comes from nature;
and this is according to the apportionment
and spinning of the thread of destiny,
and such—like coincidence and chance;
and this is from one of the same stock,
and a kin and partner,
one who knows not however
what is according to human nature.[5]
But I know;
for this reason I behave towards him or her
according to the natural law of fellowship
with benevolence and justice.
At the same time, however, in things indifferent
I attempt to ascertain the value of each.

(MARCUS AURELIUS, THE MEDITATIONS OF MARCUS AURELIUS:
SELECTIONS ANNOTATED & EXPLAINED, P. 143)

6 Nothing can happen that is not aligned with the nature of those involved in the happening. But, again, this does not mean that what happens should happen, ought to happen, or in some way furthers a plan that only a god knows.

When we say, "God works in mysterious ways," we are merely saying that we don't know why things happen as they do. When we say we don't know why things happen as they do, we are merely saying that things could happen other than they do. But can they? If they could, why don't they?

Things happen the way they happen because at the moment of their happening no other happening is possible. Take something as seemingly random as playing the lottery. You buy a ticket and wait for the numbers to be generated. Could those numbers be any number? Only before they are generated. But before they were generated there was no number at all. So in what way could it be different if it doesn't yet exist? When it does exist, it exists as it is and cannot be other than it is. You can call this randomness or chance, but the label adds nothing to the reality.

The simple fact is this: things happen. They happen because of causes over which you have little if any control. If there is any answer to the question *Why?* it is simply this: Because it cannot be other than it is. *Lama? Kakha.*

Nothing can happen to a man or woman
which is not according to the nature of a human being,
nor to an ox which is not according to the nature of an ox,
nor to a vine which is not according to the nature of a vine,
nor to a stone which is not proper to a stone.
If then there happens to each thing
both what is usual and natural,
why should you complain?
For the common nature brings nothing
which may not be borne by you.[6]
(MARCUS AURELIUS, THE MEDITATIONS OF MARCUS AURELIUS:
SELECTIONS ANNOTATED & EXPLAINED, P. 203)

7   Why is this moment the way it is? It isn't a matter of choice. After all, if it were a matter of choice, who would be doing the choosing? Not you, certainly. You didn't even know what this moment was until it arrived. If you didn't choose it, then who did? God? Lots of people would say so, but does God—the Source and Substance of *all* reality—really have a choice? No. God is the infinite field in which springs forth the possible and the probable. Everything and its opposite grows naturally from the fertile soil of the Divine: good and evil, light and dark, yin and yang. Just as a magnet cannot choose to be positive or negative rather than positive and negative, so God cannot choose to be other than God, and God is everything, including everything at this moment. So if you don't choose, and God doesn't choose, who chooses? No one. There is no choice between this and that; there is only reality manifesting as this and that.

8   Think about this: You want to lose ten pounds, or maybe fifty. But you don't. You know what to do: eat less, eat better, exercise more, that kind of thing. This isn't rocket science. Sure, the processed food industry is feeding (pun intended) your addiction to fat, sugar, and salt, but you choose what to put into your mouth, don't you? Don't you?

Maybe not. After all, if you could eat differently, you would eat differently. If you could weigh less, you would weigh less. Maybe you don't because you can't. The "you" who is overweight, addicted to food, alcohol, dope, gambling, sex, or reruns of *NCIS* is just that—addicted, trapped, a product of forces beyond its control. So don't control it; after all, how can the addicted "you" control the "you" who is addicted so that you are no longer addicted?

The key isn't to change, but to grow beyond the small and addicted self into the greater and liberated Self. That is what this anthology of texts and the practice of Passage Meditation is all about. As you plant the seeds of wisdom into your smaller self they take root—like Jesus's mustard seed—and eventually overwhelm the smaller self with the liberated larger Self.

The challenge isn't to be other than you are. The challenge is to be all that you are.

Because.
Because if this moment could be other than it is,
it would be.[7]

Because.
Because if you could be other than you are this moment,
you would be.[8]

(CONTINUED ON PAGE 277)

9 │ This moment isn't an accident. It is the necessary result of 13.8 billion years of evolution. It all goes back to the big bang. So do you. The reasons your birthday cake doesn't have 13.8 billion candles on it are three: first, a cake big enough to hold 13.8 billion candles is too big to bake; second, you just don't have the capacity to blow out 13.8 billion candles in one breath and you don't want to appear weak in front of family and friends; and third, you continually mistake yourself for your self rather than your Self.

You and this moment in which you are happening is the result of all the moments that came before. You and this moment in which you are happening is just the next domino to fall, and it falls because all the dominos before you have fallen. This is the real meaning of karma.

Don't imagine that karma is reward or punishment for deeds done in the past. Karma doesn't judge; it is a fact of nature no more or less conscious than gravity. Karma doesn't decide to do anything; it is just the fact that anything is doing. Karma is the label we give to life happening.

"Behold I place before you birthing and dying, blessing and cursing, now choose life that you and your descendants might live" (Deuteronomy 30:19). Reality—God, Brahman, Allah, Tao, Great Spirit—places everything before you: beginnings and endings, good and bad, success and failure. You aren't asked to choose between them; you are challenged to choose living, which means choosing all of them.

Because.
Because given what is at this moment,
what happens must happen.[9]

(CONTINUED ON PAGE 279)

10 You aren't powerless; you just aren't powerful enough to change the past so that the present might be other than it is. What you can do, what you must do, is choose how to engage with what is. Even in this your choosing is shaped by conditions beyond your control, but it isn't predetermined. You have some room to maneuver.

Imagine your life as a huge ship on the ocean. The course is set, but you can see that the destination toward which you are sailing is no longer one that serves your larger Self and its goal of cultivating compassion and justice. You need to turn the ship around. Grabbing the wheel and trying to turn the rudder directly turns out to be beyond your capacity. The pressure of the sea is too great, and the ship speeds on. While huge changes may be impossible, smaller ones are not. I've mentioned this before; it is called trim tabbing.

A trim tab is a smaller rudder that can be turned, and when it is turned, it shifts the pressures being placed on the main rudder. When the trim tabs are turned, you can then turn the main rudder and alter your course. Small changes can lead to major redirection.

Engage each moment as an opportunity to turn the trim tab. Turn ever more slightly in the direction of kindness, and over time you will become more kind. Shift toward justice even a little, and over time you will become more just.

Because.
Because you aren't free to change what is,
only what is next.[10]

(CONTINUED ON PAGE 281)

11 Do tsunamis have to happen, even though they can take hundreds of thousands of lives? Yes. The ocean doesn't set out to attack people, but if the planet is to survive, its plates must shift, and shifting tectonic plates can cause tsunamis, and tsunamis can take lives. This isn't the best scenario; it is simply the only possible one.

Insisting that this world is the best of all possible worlds forces you to explain why needless pain and suffering are the norm and prevents you from making the best of all possible worlds even better. After all, if this is the best world, what could be better than best?

But perennial wisdom is a call to engagement, not passivity. While it does say that what is happening is the culmination of everything that has happened, and therefore must itself happen, it doesn't say that what will happen next is fixed. You are not free to change the present, but you are free to engage it differently.

Only the smaller self is conditioned. Only the smaller self is locked into the habits of the past, making them the masters of your future. But you are so much more than the smaller self. You are God. And God is endless creativity, endless experimentation. Remembering who you really are, identifying with the Self even as you maintain the function of the self, you are free to shift how you live and, in doing so, change what comes next.

12 *Kakha.*

Because.
Because this isn't the best of all possible worlds,
it is the only possible world.[11]

Lama?[12]

Sages Cited, Annotated ☐

Prepared by Aaron Shapiro

Abba Benjamin: 590–691; thirty-eighth pope of the Coptic Church from 622 until his death in 691. Benjamin is notable for maintaining the unity of the church through three successive eras of political and social upheaval in the Eastern Mediterranean: the Persian occupation (623–638), the return of Byzantine rule (628–640), and the Arab conquest (640). Little is known of Benjamin's early years as pope, but his pontificate was essential to the survival of Egyptian Orthodox Christianity—particularly due to Benjamin's resistance to the imposition of a Chalcedonian pontiff under Byzantine rule, as well as his meeting with the Arab commander 'Amr ibn al-'As, a meeting that secured the restoration of Coptic rights when Persia fell under the control of Islam.

Abba Hierax: One of the Desert Fathers, a group of Christian ascetics who withdrew from the complexities of life under a newly Christianized Rome to seek a monastic existence in small desert communities. The Desert Fathers felt that the conversion of Rome, enacted by Constantine in 380, and the subsequent blending of the religious functions of the church and the political functions of the Roman State under Emperor Constantine, made it impossible for a truly spiritual Christian society to develop. Thus they sought out a simpler, spiritual path, developing what were, in effect, alternative Christian societies.

Abba Poeman: An Egyptian monk and saint of Eastern Christianity, Abba Poeman (Shepherd) is the most widely quoted of the Desert Fathers and is known for his tolerance and compassion, as well as for his eschewal of religious authority, disinterest in the extremes of asceticism, and emphasis on providing gentle spiritual guidance. Poeman seems to have been forced into the desert life, fleeing the monastery at Scetis when that early center of monasticism was overrun by raiders. It was Abba Poeman and his group who recorded the sayings tradition of desert monasticism in the book called *The Wisdom of the Desert Fathers.* However, some scholars—noting the sheer number of quotations attributed to Poeman— have argued that his name became a kind of catchall and that some of the sayings attributed to him were in fact the sayings of other, unnamed desert ascetics.

Abulafia, Abraham: 1240–c. 1291; kabbalist of the medieval period. Abulafia produced twenty-six literary works in his lifetime, including works of theological commentary, grammatical treatises, and poems; however, his most important works are his kabbalistic handbooks, on the techniques of meditation and study necessary to achieve the highest levels (which Abulafia terms "prophetic") of mystical comprehension and communion with God. His influence may be traced through the development of Christian Kabbalah, as well as in the ecstatic tradition of Kabbalah, which later influenced Hasidism.

Al-Ghazali: Among the most influential of Muslim philosophers, al-Ghazali (1056–1111) sought to end the Islamic fascination with Hellenistic thinkers such as Aristotle on the grounds that they were "unbelievers." The first philosophers to formalize Sufism as a succinct doctrine of thought, he also sought to unify Sufism with Shariah, Islamic law.

Al-Hallaj, Mansur: 858–922; Persian writer, mystic, and teacher of Sufism. Al-Hallaj's radical methodology of mystical universalism, which posited that one had to go beyond mere religion to find spiritual union with the Divine, resulted in his being accused of heresy and executed by Abassid Caliph al-Muqtadir. He is best known for writing *Kitab al-Tawasin*, which contains a dialogue wherein Satan refuses to recognize Adam as the image of God (this dialogue, moreover, may have influenced Milton's depiction of Satan's resentment toward humankind in *Paradise Lost*).

Amma Sarah: One of the "Desert Mothers" living in Egypt, Persia, and Palestine during the fourth and fifth centuries. The sayings tradition of the Desert Mothers is partially recorded in *The Wisdom of the Desert Fathers*, which contains forty-seven sayings attributed to various *ammas*, or mothers, of the desert monastic communities. Amma Sarah, also referred to as Sarah of the Desert, seems to have had a rather caustic wit and to have stressed purity of heart over the maintenance of social (and gender) norms.

Augustine: 354–430; Aurelius Augustinus, also known as Saint Augustine of Hippo; author of the *Confessions of Saint Augustine*. Augustine is the foremost Christian philosopher of the Middle Ages, instrumental in the merging of Neoplatonic thought with the Judeo-Christian scriptural and theological traditions.

ben Sirach, Jesus: A Jewish scribe of the early second century BCE, Ben Sira, as he is also known, is the author of the apocryphal Wisdom of Jesus ben Sirach, included in the Septuagint, the Greek translation of the Hebrew Bible. Though little is known of his life, it is thought that he authored the work while living in Alexandria sometime between 180 and 175 BCE.

ben Zoma, Simeon: A Talmudic scholar of the early second century CE, Ben Zoma was a colleague of Ben Azzai and Rabbi Akiva. It is said, in the Babylonian Talmud, that the three colleagues, along with a fourth, Elisha ben Abuyah, achieved paradise via their search for esoteric knowledge in their study of Torah. And yet, of the four, only Akiva returned unscathed. Ben Azzai died, Ben Abuyah became a heretic, and Ben Zoma went mad. The story, though apocryphal, nevertheless illustrates the depth and radicalism of Ben Zoma's thought. Although he was never ordained as rabbi, his teachings have been recorded in *Pirke Avot*, and his halachic interpretations have been handed down through the centuries. He is perhaps best known for his fourfold contrarian definitions of the wise, the rich, the powerful, and the esteemed.

Broughton, James: 1913–1999; aka Sunny Jim; poet and experimental filmmaker of the San Francisco Renaissance. Broughton is best known for his films, which examine such perennial themes as sex, death, and the search for meaning. His poetry, meanwhile, falls into the category of Beat literature, blending elements of Eastern philosophy with a countercultural sensibility.

Buber, Martin: 1878–1965; Jewish essayist, translator, and editor whose prolific writings focused primarily on philosophy, the Bible, Hasidism, and Judaism. Major themes of Buber's work include the dialogic principle, the revival of Jewish religious consciousness in the modern age, the articulation of a Jewish humanism, and Zionism. Buber's best-known work is *I and Thou*, in which he presents two fundamental relationships between the self and its various others: the I-Thou relationship, which acknowledges agency and independence, as well as divine nature, in the figure of the other, and the I-It relationship, which relegates the other to the status of mere object.

Chuang-tzu: Fourth century BCE; Chinese Taoist philosopher. Traditionally, Chuang-tzu, also known as Chuang Chou, is identified as the author of the book that bears his name, the Chuang-tzu, also called *True Classic of Southern (Cultural) Flourescence*. However, the historicity of Chuang-tzu's authorship is debated. Nevertheless, the book is a classic of Taoist philosophy, providing a skeptical, sometimes caustic, and even anarcho-individualistic philosophy quite at odds with the socially minded and duty-bound Confucianism dominant in China at the time.

Confucius: 551–479 BCE; according to Chinese tradition, Confucius was the political figure, teacher, and thinker who authored the *Analects* and founded the *Ru* school of Chinese philosophy. His work forms the foundation of ancient Chinese thought regarding the nature and comportment of the ideal human being, as well as the functioning of ideal political and social systems.

Dell, William: 1607–1679; nonconformist preacher and radical Parliamentarian who lived and taught during the period surrounding the English Civil War. Dell is notable for having refused the Act of Uniformity, which normalized all religious practice within the Anglican Church, and for promoting antinomianism, the idea that one is saved through faith and grace alone, regardless of one's adherence to the moral law as expressed in scripture.

Dutton, Anne: 1692–1764; influential and prolific English evangelical writer. Dutton published some thirteen titles and was active as the editor of *The Spiritual Magazine.* Dutton's most notable work was perhaps her first—a description in verse of the process of redemption, penned from a Calvinist perspective—though she is also noteworthy for having written "Letter to the Negroes," a text designed to welcome enslaved blacks into Christianity. Dutton's work, in general, is dominated by typical Calvinist themes, and she deals frequently with the idea of humanity's inability to avoid sin, as well as the self-sufficiency of God's redemption.

Eckhart, Meister: c. 1260–c. 1327; Eckart von Harchheim, a German philosopher, theologian, and mystic of the Dominican Order whose radical approach to Christianity brought him into conflict with the religious authorities of his time. Eckhart's theology clearly departs from accepted Christian tradition in a number of ways, most notably his integration of Neoplatonic philosophy and his insistence on contemplative practice and the cultivation of detachment from the world as a necessity for humankind's spiritual reunion with God, a concept that echoes Eastern, especially Buddhist and Zen Buddhist, notions of Nirvana.

Eriugena, John Scotus: 815–877; Irish Neoplatonist theologian and poet whose major work, *De devisione naturae*, was attacked as heretical. In it, Eriugena maps a dialectical system of the created universe as an ongoing manifestation of God that exists between two poles of divine being: the uncreated creator and that which is neither created nor creates. Eriugena's work is notable because it marks the transition in Christian thought from Neoplatonism to Scholasticism.

Gautama, Siddhartha (Buddha): c. 563–483 BCE; a sage of the Shakya republic in India and the founder of Buddhism. Siddhartha's teachings were entirely oral, and they survived in that form, as part of the Buddhist oral tradition, for many centuries before being first written down about four hundred years after the Buddha's death. Key among the tenents of Buddhism are the Four Noble Truths: (1) suffering, or dissatisfaction, is bound up naturally with life's fundamental impermanence; (2) the true cause of suffering is desire, which surfaces in three ways: as craving for sensual pleasures, craving for identity, and craving for annihilation; (3) suffering can be overcome; and (4) the way to overcome it is through an "Eightfold Path," consisting of right understanding, right thought, right speech, right action, right livelihood, right effort, right mindfulness, and right concentration.

Heller, Meshullam Feibush, of Zbarazh: An eighteenth-century mystic whose teaching helped shape the early Hasidic movement, Rabbi Heller articulated a system of Hasidism that would have a profound impact on the development of Chabad. Central to Heller's work are the ideas of faith in one's teacher and, more importantly, the notion of transforming negative thoughts and emotions into a means of achieving unity with God.

Horowitz, Aharon HaLevi: 1766–1829; Polish Talmudic scholar and kabbalist. HaLevi was the founder of the now-defunct branch of Staroselye Hasidism, created in 1812 following a disagreement between HaLevi and Rabbi Dovber over the rightful successor to Reb Shneur Zalman, the first rabbi of the CHaBaD Hasidic movement. HaLevi's major work, *Sha'arei Avodah (The Gates of Worship)*, focuses on the unity of God, the union of souls, the law, and repentance. He is also the author of a work of Torah commentary, *Avodat ha-Levi*.

Hui Hai: Eighth century CE; Zen Buddhist philosopher and author of the *Zen Teaching of Instantaneous Awakening*, which focuses on using contemplative practice to achieve the realization of the interconnectedness of all things and the recognition of the divine presence in all things.

Huineng: (638–713); the Sixth Patriarch of Chan (Zen) Buddhism. Huineng is the author of the Platform Sutra, transcripts of talks given by

Huineng. The "platform" in the title is the high seat upon which Huineng sat in order to be seen and heard by his students. His sutra is the only Chinese Buddhist text to be granted scriptural status.

Isaiah: Eighth century BCE; biblical prophet and presumed author of the book of Isaiah. Isaiah was both witness to and participant in one of the most turbulent periods in the history of Judea, a period marked by Assyrian expansionism and radical Judean political reform under Hezekiah. His prophecies emphasize a progressive vision of history, in which the suffering of the present will eventually be redeemed in an era of universal peace, justice, and prosperity. It is from Isaiah that Judaism takes its conception of its role in the development of world history: the Jews, according to Isaiah, are to be a "light unto the nations," serving as moral and spiritual guides to universal redemption.

Jeremiah: Seventh and sixth centuries BCE; the second of the major canonical Jewish prophets, traditionally thought to have authored the book of Jeremiah, 1 Kings, 2 Kings, and the book of Lamentations. Jeremiah's ministry spans the period preceding and following the Babylonian exile and the destruction of the First Temple in Jerusalem. Jeremiah's exhortations focused primarily on denouncing idolatry, corruption in the priesthood, and false prophecy.

Kabir: 1440–1518; Islamic mystical poet. Kabir's work is notable for its fusion of Islamic and Hindu influences. His major work, the *Bijak* (Seedling), posits that life is the interplay between the individual soul and God and that redemption, or enlightenment, is the result of bringing these two modes of being into harmony.

Lao Tzu: Sixth century BCE; Chinese philosopher traditionally credited with founding philosophic Taoism and authoring the Tao Te Ching. Scholars today dispute the historicity of these claims, with some arguing that Lao Tzu lived during the fourth or fifth century BCE during the Golden Age of Chinese Philosophy, a period in which a wide range of philosophical ideas were widely discussed and freely debated. Some scholars, moreover, have argued that Lao Tzu is a historical composite. Regardless, he is a central figure of Taoist philosophy, and his work has been influential to a number of anti-authoritarian movements in Chinese and world history.

Levi Yitzchak of Berdichev: 1740–1810; a leading scholar and chief rabbi of a number of Jewish communities in Poland. Reb Yitzchak became one of the most influential leaders of the early Hasidic movement in Eastern Europe. He is known primarily for his compassion in interpreting the doings of the Jews, and it was widely believed that he might act as a "defense attorney" for the Jewish people, mitigating their judgment by God. His major works include *Kedushas Levi*, a Torah commentary; the popular liturgical song *Dudele*; and a liturgical poem, "The Kaddish of Rebbe Levi Yitzchak."

Maimonides: 1135–1234; Moses ben Maimon, also known as the Rambam, one of the most influential Jewish philosophers of the Middle Ages. Maimonides's major works include the *Mishneh Torah* (a codification of Jewish law) and the *Guide for the Perplexed* (a work dealing with the nature of God and the universe and detailing Maimonides's moral philosophy). Though met with significant controversy in the time of its publication, Maimonides's work has since become an essential part of the canons of both Judaism and Western philosophy.

Meir, Yitzchak: 1798–1866; a student of the Kotzker Rebbe, prominent halachic scholar, and founder of the Ger Hasidic dynasty, today centered in Jerusalem. The Ger movement focuses on the exacting study of Torah and Talmud and stresses the pursuit of absolute honesty and authenticity in one's spiritual or religious life.

Micah: Biblical prophet whose prophetic activity spanned the period 737–690 BCE. Micah is best known for prophesying against the corruption of the ruling class and the priesthood in the Kingdom of Judah. He predicts the destruction of Jerusalem but also lays the groundwork for the Jewish messianic vision, imagining a time when Jerusalem will be restored.

Muhammad: 570–632; the founder of Islam and the political and military leader who unified Arabia into a single political and socio-religious entity.

According to Islamic tradition, Muhammad is the final prophet of Allah (God), and his revelations, recorded in the Qur'an, signify the culmination of the Judeo-Christian prophetic tradition.

Origen: 184/5–253/4; Origen Adamantius, early Christian scholar and theologian living in Alexandria. Origen was accused of apostasy for promoting the belief in the preexistence and transmigration of souls, as well as in apokatastasis, or universal salvation, the idea that all human souls will eventually be reconciled with God through divine grace.

Pelagius: 390–418; native Briton and ascetic Christian monk who opposed the notion of predestination and lionized free will as an essential part of humanity's pursuit of salvation. Pelagius's views were met with significant resistance, especially from Saint Augustine, who accused Pelagius of Judaizing, that is, of asserting the importance of works over faith and of denying the necessity of God's grace.

Plotinus: 204–270; influential Neoplatonic philosopher of the ancient world. Plotinus promoted nondualistic principles of transcendent unity, arguing that the transcendent One would exist beyond categories of subject/object, being/nonbeing, and so on. He also put forth the notion of divine "emanation" as an alternative to creation ex nihilo (from nothing). For Plotinus, creation emerges from the One as a consequence of the One's existence. Finally, Plotinus is also notable for having argued that true happiness (*eudaimonia*) is an effect of consciousness and that one attains happiness by attaining the highest levels of consciousness (those beyond the merely physical world).

Ramakrishna: 1836–1886; a leading Indian mystical teacher of the Bengali and Hindu Renaissance whose teachings fused Hindu, Islamic, and Christian theology and practice. Ramakrishna argued that all religions lead to the same God and stressed God-realization as the ultimate goal of all living beings. His teaching would, through the efforts of his student and disciple Swami Vivekenanda, lead to the foundation of the Ramakrishna Mission, a philanthropic organization devoted to humanitarian work around the world.

Rumi, Jalāl ad-Dīn Muhammad: 1207–1273; Persian poet and Sufi mystic. Rumi's major poetic works are the *Divan* and the *Mesnevi*, while his major prose works fall into the categories of discourses, letters, and sermons. As a mystic, Rumi taught that all life follows a pattern of devolution from and re-evolution toward a divine origin.

Saint Brigid of Kildare: 451–523; one of the patron saints of Ireland. Saint Brigid was a nun and abbess responsible for founding a number of convents throughout the countryside, including the legendary Kildare monestary, and she worked with Saint Patrick to evangelize the Celts.

Saint Catherine of Genoa: 1447–1510; Italian saint and mystic of the Roman Catholic Church. Catherine of Genoa began receiving visions from God at the age of twenty-six and devoted her life to the church as well as to service to the sick. Her visionary experiences were recorded late in her life by her spiritual guide Father Marabotti, who compiled them in the *Memoirs*. Her most notable works appeared only after her death and were probably edited by another party. These are the "Dialogues on the Soul and the Body" and the "Treatise on Purgatory."

Saint Gregory of Sinai: Thirteenth century to 1347 CE; Greek Orthodox monk, theologian, and mystic who advocated Hesychasm—a form of contemplative prayer intended to produce an ecstatic experience of divine union. Gregory's work is recorded in the *Philokalia*, a collection of spiritual writings ranging in date from the fourth to the fifteenth century.

Saint Isaiah the Solitary: Fourth century CE; Greek Orthodox saint whose principal treatise on contemplative worship is partially preserved in the *Philokalia*. Isaiah is best known for his treatise "On Guarding the Intellect," consisting of twenty-seven texts designed as a guide for purifying the mind.

Saint Mark the Ascetic: Fifth century CE; ascetic and Christian theologian. Mark's writings, three of which are included in the *Philokalia*, provide a detailed vision of the nature of temptation and place a great deal of emphasis on the necessity of God's grace as a prerequisite for salvation.

Among his most important treatises are "On the Spiritual Law" and "On Those Who Think They Are Made Righteous by Works."

Saint Maximos the Confessor: 586–662; Greek Orthodox monk and proponent of Neoplatonist theology, which argues that salvation consists of humankind's spiritual reunion with God. Maximos was also deeply embroiled in the Monothelite controversy, a disagreement over the nature of Christ's will. Monothelism holds that Christ had a singular will, synonymous with the will of God the Father. Maximus opposed the Monthelites, asserting that Christ had both a human and a divine will. His opposition brought him into conflict with the religious authorities of his time and resulted in his being tried and convicted of heresy, though he was later vindicated by the Sixth Ecumenical Council.

Saint Paul: First century CE; the apostle Paul, once Saul of Tarsus. Famously converted to Christianity on the road to Damascus after having been an intense opponent, Paul is one of the greatest and most influential figures of early Christianity, responsible for spreading the Gospel of Jesus throughout the gentile communities of the Roman Empire. Paul's epistles, of course, are included as a canonical part of the New Testament.

Saint Peter of Damaskos: First century CE; one of the twelve disciples of Jesus, a prominent leader of the first-century Christian movement, and a saint of the Catholic Church, which traditionally considers him to have founded the Holy See in concert with Paul. Peter's life story is told in the canonical Gospels, along with the book of Acts, the Hebrew Gospel, and other writings of the early church.

Schneerson, Menachem Mendel: 1902–1994; leader of the Lubavitch movement of Hasidic Judasim for forty years. Reb Schneerson was responsible for the recovery of the Lubavitch community following its near destruction by the Nazis during the Holocaust. Under his leadership, more than fourteen hundred Chabad-Lubavitch centers were established in thirty-six countries around the world. Moreover, Schneerson also established educational and outreach organizations offering social services and humanitarian aid to anyone in need, without regard to the recipient's religious affiliation.

Shankara, Adi: Eighth century CE; Hindu philosopher who taught that the division between Brahman and Atman (Divine Being and the individual self) is illusory. Shankara's most influential works are his commentaries on the Upanishads, the Bhagavad Gita, and the Brahma Sutras, and he is particularly notable for being the first to articulate the system of Hinduism known as Advaita (nondualism).

Stithatos, Nikitas: 1005–1090; a Christian mystic and saint of the Eastern Orthodox Church. Stithatos is famed as the author *The Life of Symeon*, a biography of his friend and teacher Symeon the Theologian. He is also noted for having defended Symeon's teaching of the hesychast prayer and for writing a number of treatises on Gnostic theology now collected in the *Philokalia*. Stithatos's most important works in this regard are "On the Soul," "On Paradise," and "On the Hierarchy."

Ta-shih, Yung-chia: 665–713 CE; Zen Buddhist poet and sage. Ta-Shih held, as does Buddhism in general, that Atman (self) and Brahman (God) are one, and he advocated contemplative practice as a way to bring the individual mind to God consciousness.

Thurman, Howard: 1899–1981; African American author, educator, minister, civil rights leader, and founder of the Howard Thurman Educational Trust. In addition to his works as director and chairman of the trust, Thurman also held posts at Howard University and, later, at Boston University. In addition, he was instrumental in the creation of the Church for the Fellowship of All Peoples, the first intercultural church in the United States, in 1945. As an author, Thurman was prolific; he wrote no fewer than twenty books dealing with cultural and ethical issues, the most famous of which, *Jesus and the Disinherited*, was cited as an influence by Martin Luther King Jr.

Winstanley, Gerrard: 1609–1676; Protestant reformer and activist during the reign of Oliver Cromwell. Winstanley authored the pamphlet

The Law of Freedom in a Platform, which pitted Christian ethics against capitalism and advocated the abolishment of both wages and property, imagining a utopian community built along what would today be called Communist lines. He is counted among the founders of the True Levellers, or Diggers, movement, which occupied public commons, cultivated them, and distributed the resulting crops free of charge.

Primary Sources, Annotated ☐

Prepared by Aaron Shapiro

Analects of Confucius: A collection of the sayings of Confucius, compiled by his students between 471 and 221 BCE, and achieving its final, complete form by the time of the early Han Dynasty (206–220 CE). The *Analects* is considered one of the principal books of ancient Chinese philosophy, and it focuses primarily on the cultivation of moral virtue, beginning with a focus on the individual and then extending that focus to one's family, one's community, and the state.

Apocryphon of James: Part of the Apocrypha of the New Testament, discovered among the codices of the Nag Hammadi library in 1945. Framed as a letter from James to an unknown correspondent, the Apocryphon of James purports to contain the teachings and parables that Jesus offered to James and Peter during the time between Jesus's resurrection and his ascension.

Bhagavad Gita: Seven-hundred-verse scripture contained in the Hindu epic *Mahabharata*. Set on the battlefield at the start of the Kurukshetra War, the Gita tells the story of Arjuna, a Pendavra prince who, faced with the prospect of fighting a civil war against his own relatives, teachers, and friends, is filled with doubt. He turns to his charioteer, secretly the Lord Krishna, who responds to his moral confusion by elaborating on concepts of duty and philosophy. The text has been read as an allegory for the moral struggle of each individual, and it offers a prescription of knowledge, devotion, and desireless action as the way to achieve personal salvation.

Carmina Gadelica: Compiled during the period 1855–1910, the *Carmina Gadelica* presents a wide-ranging collection of Gaelic songs, hymns,

prayers, blessings, incantations, poems, and tales, as collected and translated by Alexander Carmichael. Though later scholars criticized the veracity
of Carmichael's sources and the accuracy of his translations, the text is still
considered an indispensable source for those studying Scottish folklore.

Chandogya Upanishad: One of the ten principal Upanishads—the ten
major Hindu scriptures—the Chandogya Upanishad presents a system of
meditative practice designed to lead the reader to transcend the divisive
illusions of egoic self-consciousness and its experience of finite, temporal
reality (the "wheel" of birth, life, death), and thus to move beyond suffering by embracing the knowledge of ultimate Self and regaining one's
connection to the original Source of Being.

Chuang-tzu: Scholars debate its authorship, but Chinese tradition has it that
this text records the teachings and writings of Chuang-tzu, a highly influential sage of the fourth century BCE, along with the writings and teachings of his followers and related philosophers. An important precursor to
the development of Chinese Zen Buddhism, the text presents a frequently
skeptical philosophy, posing essential questions on the nature of self and
knowledge. In addition, the text includes meditations on what might be
termed an individualist form of anarchism, as well as satirical pieces tar-
geted at contemporaneous schools of philosophy, such as Confucianism.

Confessions of Saint Augustine: Thirteen-book autobiography penned
by Saint Augustine of Hippo between 397 and 398 CE. Written when
Augustine was around forty years old, the first nine books of the *Confessions* cover the saint's wayward youth—dealing with his sensual life, as
well as his flirtation with Manicheism, skepticism, and Neoplatonism—
and leading up to his conversion to Christianity. The later books contain Augustine's discourses on memory, time, and eternity, as well as an
exegesis on the book of Genesis. The primary theme emerging from the
text is that of redemption, positing that individual and universal redemption are linked and that each describes an arc of exile from and return to
Divine Being.

Crest-Jewel of Discrimination: Called the *Vivekachudmani* in Sanskrit, this eighth-century poem ascribed to Adi Shankara expounds the philosophy of Advaita Vedanta over the course of 580 metrical verses. Written as a dialogue between a master and his disciple, the text provides a step-by-step guide to reaching enlightenment. In this regard, Shankara posits that cultivating *viveka*, which refers to the intellect's ability to distinguish illusion from reality, is the central facet of spiritual development. Such cultivation leads to the realization that the world as we know it is illusion and that Divine Being (Brahman) is the ultimate Reality.

Deuteronomy: The fifth book of the *Tanakh*, or Hebrew Bible, Deuteronomy consists of three sermons delivered by Moses near the end of his life, as the Jews are about to enter into Canaan, the Promised Land. The first sermon recapitulates the narrative of the Jews wandering in the desert after the Exodus; the second reasserts the necessity of the Jews' allegiance to God and to God's law, an allegiance upon which their possession of the Promised Land depends; the third, however, offers the promise that, should the Jews prove unfaithful and the land be lost, they may restore themselves through repentance. Though tradition accepts Moses's authorship, modern scholarship suggests that the book's origins lie in the period following Assyria's destruction of the Northern Kingdom of Israel, when the Southern Kingdom (Judah) adapted Israeli traditions to a program of political and religious reform. The final form of the text, meanwhile, only emerged in the sixth century BCE, after the Jews' return to Judah from Babylonian captivity.

Dhammapada: Roughly translated as "The path of truth, harmony, and righteousness," the Dhammapada consists of 423 verses recording various sayings of the Buddha. The sayings were set down by the Buddha's disciples following his death and are organized into twenty-six chapters according to theme. By crystallizing the Buddha's teaching in this way, the Dhammapada not only preserved the Buddha's teaching, but also made it widely accessible. Today, the Dhammapada is the best known and most commonly read Buddhist scripture.

Dialogue of the Savior: Preserved in a single Coptic copy found in Codex III of the Nag Hammadi codices, and dated to approximately 150 CE, the *Dialogue of the Savior* presents the teachings of Jesus as he responds to questions from three of his disciples. Its primary theme is the achievement of salvation through mystical enlightenment, though the text also contains a creation myth, a cosmology, and an apocalyptic vision. The unevenness of the narrative and the stylistic differences among its parts have led scholars to believe that the text was likely redacted from multiple sources.

Ecclesiastes: Part of the Writings (*Ketuvim*) section of the Hebrew Bible, Ecclesiastes is traditionally attributed to King Solomon, though the text is in fact anonymous and was likely written sometime near the end of the third century BCE. The book takes the form of an autobiography, detailing the main character's investigations into the meaning of life and the best way of living. The book argues that the actions of humanity are "vain" or "empty" and that human wisdom may have no bearing on eternal truth. It concludes by saying that because both intellectual and personal ambition are rendered absurd by the inevitability and universality of death, one should forgo them and simply enjoy the small pleasures of daily life.

Epistle of James: Of uncertain authorship, but traditionally attributed to James the Just, the Epistle of James is a letter contained in the New Testament and probably composed in Jerusalem in the latter half of the first century CE (or perhaps early in the second). In the letter, James reinforces the practical duties of Christian life, warns against a range of vices, and stresses, above all, the practice of patience and faith in the coming of the Messiah.

Exodus: The second book of both the Hebrew and the Christian Bible. The book relates the story of the Jews' liberation from Egyptian slavery. Led by their prophet, Moses, the Jews journey through the desert to Mount Sinai, where they enter into a covenant with God, who gives them their laws and promises them the land of Canaan in return for their faithfulness. Jewish tradition attributes the authorship of Exodus, along with that of the entire Torah, to Moses; modern scholars, however, see the book as a product of the Babylonian exile.

The Forty Foundations of Religion: Written by the Sufi sage Imam Abu Hamid al-Ghazali (1058–1111), *The Forty Foundations of Religion* presents al-Ghazali's own summation of his major philosophical and theological work *The Revival of Religious Knowledge* and provides a guide to Islamic principals on issues of law, worship, spirituality, and mysticism.

Genesis: The first book of the Hebrew and Christian Bibles, Genesis relates the story of God's creation of the world and humanity, as well as the story of the formation of the people of Israel. The basic narrative moves from the initial act of creation through the Fall of Man in the Garden of Eden, and on to the story of the Flood, in which God, horrified at the wickedness of humankind, attempts to unmake the world, saving only Noah and his family. The post-Flood narrative tracks the story of the Patriarchs, as Abraham is told by God to leave his home and to go into Canaan. There Abraham makes a covenant with God, who promises the land to Abraham and his descendants, who live there for three generations, from Abraham to Isaac to Jacob. Following another encounter with God, Jacob's name is changed to Israel, and through the agency of Jacob's son Joseph, the entire people is moved into Egypt, where they (briefly) prosper. Like the book of Exodus (see above) the authorship of Genesis is attributed to Moses, though scholars date the redaction of the book to around the sixth century BCE.

Gospel according to John: The fourth canonical Gospel of the New Testament, the Gospel according to John provides an account of the life and ministry of Jesus. The text opens with John the Baptist's affirmation of Jesus and closes with Jesus's death, resurrection, and final appearances. John presents a unique vision of Jesus, describing him as the incarnation of Logos, or the Divine Word.

Gospel according to Luke: The third canonical Gospel of the New Testament, the Gospel according to Luke (like John) bears witness to the life of Jesus, tracing his story from birth to ascension. The text emphasizes Jesus's compassion and contains some material—such as the Prodigal Son and Good Samaritan stories—not present in the other Gospels.

Gospel according to Matthew: The first of the canonical Gospels of the New Testament, the Gospel according to Matthew begins with the baptism of Jesus and moves on to record his ministry, his trial, the crucifixion, the resurrection, and the giving of the Great Commission. Matthew also contains five discourses of Jesus, including the Sermon on the Mount.

Gospel of Eve: A lost, Gnostic book of the New Testament Apocrypha; the only surviving elements of the text appear as quotations in the *Panarion* of Epiphanius.

Gospel of the Hebrews: Composed in Greek for use by Jewish-Christians living in Egypt in the second century CE, the Gospel of the Hebrews contains sayings of Jesus alongside discussions and descriptions of Jesus's preexistence, birth, baptism, and temptation. The full extent of the Gospel is unknown, and no extant manuscript exists. It survives in fragments quoted by the early church fathers.

Gospel of Mary: Part of the Apocrypha of the New Testament, the Gospel of Mary appears in the codex Papyrus Berolinensis 8502, discovered in Cairo in 1896 and dated to the second century CE. The text contains two dialogues of Jesus, related by Mary Magdalene to the apostles sometime between the resurrection and the ascension. Considered a Gnostic text, the Gospel of Mary's dialogues are each largely concerned with relating a vision of humanity's true identity—as the image and likeness of God—and arguing that salvation rests in return to or reconciliation with God.

Gospel of Philip: A noncanonical Gnostic Gospel of the Nag Hammadi library, the Gospel of Philip dates to the third century CE and takes the form of an anthology of Gnostic teachings presented without narrative context. The primary theme of the text seems to be sacrament, but the text is best known for being the source of the theory that Mary Magdalene was, in fact, Jesus's wife or partner.

Gospel of Thomas: A noncanonical gospel discovered among the codices of the Nag Hammadi library, the Gospel of Thomas records 116 sayings of Jesus, sometimes embedded in brief parables or dialogues. Some scholars have seen Thomas as a record of the early Christian oral tradition and proof of the existence of the Q Gospel—the theoretical source of the sayings of Jesus that appear, at times word for word, across the canonical Gospels.

Hadith, Sayings of Prophet Muhammad: Collective sayings of Muhammad taken from *Mishkat al-Masabih*, presenting an introductory guide to Islamic belief and practice, touching on issues of purification, prayer, mourning, pilgrimage, jihad, compassion, and so forth.

Heart Sutra: The most widely known book of Buddhist scripture, the Heart Sutra presents the essence of Buddhist philosophy. In brief, it narrates the path to enlightenment of Avalokitesvara, the Bodhisattva of compassion, using a method of meditation to awaken inner wisdom and thereby recognize the fundamental "emptiness" of all perceived phenomena.

Homilies on the Gospel of John (Saint Augustine): Comprising 124 tractates, this text presents Augustine's commentary on the Gospel of John in a dialogic, question-and-answer style. While some of the tractates were dictated to copyists, many were in fact delivered as sermons, and so much of the text is pastoral in its concerns, rather than overtly theological. And yet, it is nevertheless the most theologically profound of the commentaries on John written by ancient authors. Its primary themes include the incarnation of the Word in the person of Christ, the nature of the church and its sacraments, and the fulfillment of the divine plan.

Job: Perhaps the most disturbing of the books of the Hebrew Bible, the book of Job examines the problems of suffering and injustice in the world. It details the trials of Job, his discussions with his friends over the nature and cause of suffering, his challenge to God, and God's response.

Katha Upanishad: One of the primary Upanishads, often also referred to by the alternate title "Death as Teacher," the Katha Upanishad tells the story of a boy, Nachiketa, who, in a conversation with Yama, the God of Death, learns the secret of life. According to Yama, there are two paths in life: One focuses on the pleasures of the senses and the things of this world; this path leads only to death. The second path focuses on an inward, spiritual journey, whose end is union with the Divine and immortality.

Letter to an Elderly Friend: From the collected letters of Palagius, in which Palagius puts forth his views on the divine nature of all life, arguing that God is both immanent and transcendent, both present in and as the world, and beyond it.

Liber Graduum: Also known as the *Book of Steps*, this text is an anonymous Syriac Christian treatise dated to the late fourth or early fifth century CE. Divided into thirty discourses, the book is addressed to the author's Persian Christian community, dividing the community into two groups—the perfect and the upright—and laying out the basic ethical and spiritual precepts for members of each group. The precepts are also divided into two segments: the major commandments, applying to those who wish to be perfect, and the minor commandments, applying to the upright remainder of the community.

Meditations of Marcus Aurelius: A series of personal writings and aphorisms written in Koine Greek by the Roman general Marcus Aurelius. The *Meditations* is divided into twelve books, each corresponding with a different period in the author's life; the work presents an essentially Stoic philosophy, advocating an analytical approach to the knowledge of self and other, the development of a cosmic, rather than egoic, perspective, the avoidance of indulgence in sensory pleasure, the stripping away of distraction, and the maintenance of a strong ethical code.

Mesnevi: A 25,000-verse poem written in six books over the period 1258–1273 CE by the Sufi mystic Jalāl ad-Dīn Muhammad Rumi. The text presents the various aspects of Sufi religious life and offers spiritual advice to Sufi adherents. Books 1 and 2 are primarily concerned with a discussion of self-delusional tendencies of the carnal self; books 3 and 4 investigate the themes of Reason and Knowledge, as personified in the figure of Moses; books 5 and 6 lay out the argument that, in order to comprehend God, humanity must learn to see beyond the limitations of physical being.

Mishneh Torah, **The Book of Knowledge:** Book 1 of Maimonides's monumental *Mishneh Torah,* the Book of Knowledge lays out the theological and philosophical foundations of Judaism. It includes meditations on the nature of God; an examination of the problem of anthropomorphism in religious language; theories of physics, metaphysics, prophecy, and ethics; an argument for the importance of Torah study as both a devotional act and an act of critical thinking; an argument against paganism; and investigations of issues of free will, repentance, and divine providence.

Mundaka Upanishad: Couched as a conversation between Shaunaka and Angiras, the Mundaka Upanishad is a mantra Upanishad, written in verse, and designed to teach the knowledge of Brahman (the Godhead). The text divides knowledge into two broad categories: *Apara Vidya* (knowledge of the material world) and *Para Vidya* (knowledge of Eternal Truth). Both are necessary: *Apara Vidya* enables the accomplishments of the sciences and rationality, but it cannot make known the origins of reality or the root cause of being; this is the province of *Para Vidya,* which opens the doors of perception to the underlying fabric of creation. The text discusses the path by which one may comprehend *Para Vidya* and includes such injunctions as the renouncement of all action, and the practice of yoga for self-realization. Finally, the text discusses the passage of the soul into Brahman and the annihilation of the perspective of the egoic self within the larger cosmic selfhood of God.

Papyrus Oxyrhynchus: Two manuscripts in vellum found among a group of manuscripts in Greek, Latin, and Arabic, discovered in Egypt and dating from the first to the sixth century CE. The two papyri that most concern us here are Oxyrhynchus 840 and Oxyrhynchus 1224, which each contain narratives and lines relating to the Gospels. Oxyrhynchus 840 is the more complete of the two texts and contains a unique narrative detailing an encounter between Jesus and a Pharisee in which the two argue over the notion of ritual cleanliness. The text is dated around 150–200 CE. Oxyrhynchus 1224, meanwhile, is dated from the third or fourth century and contains six highly damaged lines that roughly parallel Mark and Luke but appear to have been written independently of the canonical Gospels.

Pesikta de-Rav Kahana: A compendium of thirty-three Rabbinic homilies. The homilies fall into three groups: the Pentateuchal, dealing with special Sabbaths and feast days; the Prophetic, dealing specifically with the prophetic lessons for Sabbaths of mourning and comfort; and the Tishri, dealing with penitence. The date of completion for the *Pesikta* is uncertain but can be placed around the fifth or sixth century CE.

Philokalia: An anthology of texts written between the fourth and fifteenth centuries CE by spiritual masters of the Eastern Orthodox Church and intended as guides for monks. The texts offer instruction on meditative and contemplative practices in the hesychast tradition, wherein one focuses inward during prayer, seeking to minimize sensory perception.

Pirke Avot: Also known as Ethics of the Sages, *Pirke Avot* is a collection of the ethical teachings and maxims of the early Rabbinic sages divided into six chapters. It appears in the Talmud within Tractate *Avot* and is unique among Talmudic writings in that it is not augmented with commentary by later scholars or sages.

Proverbs: One of the twenty-four books composing the *Tanakh*, or Hebrew Bible, Proverbs appears as the second book in *Ketuvim* (Writings). Traditionally attributed to Solomon but thought to have been compiled long after his time, Proverbs is classified as a work of wisdom literature, in which wisdom is frequently personified and defined by contrast to a "fool" character. Proverbs, like much wisdom literature, is specifically interested in examining the relationship between the mundane and the sublime (or divine).

Pseudo-Clemintine Homilies: A third-century romance narrating, over the course of twenty books, the religious experiences and questioning of experiences of a character named Clement (whom the text identifies alternatively as Pope Clement I and Titus Flavious Clements). The story, however, is largely a framework for sense theological and philosophical discourse framed as discourses with the apostle Peter.

Qur'an: The central religious text of Islam; within Islamic tradition, the Qur'an is considered to be the record of a series of revelations given to the prophet Muhammad by the angel Gabriel over a period of twenty-three years, from 609 to 632 CE. Muslims regard the Qur'an as the culmination of an ancient lineage of prophetic revelations beginning with Adam and including Abraham, Moses, David, and Jesus.

Rig Veda: One of the four canonical scriptures, called the Vedas, at the heart of Hinduism. The Rig Veda is one of the oldest extant texts in an Indo-European language and is dated to between 1700 and 1100 BCE. The text is organized into ten mandalas (books) containing multiple accounts of the origin of the world, hymns to the gods as well as hymns for life events such as marriage and death, and a wide range of prayers.

Svetasvatara Upanishad: One of the primary Upanishads, containing 113 verses in six chapters and detailing a system of Hindu philosophy wherein God (the ultimate being, generally called Brahman, though referred to as Rudra in the text) is figured as being transcendent while still maintaining cosmological functions. Some scholars have argued that the text is the earliest example of Shaivism, today one of the most widespread sects of Hinduism.

Talmud: From the Hebrew root word *l-m-d*, to teach, the Talmud is an anthology of Rabbinic teaching that, along with the Hebrew Bible, forms the bedrock of Judaism. The Talmud consists of two parts, the *Mishnah*, the earliest collection of Rabbinic teaching compiled around 200 CE, and the *Gemara*, a commentary on the *Mishnah*, the Hebrew Bible, and other subjects pertinent to Jewish life, compiled around 500 CE. More a library of diverse opinions about Judaism than a cohesive presentation of Judaism, the Talmud deals with Jewish law, ethics, customs, folklore, history, theology, and philosophy.

Talmud, *Kiddushin*: A treatise of the *Mishnah* that also appears in both the Babylonian and the Jerusalem Talmuds; the text deals primarily with the conditions required to validate a marriage.

Talmud, *Shabbat*: A treatise of the *Mishnah* that also appears in both the Babylonian and the Jerusalem Talmuds; the text deals primarily with the laws for proper observance of the Sabbath.

Tao Te Ching: Classic Chinese philosophical text written in the sixth century BCE and attributed to the sage Lao Tzu; the actual authorship and dating of the text are still debated, though some have postulated that parts of the text may date to the fourth century BCE. The Tao Te Ching is essential to philosophical and religious Taoism and has had wide-ranging influence on other schools of thought, including Buddhism. The text is organized into eighty-one short poems and contains a total of five thousand characters. The poems deal with a series of profound themes including the ineffability of the source of life, the (feminine) creative aspect of the soul, achieving unity with the source of being, and the methods of discovering wisdom and maintaining humility.

Wisdom of Jesus ben Sirach: A work of the second-century scribe Joshua ben Sira. Originally a Hebrew text, the Wisdom of Jesus ben Sirach was not accepted into the Jewish liturgical canon; it survived in Greek translation as part of the Septuagint, however, and some original Hebrew texts have been now discovered. The book seems to be modeled on Proverbs; it is written in verse and contains a set of maxims dealing with an individual's duty to self, family, society, the state, the poor, and most especially God.

Wisdom of Solomon: One of the books of Deuteronomy included in the Septuagint. Though noncanonical in Rabbinic Judaism, the book has been canonized as part of the Christian Bible. Traditionally ascribed to Solomon, the text is thought to have been written in the Hellenistic period around 70 CE by an Alexandrian Jew. As a book of wisdom literature, the Wisdom of Solomon presents the character of wisdom in personified form. The book is divided into six chapters and two parts. The first part deals largely with an address, or rebuke, to the rulers of the earth. The second contains an address by Wisdom to King Solomon, in which Solomon's life is recounted.

Notes ☐

Preface

1. "Nones on the Rise," Pew Forum on Religion & Public Life, pewforum .org, October 9, 2012.
2. Eknath Easwaran, *Passage Meditation: Bringing the Deep Wisdom of the Heart into Daily Life* (Tomales, CA: Nilgiri Press, 2008), 13.

What Is Perennial Wisdom?

1. Kalama Sutra, my translation.
2. Aldous Huxley, *The Perennial Philosophy: An Interpretation of the Great Mystics, East and West* (New York: Harper Perennial, 2009), vii.
3. Aldous Huxley, introduction to *Bhagavad-Gita: The Song of God*, trans. Swami Prabhavananda and Christopher Isherwood (New York: Signet Classics, 2002), 14–15.
4. Eknath Easwaran, *Original Goodness: Eknath Easwaran on the Beatitudes* (Tomales, CA: Nilgiri Press, 1996), 8–9.

How Shall I Live?

1. Albert Einstein, *New York Times*, March 13, 1940.

Why?

1. Stephen Mitchell, *The Book of Job* (San Francisco: North Point Press, 1987), xxviii.

☐ Bibliography and Suggestions for Further Reading

Angel, Marc D. *Maimonides—Essential Teachings on Jewish Faith and Ethics: The Book of Knowledge and the Thirteen Principles of Faith—Annotated & Explained*. Woodstock, VT: SkyLight Paths, 2012.

Azevedo, Mateus Soares. *Ye Shall Know the Truth: Christianity and the Perennial Philosophy*. Bloomington, IN: World Wisdom, 2005.

Broughton, James. *Packing Up for Paradise: Selected Poems 1946–1966*. Boston: Black Sparrow Press, 1997.

Buber, Martin. *The Way of Man according to the Teachings of Hasidism*. London: Vincent Stuart LTD, 1963.

Burleson, Blake, and Michael Sciretti Jr., eds. *Baptist Wisdom for Contemplative Prayer*. Telephone, TX: Praxis, 2012.

Burroughs, Kendra Crossen, annotator. *Bhagavad Gita: Annotated & Explained*. Translated by Shri Purohit Swami. Woodstock, VT: SkyLight Paths, 2001.

———. *Selections from the Gospel of Sri Ramakrishna: Annotated & Explained*. Translated by Swami Nikhilananda. Woodstock, VT: SkyLight Paths, 2002.

D'Arcy, Martin C. *The Meeting of Love & Knowledge*. New York: Harper & Brothers, 1957.

Davies, Stevan, trans. and annotator. *The Gospel of Thomas: Annotated & Explained*. Woodstock, VT: SkyLight Paths, 2013.

Earle, Mary C. *Celtic Christian Spirituality: Essential Writings—Annotated & Explained*. Woodstock, VT: SkyLight Paths, 2011.

Eknath, Easwaran. *God Makes the Rivers to Flow*. Tomales, CA: Nilgiri Press, 2003.

———. *Original Goodness*. Tomales, CA: Nilgiri Press, 1996.

Ferraro, Jennifer, and Latif Bolat. *Quarreling with God*. Ashland, OR: White Cloud Press, 2007.

Garmard, Ibrahim, trans. and annotator. *Rumi and Islam: Selections from His Stories, Poems, and Discourses—Annotated & Explained*. Woodstock, VT: SkyLight Paths, 2004.

Griffin, David. *Primordial Truth and Postmodern Theology*. Albany: State University of New York, 1989.

Guenon, Rene. *The Essential Rene Guenon*. Edited by John Herlihy. Bloomington, IN: World Wisdom, 2009.

HaLevi, Aharon. *Avodat ha-Levi*. Jerusalem, 1972.

———. *Sha'arei ha-Yihud ve-ha-Emunah*. Jerusalem, 1982.

Holman, John. *The Return of the Perennial Philosophy*. London: Watkins, 2008.

Huxley, Aldous. *The Perennial Philosophy: An Interpretation of the Great Mystics, East and West*. New York: Harper Perennial, 2009.

Huynh, Thomas. *Art of War—Spirituality for Conflict: Annotated and Explained*. Woodstock, VT: SkyLight Paths, 2008.

Idel, Moshe. *The Mystical Experience of Abraham Abulafia*. Albany: State University of New York, 1988.

Kelly, Joseph T., annotator. *Saint Augustine of Hippo: Selections from Confessions and Other Essential Writings—Annotated & Explained*. Translation from the Augustinian Heritage Institute, *The Works of Saint Augustine: A Translation for the 21st Century*. Woodstock, VT: SkyLight Paths, 2010.

Kohn, Livia, trans. and annotator. *Chuang-tzu: The Tao of Perfect Happiness—Selections Annotated & Explained*. Woodstock, VT: SkyLight Paths, 2011.

Lakhani, Ali M. *The Timeless Relevance of Traditional Wisdom*. Bloomington, IN: World Wisdom, 2010.

Lin, Derek, trans. and annotator. *Tao Te Ching: Annotated & Explained*. Woodstock, VT: SkyLight Paths, 2007.

Lings, Martin, ed. *The Underlying Religion: An Introduction to the Perennial Philosophy*. Bloomington, IN: World Wisdom, 2007.

Maguire, Jack, annotator. *Dhammapada: Annotated & Explained*. Translated by Max Muller. Woodstock, VT: SkyLight Paths, 2005.

Matt, Daniel, trans. and annotator. *Zohar: Annotated & Explained*. Woodstock, VT: SkyLight Paths, 2004.

McNeil, Russell, annotator. The Meditations of Marcus Aurelius: *Selections Annotated & Explained*. Translated by George Long. Woodstock, VT: SkyLight Paths, 2012.

Miller, John, ed. *God's Breath: Sacred Scripture of the World*. New York: Marlowe & Company, 2000.

———. *God's Light: Prophets of the World's Great Religions*. New York: Marlowe & Company, 2003.

Mitchell, Stephen. *The Book of Job*. San Francisco: North Point Press, 1987.

Oldmeadow, Harry. *Crossing Religious Frontiers: Studies in Comparative Religion*. Bloomington, IN: World Wisdom, 2010.

Oldmeadow, Harry. *Frithjof Schuon and the Perennial Philosophy*. Bloomington, IN: World Wisdom, 2010.

Paintner, Christine. *Desert Fathers and Mothers: Early Christian Wisdom Sayings—Annotated & Explained*. Woodstock, VT: SkyLight Paths, 2012.

Perry, Whitall. *A Treasury of Traditional Wisdom*. New York: Simon and Schuster, 1971.

Pine, Red. *The Platform Sutra: The Zen Teaching of Hui-neng*. Berkeley, CA: Counterpoint Press, 2008.

Prabhavananda, Swami. Shankara's Crest-Jewel of Discrimination. Los Angeles: Vedanta Society, 1975.

Prabhavananda, Swami, and Christopher Isherwood, trans. *Bhagavad-Gita: The Song of God*. New York: Signet Classics, 2002.

Rosemont, Henry. *Is There a Universal Grammar of Religion?* Chicago: Open Court, 2008.

Schneerson, Menachem Mendel. *Toward a Meaningful Life*. Edited by Simon Jacobson. New York: William Morrow, 1995.

Schuon, Frithjof. *The Transcendent Unity of Religions*. Wheaton, IL: Quest Books, 2011.

Sefik, Can. *Fundamentals of Rumi's Thought: A Mevlevi Sufi Perspective*. Edited and translated by Zeki Saritoprak. Clifton, NJ: Tughra Books, 2006.

Shapiro, Rami. *Amazing Chesed: Living a Grace-Filled Judaism*. Woodstock, VT: SkyLight Paths, 2012.

Shapiro, Rami, trans. and annotator. *The Divine Feminine in Biblical Wisdom Literature: Selections Annotated & Explained*. Woodstock, VT: SkyLight Paths, 2013.

———. *Ecclesiastes: Annotated & Explained*. Woodstock, VT: SkyLight Paths, 2010.

———. *Ethics of the Sages:* Pirke Avot—*Annotated & Explained*. Woodstock, VT: SkyLight Paths, 2006.

———. *The Hebrew Prophets: Selections Annotated & Explained*. Woodstock, VT: SkyLight Paths, 2004.

———. *Proverbs: Annotated & Explained*. Woodstock, VT: SkyLight Paths, 2011.

———. Tanya: *The Masterpiece of Hasidic Wisdom—Annotated & Explained*. Woodstock, VT: SkyLight Paths, 2010.

Smith, Allyne. Philokalia: *The Eastern Christian Spiritual Texts—Selections Annotated & Explained*. Woodstock, VT: SkyLight Paths, 2008.

Smith, Andrew Philip. *The Lost Sayings of Jesus: Teachings from Ancient Christian, Jewish, Gnostic and Islamic Sources—Annotated & Explained.* Woodstock, VT: SkyLight Paths, 2006.

Smith, Huston. *Forgotten Truth: The Common Vision of the World's Religions.* San Francisco: HarperSanFrancisco, 1976.

Sotillos, Samuel Bendeck, ed. *Psychology and the Perennial Philosophy.* Bloomington, IN: World Wisdom, 2013.

Spevack, Aaron. *Ghazali on the Principles of Islamic Spirituality: Selections from The Forty Foundations of Religion—Annotated & Explained.* Woodstock, VT: SkyLight Paths, 2012.

Stoddart, William. *Remembering in a World of Forgetting.* Bloomington, IN: World Wisdom, 2008.

Sultan, Sohaib N., annotator. *The Qur'an and Sayings of Prophet Muhammad: Selections Annotated & Explained.* Translated by Yusuf Ali. Woodstock, VT: SkyLight Paths, 2007.

Taylor, Rodney L., annotator. *Confucius, the Analects: The Path of the Sage—Selections Annotated & Explained.* Translated by James Legge. Woodstock, VT: SkyLight Paths, 2011.

Wang, Robin. *Yinyang: The Way of Heaven and Earth in Chinese Thought and Culture.* New York: Cambridge University Press, 2012.

Wilson, Andrew, ed. *World Scripture.* New York: Paragon House, 1991.

Inspiration

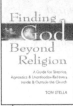

Finding God Beyond Religion: A Guide for Skeptics, Agnostics & Unorthodox Believers Inside & Outside the Church
By Tom Stella; Foreword by The Rev. Canon Marianne Wells Borg
Reinterprets traditional religious teachings central to the Christian faith for people who have outgrown the beliefs and devotional practices that once made sense to them.
6 x 9, 160 pp, Quality PB, 978-1-59473-485-4 $16.99

How Did I Get to Be 70 When I'm 35 Inside?: Spiritual Surprises of Later Life   *By Linda Douty*
Encourages you to focus on the inner changes of aging to help you greet your later years as the grand adventure they can be.   6 x 9, 208 pp, Quality PB, 978-1-59473-297-3 **$16.99**

Fully Awake and Truly Alive: Spiritual Practices to Nurture Your Soul
By Rev. Jane E. Vennard; Foreword by Rami Shapiro
Illustrates the joys and frustrations of spiritual practice, offers insights from various religious traditions and provides exercises and meditations to help us become more fully alive.
6 x 9, 208 pp, Quality PB, 978-1-59473-473-1 **$16.99**

Saving Civility: 52 Ways to Tame Rude, Crude & Attitude for a Polite Planet
By Sara Hacala
Provides fifty-two practical ways you can reverse the course of incivility and make the world a more enriching, pleasant place to live.
6 x 9, 240 pp, Quality PB 978-1-59473-314-7 **$16.99**

Spiritually Healthy Divorce: Navigating Disruption with Insight & Hope
By Carolyne Call
A spiritual map to help you move through the twists and turns of divorce.
6 x 9, 224 pp, Quality PB, 978-1-59473-288-1 **$16.99**

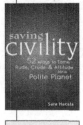

Who Is My God? 2nd Edition
An Innovative Guide to Finding Your Spiritual Identity
By the Editors at SkyLight Paths
Provides the Spiritual Identity Self-Test™ to uncover the components of your unique spirituality.   6 x 9, 160 pp, Quality PB, 978-1-59473-014-6 **$15.99**

Journeys of Simplicity
Traveling Light with Thomas Merton, Bashō, Edward Abbey, Annie Dillard & Others
By Philip Harnden
Invites you to consider a more graceful way of traveling through life.
PB includes journal pages to help you get started on your own spiritual journey.
5 x 7¼, 144 pp, Quality PB, 978-1-59473-181-5 **$12.99**
5 x 7¼, 128 pp, HC, 978-1-893361-76-8 **$16.95**

Or phone, fax, mail or e-mail to: SKYLIGHT PATHS Publishing
Sunset Farm Offices, Route 4 • P.O. Box 237 • Woodstock, Vermont 05091
Tel: (802) 457-4000 • Fax: (802) 457-4004 • www.skylightpaths.com
Credit card orders: (800) 962-4544 (8:30AM–5:30PM EST Monday–Friday)
Generous discounts on quantity orders. SATISFACTION GUARANTEED. Prices subject to change.

Judaism / Christianity / Islam / Interfaith

Spiritual Gems of Islam: Insights & Practices from the Qur'an, Hadith, Rumi & Muslim Teaching Stories to Enlighten the Heart & Mind
By Imam Jamal Rahman
Invites you—no matter what your practice may be—to access the treasure chest of Islamic spirituality and use its wealth in your own journey.
6 x 9, 256 pp, Quality PB, 978-1-59473-430-4 **$16.99**

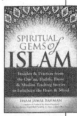

All Politics Is Religious: Speaking Faith to the Media, Policy Makers and Community   *By Rabbi Dennis S. Ross; Foreword by Rev. Barry W. Lynn*
Provides ideas and strategies for expressing a clear, forceful and progressive religious point of view that is all too often overlooked and under-represented in public discourse.   6 x 9, 192 pp, Quality PB, 978-1-59473-374-1 **$18.99**

Religion Gone Astray: What We Found at the Heart of Interfaith
By Pastor Don Mackenzie, Rabbi Ted Falcon and Imam Jamal Rahman
Welcome to the deeper dimensions of interfaith dialogue—exploring that which divides us personally, spiritually and institutionally.
6 x 9, 192 pp, Quality PB, 978-1-59473-317-8 **$16.99**

Getting to the Heart of Interfaith: The Eye-Opening, Hope-Filled Friendship of a Pastor, a Rabbi & an Imam   *By Pastor Don Mackenzie, Rabbi Ted Falcon and Imam Jamal Rahman*
6 x 9, 192 pp, Quality PB, 978-1-59473-263-8 **$16.99**

Hearing the Call across Traditions: Readings on Faith and Service
Edited by Adam Davis; Foreword by Eboo Patel
6 x 9, 352 pp, Quality PB, 978-1-59473-303-1 **$18.99**

How to Do Good & Avoid Evil: A Global Ethic from the Sources of Judaism
By Hans Küng and Rabbi Walter Homolka; Translated by Rev. Dr. John Bowden
6 x 9, 224 pp, HC, 978-1-59473-255-3 **$19.99**

Blessed Relief: What Christians Can Learn from Buddhists about Suffering
By Gordon Peerman 6 x 9, 208 pp, Quality PB, 978-1-59473-252-2 **$16.99**

Christians & Jews—Faith to Faith: Tragic History, Promising Present, Fragile Future *By Rabbi James Rudin* 6 x 9, 288 pp, HC, 978-1-58023-432-0 **$24.99***

Christians & Jews in Dialogue: Learning in the Presence of the Other *By Mary C. Boys and Sara S. Lee; Foreword by Dorothy C. Bass* 6 x 9, 240 pp, Quality PB, 978-1-59473-254-6 **$18.99**

InterActive Faith: The Essential Interreligious Community-Building Handbook
Edited by Rev. Bud Heckman with Rori Picker Neiss; Foreword by Rev. Dirk Ficca
6 x 9, 304 pp, Quality PB, 978-1-59473-273-7 **$16.99**; HC, 978-1-59473-237-9 **$29.99**

The Jewish Approach to God: A Brief Introduction for Christians
By Rabbi Neil Gillman, PhD 5½ x 8½, 192 pp, Quality PB, 978-1-58023-190-9 **$16.95***

The Jewish Approach to Repairing the World (Tikkun Olam): A Brief Introduction for Christians *By Rabbi Elliot N. Dorff, PhD, with Rev. Cory Willson*
5½ x 8½, 256 pp, Quality PB, 978-1-58023-349-1 **$16.99***

The Jewish Connection to Israel, the Promised Land: A Brief Introduction for Christians *By Rabbi Eugene Korn, PhD* 5½ x 8½, 192 pp, Quality PB, 978-1-58023-318-7 **$14.99***

Jewish Holidays: A Brief Introduction for Christians *By Rabbi Kerry M. Olitzky and Rabbi Daniel Judson* 5½ x 8½, 176 pp, Quality PB, 978-1-58023-302-6 **$16.99***

Jewish Ritual: A Brief Introduction for Christians
By Rabbi Kerry M. Olitzky and Rabbi Daniel Judson 5½ x 8½, 144 pp, Quality PB, 978-1-58023-210-4 **$14.99***

Jewish Spirituality: A Brief Introduction for Christians *By Rabbi Lawrence Kushner*
5½ x 8½, 112 pp, Quality PB, 978-1-58023-150-3 **$12.95***

* A book from Jewish Lights, SkyLight Paths' sister imprint

Spiritual Practice

Fly-Fishing—The Sacred Art: Casting a Fly as a Spiritual Practice
*By Rabbi Eric Eisenkramer and Rev. Michael Attas, MD; Foreword by Chris Wood, CEO,
Trout Unlimited; Preface by Lori Simon, executive director, Casting for Recovery*
Shares what fly-fishing can teach you about reflection, awe and wonder; the benefits of solitude; the blessing of community and the search for the Divine.
5½ x 8½, 160 pp, Quality PB, 978-1-59473-299-7 **$16.99**

Lectio Divina—The Sacred Art: Transforming Words & Images into
Heart-Centered Prayer *By Christine Valters Paintner, PhD*
Expands the practice of sacred reading beyond scriptural texts and makes it
accessible in contemporary life. 5½ x 8½, 240 pp, Quality PB, 978-1-59473-300-0 **$16.99**

Writing—The Sacred Art: Beyond the Page to Spiritual Practice
By Rami Shapiro and Aaron Shapiro
Push your writing through the trite and the boring to something fresh, something
transformative. Includes over fifty unique, practical exercises.
5½ x 8½, 192 pp, Quality PB, 978-1-59473-372-7 **$16.99**

Conversation—The Sacred Art: Practicing Presence in an Age of Distraction
By Diane M. Millis, PhD; Foreword by Rev. Tilden Edwards, PhD
Cultivate the potential for deeper connection in every conversation.
5½ x 8½, 192 pp, Quality PB, 978-1-59473-474-8 **$16.99**

Pilgrimage—The Sacred Art: Journey to the Center of the Heart
By Dr. Sheryl A. Kujawa-Holbrook
Explore the many dimensions of the experience of pilgrimage—the yearning heart,
the painful setbacks, the encounter with the Divine and, ultimately, the changed
orientation to the world. 5½ x 8½, 240 pp, Quality PB, 978-1-59473-472-4 **$16.99**

Dance—The Sacred Art: The Joy of Movement as a Spiritual Practice
By Cynthia Winton-Henry 5½ x 8½, 224 pp, Quality PB, 978-1-59473-268-3 **$16.99**

Giving—The Sacred Art: Creating a Lifestyle of Generosity
By Lauren Tyler Wright 5½ x 8½, 208 pp, Quality PB, 978-1-59473-224-9 **$16.99**

Haiku—The Sacred Art: A Spiritual Practice in Three Lines
By Margaret D. McGee 5½ x 8½, 192 pp, Quality PB, 978-1-59473-269-0 **$16.99**

Hospitality—The Sacred Art: Discovering the Hidden Spiritual Power of Invitation
and Welcome *By Rev. Nanette Sawyer; Foreword by Rev. Dirk Ficca*
5½ x 8½, 208 pp, Quality PB, 978-1-59473-228-7 **$16.99**

Labyrinths from the Outside In, 2nd Edition: Walking to Spiritual Insight—A
Beginner's Guide *By Rev. Dr. Donna Schaper and Rev. Dr. Carole Ann Camp*
6 x 9, 208 pp, b/w illus. and photos, Quality PB, 978-1-59473-486-1 **$16.99**

Practicing the Sacred Art of Listening: A Guide to Enrich Your Relationships
and Kindle Your Spiritual Life *By Kay Lindahl* 8 x 8, 176 pp, Quality PB, 978-1-893361-85-0 **$16.95**

Recovery—The Sacred Art: The Twelve Steps as Spiritual Practice *by Rami Shapiro;
Foreword by Joan Borysenko, PhD* 5½ x 8½, 240 pp, Quality PB, 978-1-59473-259-1 **$16.99**

Running—The Sacred Art: Preparing to Practice *By Dr. Warren A. Kay; Foreword by
Kristin Armstrong* 5½ x 8½, 160 pp, Quality PB, 978-1-59473-227-0 **$16.99**

The Sacred Art of Chant: Preparing to Practice
By Ana Hernández 5½ x 8½, 192 pp, Quality PB, 978-1-59473-036-8 **$16.99**

The Sacred Art of Fasting: Preparing to Practice
By Thomas Ryan, CSP 5½ x 8½, 192 pp, Quality PB, 978-1-59473-078-8 **$15.99**

The Sacred Art of Forgiveness: Forgiving Ourselves and Others through God's Grace
By Marcia Ford 8 x 8, 176 pp, Quality PB, 978-1-59473-175-4 **$18.99**

The Sacred Art of Listening: Forty Reflections for Cultivating a Spiritual Practice
By Kay Lindahl; Illus. by Amy Schnapper 8 x 8, 160 pp, b/w illus., Quality PB, 978-1-893361-44-7 **$16.99**

The Sacred Art of Lovingkindness: Preparing to Practice
By Rabbi Rami Shapiro; Foreword by Marcia Ford 5½ x 8½, 176 pp, Quality PB, 978-1-59473-151-8 **$16.99**

Thanking & Blessing—The Sacred Art: Spiritual Vitality through Gratefulness
By Jay Marshall, PhD; Foreword by Philip Gulley 5½ x 8½, 176 pp, Quality PB, 978-1-59473-231-7 **$16.99**

Spirituality

The Passionate Jesus: What We Can Learn from Jesus about Love, Fear, Grief, Joy and Living Authentically
By The Rev. Peter Wallace
Reveals Jesus as a passionate figure who was involved, present, connected, honest and direct with others and encourages you to build personal authenticity in every area of your own life.
6 x 9, 208 pp, Quality PB, 978-1-59473-393-2 **$18.99**

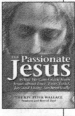

Gathering at God's Table: The Meaning of Mission in the Feast of Faith
By Katharine Jefferts Schori
A profound reminder of our role in the larger frame of God's dream for a restored and reconciled world. 6 x 9, 256 pp, HC, 978-1-59473-316-1 **$21.99**

The Heartbeat of God: Finding the Sacred in the Middle of Everything
By Katharine Jefferts Schori; Foreword by Joan Chittister, OSB
Explores our connections to other people, to other nations and with the environment through the lens of faith. 6 x 9, 240 pp, HC, 978-1-59473-292-8 **$21.99**

A Dangerous Dozen: Twelve Christians Who Threatened the Status Quo but Taught Us to Live Like Jesus
By the Rev. Canon C. K. Robertson, PhD; Foreword by Archbishop Desmond Tutu
Profiles twelve visionary men and women who challenged society and showed the world a different way of living. 6 x 9, 208 pp, Quality PB, 978-1-59473-298-0 **$16.99**

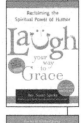

Decision Making & Spiritual Discernment: The Sacred Art of Finding Your Way *By Nancy L Bieber*
Presents three essential aspects of Spirit-led decision making: willingness, attentiveness and responsiveness. 5½ x 8½, 208 pp, Quality PB, 978-1-59473-289-8 **$16.99**

Laugh Your Way to Grace: Reclaiming the Spiritual Power of Humor
By Rev. Susan Sparks A powerful, humorous case for laughter as a spiritual, healing path. 6 x 9, 176 pp, Quality PB, 978-1-59473-280-5 **$16.99**

Bread, Body, Spirit: Finding the Sacred in Food
Edited and with Introductions by Alice Peck 6 x 9, 224 pp, Quality PB, 978-1-59473-242-3 **$19.99**

Claiming Earth as Common Ground: The Ecological Crisis through the Lens of Faith
By Andrea Cohen-Kiener; Foreword by Rev. Sally Bingham
6 x 9, 192 pp, Quality PB, 978-1-59473-261-4 **$16.99**

Creating a Spiritual Retirement: A Guide to the Unseen Possibilities in Our Lives
By Molly Srode 6 x 9, 208 pp, b/w photos, Quality PB, 978-1-59473-050-4 **$14.99**

Creative Aging: Rethinking Retirement and Non-Retirement in a Changing World
By Marjory Zoet Bankson 6 x 9, 160 pp, Quality PB, 978-1-59473-281-2 **$16.99**

Keeping Spiritual Balance as We Grow Older: More than 65 Creative Ways to Use Purpose, Prayer, and the Power of Spirit to Build a Meaningful Retirement
By Molly and Bernie Srode 8 x 8, 224 pp, Quality PB, 978-1-59473-042-9 **$16.99**

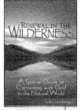

Hearing the Call across Traditions: Readings on Faith and Service
Edited by Adam Davis; Foreword by Eboo Patel 6 x 9, 352 pp, Quality PB, 978-1-59473-303-1 **$18.99**

Honoring Motherhood: Prayers, Ceremonies & Blessings
Edited and with Introductions by Lynn L. Caruso
5 x 7¼, 272 pp, Quality PB, 978-1-58473-384-0 **$9.99**; HC, 978-1-59473-239-3 **$19.99**

The Losses of Our Lives: The Sacred Gifts of Renewal in Everyday Loss
By Dr. Nancy Copeland-Payton 6 x 9, 192 pp, HC, 978-1-59473-271-3 **$19.99**

Renewal in the Wilderness: A Spiritual Guide to Connecting with God in the Natural World *By John Lionberger* 6 x 9, 176 pp, b/w photos, Quality PB, 978-1-59473-219-5 **$16.99**

Soul Fire: Accessing Your Creativity
By Thomas Ryan, CSP 6 x 9, 160 pp, Quality PB, 978-1-59473-243-0 **$16.99**

A Spirituality for Brokenness: Discovering Your Deepest Self in Difficult Times
By Terry Taylor 6 x 9, 176 pp, Quality PB, 978-1-59473-229-4 **$16.99**

A Walk with Four Spiritual Guides: Krishna, Buddha, Jesus, and Ramakrishna
By Andrew Harvey 5½ x 8½, 192 pp, b/w photos & illus., Quality PB, 978-1-59473-138-9 **$15.99**

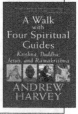

About SKYLIGHT PATHS Publishing

SkyLight Paths Publishing is creating a place where people of different spiritual traditions come together for challenge and inspiration, a place where we can help each other understand the mystery that lies at the heart of our existence.

Through spirituality, our religious beliefs are increasingly becoming a part of our lives—rather than *apart* from our lives. While many of us may be more interested than ever in spiritual growth, we may be less firmly planted in traditional religion. Yet, we do want to deepen our relationship to the sacred, to learn from our own as well as from other faith traditions, and to practice in new ways.

SkyLight Paths sees both believers and seekers as a community that increasingly transcends traditional boundaries of religion and denomination—people wanting to learn from each other, *walking together, finding the way.*

For your information and convenience, at the back of this book we have provided a list of other SkyLight Paths books you might find interesting and useful. They cover the following subjects:

Buddhism / Zen	Global Spiritual	Monasticism
Catholicism	Perspectives	Mysticism
Children's Books	Gnosticism	Poetry
Christianity	Hinduism /	Prayer
Comparative	Vedanta	Religious Etiquette
Religion	Inspiration	Retirement
Current Events	Islam / Sufism	Spiritual Biography
Earth-Based	Judaism	Spiritual Direction
Spirituality	Kabbalah	Spirituality
Enneagram	Meditation	Women's Interest
	Midrash Fiction	Worship

Or phone, fax, mail or e-mail to: SKYLIGHT PATHS Publishing
Sunset Farm Offices, Route 4 • P.O. Box 237 • Woodstock, Vermont 05091
Tel: (802) 457-4000 • Fax: (802) 457-4004 • www.skylightpaths.com
Credit card orders: (800) 962-4544 (8:30AM–5:30PM EST Monday–Friday)
Generous discounts on quantity orders. SATISFACTION GUARANTEED. Prices subject to change.